10 0106025 2
D0302784
WITHDRAWN
FROM THE
OWL

RUSH TO UNION

RUSH TO UNION

Understanding the
European Federal Bargain

DAVID McKAY

CLARENDON PRESS · OXFORD
1996

Oxford University Press, Walton Street, Oxford OX2 6DP

Oxford New York
Athens Auckland Bangkok Bombay
Calcutta Cape Town Dar es Salaam Delhi
Florence Hong Kong Istanbul Karachi
Kuala Lumpur Madras Madrid Melbourne
Mexico City Nairobi Paris Singapore
Taipei Tokyo Toronto

and associated companies in
Berlin Ibadan

Oxford is a trade mark of Oxford University Press

Published in the United States
by Oxford University Press Inc., New York

British Library Cataloguing in Publication Data
Data available

Library of Congress Cataloging in Publication Data
McKay, David H.
Rush to union : understanding the European federal bargain / David McKay.
Includes bibliographical references.
1. European federation. 2. European Union. I. Title.
JN15.M37 1996 341.24'2—dc20 96–13512

ISBN 0–19–828058–0

1 3 5 7 9 10 8 6 4 2

Typeset by Graphicraft Typesetters Ltd., Hong Kong
Printed in Great Britain
on acid-free paper by
Biddles Ltd, Guildford and King's Lynn

For Sherri Singleton,
chef and restauranteur extraordinary

PREFACE

This book owes its origins at least in part to an article by Martin Feldstein in *The Economist* newspaper on 13 June 1992. In summarizing the research of a number of American economists, Feldstein's piece alerted me to the contradictions and anomalies inherent in the Maastricht Treaty on European Union. In spite of having worked on the subject of American federalism for some years, it did not occur to me until that time that what the Europeans were doing at Maastricht was close to the equivalent of the deliberations of the Founding Fathers of the United States at Philadelphia between 1787 and 1788. As a long-standing enthusiast of European integration, I became aware that the introduction of a single currency in the European Community carried with it important costs as well as benefits. I was also struck by the fact that Maastricht represented a sea change in the history of European integration. In effect, the negotiating parties were in the business of creating a new federal state, and while economists were beginning to understand the full ramifications of this decision, few of my fellow political scientists had, until that time, complemented the economists' work with theoretically informed research on the political consequences of the Treaty.

By adapting William Riker's theory of federalism, this book strives to extend the analysis of the origins and the viability of political unions to the European case. All too often, academics and others have assumed an inevitability to European integration, and have implied that the nations of Europe were somehow pre-ordained to evolve into a single nation state. The central argument of this book is that federations are not simply willed; they are forged out of political and economic necessity. Ultimately they are the products of interests rather than ideas.

Among those with whom I have exchanged views or who have read parts of the manuscript, I would like to thank Norman Schofield, David Sanders, Wayne Sandholtz and Finn Ostrup. I am also grateful to the participants at the European Consortium for Political Research Workshop on the Origins and Viability of Political Unions at Bordeaux in May 1995, and especially to Kenneth Dyson, Kevin Featherstone, and

Graham Wilson, who commented so constructively on my work. Thanks also to two of my Ph.D. students, Michael Smith and Andy Wroe, for providing invaluable research assistance. Finally, thanks to the Department of Government, University of Essex, which, even after twenty years, continues to amaze me with its intellectual eclecticism and adaptabitity.

DAVID MCKAY

September 1995

CONTENTS

LIST OF TABLES

ABBREVIATIONS

CAP	Common Agricultural Policy
CPSU	Communist Party of the Soviet Union
ECB	European Central Bank
ECPR	European Consortium for Political Research
ECSC	European Coal and Steel Community
ECU	European Currency Unit
EDC	European Defence Community
EEC	European Economic Community
EFTA	European Free Trade Association
EMI	European Monetary Institute
EMS	European Monetary System
EMU	European Monetary Union
EP	European Parliament
EPC	European Political Community; European Political Co-operation
EPP	European People's Party
ERM	Exchange Rate Mechanism
GATT	General Agreement on Tariffs and Trade
IMF	International Monetary Fund
MEP	Member of the European Parliament
NAFTA	North America Free Trade Agreement
NATO	North Atlantic Treaty Organization
OECD	Organization for Economic Co-operation and Development
PES	Party of European Socialists
SEA	Single European Act
WEU	Western European Union

PART I

On the Origins of European Union

1

The Puzzle of European Union

INTRODUCTION

When the countries of the European Community signed the Maastricht Treaty on 7 February 1992 they were embarking on a remarkable political experiment. Twelve countries had come together and voluntarily agreed to cede responsibility for major areas of government to a supranational authority. Moreover, by granting control over macroeconomic policy to the federal level, they were creating a union that was very much more than a loose confederation of countries. Macroeconomic policy is one of the most vital functions of the modern state (possibly *the* most vital function) so potentially Maastricht involved the creation of a genuine political union or federation. By implication, at least, the Twelve were setting out down a road that would lead to a United States of Europe.

It is the major claim of this book that the literature on European union has yet to generate a theoretical framework powerful enough to explain these events and to provide pointers as to whether the great experiment will succeed. Enough books and articles on the origins and development of European Union have been written to fill a small library, but the vast majority are devoted to historical description or provide a textbook treatment of the Union's economy, society, or political arrangements.[1] Theoretically informed studies are few and far between; often they are written by commentators or scholars intent on advancing a particular political position.[2]

[1] Four recent histories of the development of European integration are David Arter, *The Politics of European Integration in the Twentieth Century*, Aldershot, Dartmouth, 1993; Martin Holland, *European Integration: From Community to Union*, London, Pinter, 1994; David Weigall and Peter Stirk (eds.), *The Origins and Development of the European Community*, Leicester, Leicester University Press, 1992; Derek W. Urwin, *The Community of Europe: A history of European Integration Since 1945*, London, Longman, 1991.

[2] For an example of a study taking a strong pro-federalist position, see Andrew Duff *et al.* (eds.), *Maastricht and Beyond: Building the European Union*, London, Routledge, 1994. An example of the anti-federalist position is James M. Buchanan *et al.*, *Europe's Constitutional Future*, London, Institute of Economic Affairs, 1990.

At the core of the present volume's analysis is the assumption that politicians do not cede authority (or give up some part of their power resources) voluntarily unless they believe that the benefits of doing so exceed the costs. Similarly, the book assumes that federations will succeed only if the benefits to the component states of remaining in a federation exceed the costs. Once this calculus changes, and the costs exceed the benefits, the federation (or part of the federation) will break up. We cannot, of course, test the second proposition as far as the European Union is concerned. What we can do, however, is, given the information we have about the countries of the EU, provide political and economic scenarios which point to potential successes or failures. As far as both the creation and the viability of union is concerned, comparisons will be drawn with other political unions and federations. As, in terms of size, political and economic development, the United States is, of all the world's federations, closest to Europe, it will be used as the principal comparator nation.

Although a rational choice (or realist) perspective is at the centre of the analysis, other perspectives are examined and tested in turn. The author concedes at the outset that no single explanation is sufficient to explain the Maastricht phenomenon. The claim is, merely, that the rational choice perspective is the single most convincing approach to what for many observers—and especially those from outside Europe—is a genuine intellectual puzzle.[3]

There are two dimensions to this puzzle. The first concerns the *timing* of European union. A priori we should have expected European union to have occurred in the 1950s rather than the late 1980s and the early 1990s. As judged by historical precedent, countries are most likely to come together to form political unions when enlargement results in a strengthening of any response to an actual or potential military threat or opportunity.[4] In the 1950s both an external and an internal threat were present. Internally, fears of German irredentism were still very

[3] One the more theoretically informed studies of European union concludes that the phenomenon is indeed an intellectual puzzle. Wayne Sandholz, 'Choosing Union: Monetary Politics and Maastricht', *International Organization*, 47/1, Winter 1993, 1–39. Further insightful theoretical perspectives are provided by Kenneth Dyson, *Elusive Union: The Process of Economic and Monetary Union in Europe*, London, Longman, 1994, and Robert O. Keohane and Stanley Hoffman (eds.), *The New European Community: Decision Making and Institutional Change*, Boulder, Colo., Wesview Press, 1991.

[4] See in particular William Riker's *Federalism: Origin, Operation, Significance*, Boston, Little Brown, 1964, ch. 2.

much present. Externally, the Soviet Union posed an unambiguous threat not only to West Germany but to most of the other countries of Western Europe. Electorally powerful Communist parties in France and Italy also actively supported Soviet expansionism, thus strengthening the Soviets' strategic resources.

In the event, the European Defence Council, which would have created a set of supranational and democratically accountable institutions responsible for a common policy in the defence field, came to nothing. And the European Coal and Steel Community (ECSC) and the original European Economic Community (EEC) of the Six, had limited memberships, narrow policy briefs, and very rudimentary institutional structures. The North Atlantic Treaty Association (NATO) did, of course, provide for the sort of military co-operation necessary to help meet the Soviet threat, but only in the context of an overwhelming American military capacity and it totally lacked the sort of supranational institutional structure necessary to meet the most minimal conditions of a political union.

By the late 1980s fears of German expansionism had evaporated, indigenous Communist parties were in disarray, and the Soviet Empire was on the brink of dissolution. Yet it was precisely at this time that the countries of the EC decided on political union.

It could be argued that by the 1980s economic conditions had changed to such an extent that they, rather than military and defence factors, became the driving force behind union. In particular, the internationalization of capital, together with the emergence of competing trading blocs, was forcing the countries of Europe into ever closer economic integration, culminating in the proposals for a single currency. Although intuitively feasible, this perspective fails two basic empirical tests: (*a*) Why was it that Europe's competitors (Japan and the United States) welcomed rather than opposed European union? If, as some of the more alarmist commentators have put it, we are in for an economic *battle* among the major blocs,[5] The Americans and Japanese should have resisted European union at every turn. (*b*) Moreover, although moves towards economic integration in both East Asia and North America were taken in the 1990s, in neither of these areas (nor anywhere else of significance) have serious moves towards monetary integration been taken, and no group of nations has embarked on a timetable of full

[5] A stimulating polemic arguing this case is Lester Thurow's *Head to Head: The Coming Economic Battle Among Europe and America*, New York, William Morrow, 1992.

economic and *political* integration. The second aspect to the puzzle is, then, the uniquely radical *European* response to the changed economic circumstances of the 1980s and 1990s. To make better sense of this puzzle some reference to the broader social science literature on European union is necessary.

SOCIAL SCIENCE AND EUROPEAN UNION

Theoretical perspectives on European union tend to follow the disciplinary boundaries in the social sciences. Very generally, the major intellectual divide is between scholars working in international relations and those researching in history and political science. The latter tend to stress the role of individuals, interests, and domestic political institutions. The former take the nation state and international institutions as the basic units. The major debate within international relations, between realists and idealists (or neo-realists and neo-liberals), dwells on the possibility of international co-operation and whether the actors engaged in international affairs are concerned with relative or absolute gains.[6] As suggested above, European union presents the realists with something of a puzzle. If self-interested states co-operate only if they can gain relative to others—as with NATO member states in relation to the Soviet bloc in the bi-polar post-war world—why are the countries of Europe co-operating so effectively in the 1990s?[7] On the face of it, European union seems to endorse the neo-liberal perspective—the countries of Europe are co-operating because they believe it will result in absolute gains or an increase in the general welfare in a multi-polar world. We do not *know* that such gains will follow, however. Idealists might *wish* such consequences but their theoretical perspective does not demonstrate that such benefits *must* follow from co-operation.

Within history and political science the theoretical debate has taken a somewhat different path. Most political science accounts of European integration concentrate on the historical evolution of integration, and evaluate the role in the process played by domestic political actors and interests and supranational institutions—not least the Commission of the European Community. Much of this literature is in the idealist or

[6] For a useful review of this debate, see David A. Baldwin (ed.), *Neorealism and Neoliberalism: The Contemporary Debate*, New York, Columbia University Press, 1993.

[7] For a discussion, see Joseph M. Grieco, 'The Maastricht Treaty, Economic and Monetary Union and the Neorealist Research Programme', *Review of International Studies*, 21, 1995, pp. 21–40.

neo-liberal tradition. It assumes that common interest will lead to co-operation and improved welfare for all the participating countries.[8] Working from within a slightly different tradition, much of the early literature on the evolution of federal states makes similar value assumptions: co-operation is *ipso facto* a good thing and federal-like arrangements are the optimal institutional structures for the governance of culturally diverse states which share some common interest.[9] Although intuitively plausible, these approaches have limited explanatory power. As with the idealists working in the international relations tradition, simply wishing union is not enough, as the experience of the 1950s shows. Neither the timing nor the nature of the trade-offs involved in the creation of unions is explained by the desirability of co-operation between states sharing common interests. We will return to this point in Chapter 2.

Within political science, rational choice theory is the direct analogue of the realist perspective in international relations. Self-interested politicians, voters, and interest groups are the basic units of analysis and all will do what they can to maximize votes and/or economic and other benefits. As far as European integration is concerned, most of the relevant work dwells on the bargaining strategies employed by the participants at Maastricht. Although quite sophisticated, this research emphasizes process rather than substance. Quite rightly, scholars have been quick to note the complexity of the bargaining process. They have also identified the contrasting interests and motives of those politicians representing different nation states and supra- and international institutions. Some of the better contributions recognize the two-level nature of the bargaining game: politicians bargain both at the supranational level and with domestic interests. And because politicians both within and between different countries have different interests and motivations, the bargaining outcome must be an elaborate compromise following complex negotiations.[10] That Maastricht represented a compromise seems incontrovertible. However, it also represented much more than this, for

[8] See Duff *et al.*, *Maastricht and Beyond*. Even many of those studies laying claim to an objective view of European union show some bias towards integration. See e.g. Arter, *The Poltics of European Integration*, ch. 9 and Holland, *European Integration*, ch. 9.

[9] See in particular, T. M. Franck (ed.), *Why Federations Fail: An Enquiry into the Requisites for Successful Federalism*, New York, New York University Press, 1968. For a general discussion of this literature, see Preston King, *Federalism and Federation*, London, Croom Helm, 1982, ch. 6.

[10] See Dyson, *Elusive Union*; also Kenneth Dyson, Kevin Featherstone, and George Michalopolous, 'The Politics of EMU: The Maastricht Treaty and the Relevance of Bargaining Models', Paper before the Annual Meeting of the American Political Science Association, New York, 1994; Sandholz, 'Choosing Union'.

what the countries of the European Community were engaged in was the creation of a new political entity. Put another way, the result of the bargaining process was the creation of something resembling a federal state. In historical and comparative perspective what they were doing was much more akin to the proceedings at Philadelphia in 1787 than to the negotiations over the General Agreement on Tariffs and Trade, or the adoption of the Single European Act, which are often used as comparators for the decision-making process at Maastricht.

Given the scope and scale of Maastricht, we have to go much further than analysing the complexities of the bargaining process, or attempting to explain this process in terms of the disaggregated motives of the leading participants. As Maastricht led to the adoption of a federal-like constitution involving the acceptance of common policies, focusing on what the participants shared in common rather than what separated them may be of great heuristic value.

Although largely ignored by students of European union, there is a body of literature which attempts to synthesis the common motivations of politicians with the specific question of why states decide to form political unions.[11] William Riker's work on federalism explains the decision to form federations in terms of the perceived costs and benefits to the negotiating parties. Federations emerge when the benefits of enlargement exceed the costs. Nascent federations are in danger of failing (or breaking up) when the costs borne by the component states are perceived to be greater than the benefits derived from remaining in the federation.[12] Although Riker's work is firmly in the realist school—early versions of his thesis considered the aversion of external threats as the *only* factor in the cost/benefit calculus—he does not take some abstract notion of the nation state as the basic unit of analysis. For him rationally calculating *individuals* are the key actors. He explains the creation of the United States, therefore, not in terms of the interests of the original thirteen states, but in terms of the perceptions of a group of politicians—the Founding Fathers—who represent both the thirteen states and the emergent Union.[13]

[11] But see Michael Burgess and Alain-G. Gagnon (eds.), *Comparative Federalism and Federation: Competing Traditions and Future Directions*, London, Harvester Wheatsheaf, 1993, chs. 1 and 6.

[12] Riker, *Federalism*, ch. 3. See also his 'Federalism', in Fred I. Greenstein and Nelson W. Polsby, *The Handbook of Political Science*, vol. v: *Government Institutions and Processes*, Reading, Mass., Addison Wesley, 1975, 93–172.

[13] Riker, *Federalism*, 20–5.

Riker's work has the advantage, therefore, of synthesizing the realist perspectives of international relations theory with the rational choice tradition in political science. It also had the advantage of stressing the agreed interest which the participants *must* have (or believe they have) before they cede power to a higher political authority. In addition, Riker provides a coherent framework for the analysis not only of the origins of unions but also for identifying those conditions under which they are likely to survive. No other theoretical perspective provides us with such potentially powerful analytic tools.

Most of his work on federalism was written in the 1950s and 1960s, however, and as a result reflects both the political events and the intellectual fashions of that period. As will be developed in Chapter 2, he underplays the role of mass-élite linkages in the formation of unions, and much in the mould of the dominant realist thinkers of the time, reduces explanation to a single cause: the presence or absence of an external military or diplomatic threat or opportunity for aggrandizement. As already suggested, such a perspective is clearly inappropriate to the conditions prevalent in Europe in the 1980s and 1990s. The present volume adapts Riker's framework by developing his conception of threat and opportunity to include internal[14] or domestic political threats and opportunities. In other words, the events leading up to the adoption of the Maastricht Treaty are characterized in terms of the presence of political threats and opportunities which, in varying degrees, were perceived to be present in all the signatory countries in the late 1980s and early 1990s. Politicians agreed to European Union because they believed that the political benefits of doing so exceeded the political costs involved in remaining in a loose confederation of states.

This calculation was not the same for actors in all countries. In most, the electoral consequences of inflation and competitive devaluations were paramount. In others these considerations were conflated into a wider concern that a failure to control inflation might threaten not just incumbent governments but political stability. Put another way, by the late 1980s a new paradigm of economic management had emerged which made the fight against inflation the highest priority for all member states. What then were the motives of the Germans who had little to gain through association with high inflation states? On the face of it, understanding German motives in agreeing to monetary union presents

[14] In his later work Riker accepted that internal *military* threats could become part of the federal contract, but he never addressed the question of internal non-military political threats. See Riker, 'Federalism'.

a number of difficulties. It may be that the Germans see European Union as a way of reasserting a foreign policy role commensurate with their economic power. A more cynical interpretation is that the Germans never expected the European federal bargain to apply to more than a core of fiscally sound states, most of whom were already integrated with the German economy.

This book assigns pride of place to *political* explanations of European union and rejects both the economistic and ideological perspectives. Of course the economic context of the period is crucial to understanding the move towards union, and of course some degree of common cultural, economic, and political interest exists among the countries of Europe. But on their own these phenomena explain little. Common interest among the European family of nations is centuries old, and in this century alone, inflation has wrought havoc in many of the countries of the EU. Yet it was only in the late 1980s and early 1990s that the political trade-offs fell the right way for the acceptance of the need for federal-like arrangements. In other words, political unions do not emerge automatically because of some common interest, nor do particular economic conditions—however extreme—produce this result.

The Rikerian perspective can also be adapted to cast light on the prospects for the European Union's survival. By definition this exercise must be limited: Maastricht marked the *beginning* of a process that would lead to full union. What will happen over the next few years in terms of the achievement of specific goals, and indeed whether full union will emerge, is anybody's guess. According to the rational choice approach, emerging unions will not survive if the original conditions necessary for the creation of the union prove either (*a*) to be invalid; or (*b*) are removed or disappear soon after the act of union.[15] In the European context it may be that the politicians responsible for the Treaty misperceived the nature of the internal and external political threats. Or it may be that these threats will soon evaporate, thus removing the union's *raison d'être*. While we can speculate on these questions we obviously cannot answer them.

What we can do, however, is follow through the logic implicit in the rational choice framework and then speculate on the likely political problems which the EU may encounter. We can also make some judgements as to whether these problems will be sufficiently great to constitute

[15] Riker, *Federalism*, ch. 3.

a challenge to the integrity of the newly formed union. There are two dimensions to this exercise. There is, first, the natural tension that exists between what might be called centralists (or nationalists) and decentralists (or anti-nationalists). Centralists assign the highest priority to the union's main political goal: the avoidance of electoral and political instability. Decentralists assign top priority to other values: distributional questions of wealth, income, cultural or linguistic identity, and equality. This tension is at the heart of most of the debate about the allocation of governmental functions not just in the European Union but in all other unions or federations.[16] The Maastricht Treaty's major device for stabilizing politics in the member states was to give the central government control over a range of economic policies and in particular macroeconomic policy. By so doing the Treaty's provisions reduced the potential capacity of national governments to deal with some aspects of distributional policy by removing individual countries' freedom to vary interest rates and money supplies and to devalue or revalue their currencies. By implication, at least, after monetary union is achieved, national governments will be obliged either to use fiscal policy alone when dealing with inequalities and the distributional consequences of asymmetric economic and political shocks (such as energy crises), or will have to rely on the largesse of Brussels as a source of redistribution.[17]

Later chapters will develop this theme by comparing the potential nature and extent of these tensions in the EU with the actual pattern prevalent in other federations and in particular the United States.

Second, as a number of students of federalism have pointed out, the major device for mediation in federal systems is the party system.[18] Through their interaction with the federation's institutional structures, political parties perform crucial representational and allocational

[16] This was, of course, the essence of much of the debate at the constitutional convention at Philadelphia in 1787 and it dominated the ratification process. For a general review of the American and other cases, see S. Rufus Davis, *The Federal Principle: A Journey Through Time in Quest of a Meaning*, Berkeley and Los Angeles, University of California Press, 1978.

[17] A growing economics literature is aware of the political problems associated with monetary integration, but political scientists have so far paid little attention to the problem. See e.g. Michael Emerson *et al.*, *One Market, One Money: An Evaluation of the Potential Benefits and Costs of Forming an Economic and Monetary Union*, Oxford, OUP, 1992; J.-P. Fitoussi *et al.*, *Competitive Disinflation: The Mark and Budgetary Politics in Europe*, Oxford, OUP, 1993; C. A. E. Goodhart, *EMU and ESCB After Maastricht*, London, LSE Financial Markets Group, 1992.

[18] Riker, 'Federalism', 137–41.

functions. Generally speaking, the more decentralized the party system the more decentralized the union. In this context, the EU is a very unusual political union. It lacks a fully developed range of representative institutions and its political parties are so decentralized that it is difficult to see how they can perform a mediating representational and allocational role. An undeveloped and highly peripheralized institutional structure would not matter if the public functions assigned to the centre were also undeveloped. But they are not. It is this disjunction between highly centralized policy formation and implementation (in selected areas) and highly decentralized representational institutions and processes that make the European such an odd political animal. Again, by drawing on the historical and contemporary experience of other federations, and particularly the United States, the problems of the emerging European Union can be placed in perspective.

THE CHAPTERS TO COME

Chapter 2 has two objectives. It deals first with problems of definition and establishes that, by the most commonly accepted definitions, the European Union is indeed a species of federal state. Second, the chapter presents an intellectual justification for studying the origins and viability of political union in terms of a rational choice framework. This is accomplished by reviewing competing explanations, most of which are drawn from the comparative politics literature on federalism. The shortcomings of the Rikerian model are also exposed, and adaptations are suggested, which go some way towards meeting these failings.

Chapter 3 places the origins and development of the European Community in this theoretical context. Particular emphasis is placed on the early history of the Community, and to explaining why it was that European union failed to emerge in the 1950s and the 1960s. Later developments are also covered, including the response of the Community to the economic dislocations of the 1970s when, rather than the Community coming together, it seemed in danger of falling apart. Chapter 4 highlights the quite startling moves towards greater integration—and eventually union—as represented by the Single European Act and, in particular, the Maastricht Treaty. A clear distinction is drawn between the two initiatives. While the former was in the tradition of the original Treaty of Rome, proposing a genuine customs union for member states, the latter was a patently political act driven by a perception among national and Community-level élites that only political union could prevent domestic electoral and political instability. While these domestic political pressures stemmed from structural changes in national and international economies, economic factors are not, on their own, sufficient to explain the move to union. Chapter 5 will provide evidence of the commitment to what was expected to be the low inflation regime of the European Monetary System, membership of which was viewed as an essential prelude to full monetary union, by reviewing the turmoil on the foreign exchange markets in 1992 and 1993. Special attention is paid to the behaviour of the Nordic countries, all of whom had adopted a strategy of 'shadowing' the Deutschmark and all of whom were applicants for EU membership. Their actions provide further evidence of the extent to which politicians in a range of countries were prepared to make sacrifices in order to ensure price stability.

Chapters 6 and 7 are concerned with the potential viability of European Union. Chapter 6 synthesizes those theories, drawn both from political science and economics, which attempt to explain the relationship between fiscal or economic centralization and political centralization. The chapter also points to those conditions which are likely to determine a particular level of centralization in any federation by highlighting the role played by political parties as mediators between the centre and the periphery. Ultimately, this role depends on the extent to which citizens identify with the federal (or central) government as opposed to the governments of the component states. Chapter 7 attempts to apply some of these theories to the European context. As monetary union is as yet only a prospect, this exercise must, by definition, be hypothetical in nature. None the less an attempt is made to draw systematic comparisons with other federal systems, and in particular the United States. Comparisons focus on the union's vulnerability to external shocks, the conditions under which fiscal centralization is likely to occur, the level of public support for Europe-wide institutions, and the role played by political parties as mediators between the centre and the periphery.

The final chapter provides an audit on the future prospects of the EU, with particular attention focused on the likely scenarios under which the union, or parts of the union, might break up. Although by definition speculative, this exercise will at all times be informed by the book's theoretical framework.

2

Federal Theory and European Union

INTRODUCTION

Although the study of federalism as a form of political organization has been a topic in political philosophy at least since the publication of Althusius's *Politica* in 1603,[1] it was not until the creation of the United States that the conception of federalism as political *community* was established. Hitherto, federalism had been defined in terms of leagues or collectivities of states each with a separate identity and distinct citizenry. In contrast, the Founding Fathers stressed the need for citizens to hold a dual identity; to become citizens both of the component states and to hold a common national identity. Samuel Beer has made this point well:

> In the national perspective, although we are one people who enjoy a common life as one nation, we have set up not a unitary but a dual system of government. In establishing this system, the American people authorized and empowered two sets of governments: a general government for the whole, and state governments for the parts.[2]

Constitutional arrangements reflected this dual status. Taxes could be levied at both the federal and at the state levels; the federal government was assigned carefully enumerated powers, with those powers not enumerated 'reserved' to the states.[3] Put another way, the Founding Fathers established that an essential feature of a federal system was that the activities of government would be divided between a central authority and regional authorities and that each would make final decisions in its assigned sphere of activity. Crucially, the Founding Fathers were clever enough not to be too rigid as to the precise delineation of powers between the different levels of government. In all federal systems the balance between central and regional governments ebbs and flows. In

[1] For a full discussion, see Carl J. Friedrich, *Trends of Federalism in Theory and Practice*, London, Pall Mall Press, 1968, ch. 2.

[2] Samuel H. Beer, *To Make A Nation: The Rediscovery of American Federalism*, Cambridge, Mass., Harvard University Press, 1993, 1.

[3] For a full discussion, see James Madison, Alexander Hamilton, and John Jay, *The Federalist Papers*, Harmondsworth, Penguin, 1987, also Isaac Kramnick's 'Editor's Introduction'.

this sense it is misleading to interpret federalism as a system characterized by dual sovereignty. Sovereignty is indivisible; it implies a constellation of fixed and irrevocable powers reserved to a particular level of government.[4] In reality, no government, whether national or regional, has sovereignty over its activities. All are constrained to a greater or lesser degree whether by external or internal political and economic forces. The modern conception of federalism is, rather, that the principle of the division of powers between centre and regions is established constitutionally and that citizens hold an identity at both levels. At the minimum the component states should have the right to territorial integrity, to some representation in the institutions of the central or federal government, and to be protected by the federal authority from external aggression. Given that federalism is a constantly adapting process rather than a system of government amenable to some fixed definition, it should come as no surprise that considerable variations on the theme exist or that scholars have devoted a great deal of time to questions of definition.[5] Some have argued that a true federation exists only if the federal government provides for the common defence.[6] Others have stressed the economic dimension—all 'true' federations are characterized by some degree of fiscal centralization with the federal government engaged in redistribution via centrally collected tax revenues.[7] Certainly all of the world's major federations in the late twentieth century display both of these features. In the light of this literature, to what extent does the European Union (EU) qualify as a form of federal state?

THE EUROPEAN UNION: FEDERATION OR SUPRANATIONAL COMMUNITY?

Until the signing of the Maastricht Treaty, few observers characterized the European Community (EC) as a federation. For although the Community had, by the late 1980s, acquired what looked like the institutional

[4] For a discussion of sovereignty and federalism, see Preston King, *Federalism and Federation*, London, Croom Helm, 1982, ch. 9.

[5] For a review of the definitional problems involved, see William H. Riker, *Federalism: Origins, Operation, Significance*, Boston, Little Brown, 1964, chs. 2 and 3; also Alain-G. Gagnon, 'The Political Uses of Federalism', in Michael Burgess and Alain-G. Gagnon (eds.), *Comparative Federalism and Federation: Competing Traditions and Future Directions*, London, Harvester Wheatsheaf, 1993, 15–44.

[6] John Pinder, 'The New European Federalism', in Burgess and Gagnon, *Comparative Federalism*, 46.

[7] Ivo D. Duchacek, *Comparative Federalism: The Territorial Dimension of Politics*, New York, Holt, Rinehart and Winston, 1970, 222–30.

structure typical of a federal state, in practical terms it fell far short of meeting the minimal conditions for federation. The Council of Ministers did have real power to make policy, and the bureaucracy (the Commission) had also acquired considerable power to issue directives in line with the broad principles laid down by the Council of Ministers. Moreover, the Court of Justice was widely accepted as supreme over national courts and was accepted as the body responsible for adjudicating disputes. Finally, the European Parliament was a directly elected body with increasingly important powers over budgetary measures.

On closer examination, however, it becomes clear that almost all of the EC's functions were infused with the influence of national governments. In effect, no area of governmental activity was unambiguously the responsibility of EC institutions and policy makers. Even after the changes following the implementation of the Single European Act (SEA) which generally strengthened Community institutions, 'federation' would have been an inappropriate appellation for the EC. The Council of Ministers was not a unitary executive (or possibly the upper house of the legislature) but 'an intergovernmental negotiating forum',[8] made up of a collection of national politicians and diplomats. Most EC policies emanated from the Commission itself which was in turn penetrated by national governments and national interest groups. The EP had but a marginal role to play in policy-making. In no sense was it the main source of legislation acting on the mandate of the voters. Indeed, if one had to identify legitimate and accountable bodies with real power it would have to be the Commission and the Council given that their make-up was determined by democratically elected national politicians. Finally, although increasing quite rapidly, the scope of the EC's activities was quite limited in relation to the scope of national government activity. Agriculture remained the single most important area of EC activity in financial terms with regulation (on environmental, consumer, trade, and transportation matters) gaining rapidly in importance.

Given these strictures it is not surprising that commentators have talked not of federalism, but of 'intergovernmentalism' or 'supranationalism'.[9] What can be concluded is that by the late 1980s the EC had evolved into a very odd political animal—and certainly one

[8] Andrew Duff *et al.*, *Maastricht and Beyond: Building the European Union*, London, Routledge, 1994, 192.

[9] For a discussion of this point, see Robert O. Keohane and Stanley Hoffman (eds.), *The New Community of Europe: Decision Making and Institutional Change*, Boulder, Colo., Westview Press, 1991, 12–13.

with no parallel elsewhere. With the passage of the SEA it appeared to be moving towards a more federal-like structure. Qualified majority voting in the Council was introduced for some policy areas, thus limiting the use of national vetoes. The Commission was also given greater independence in relation to the Council, and the Parliament's role as a consultative, assenting, and amending body was strengthened.

As significant were pledges to work towards the adoption of a European foreign policy and 'to transform the relations as a whole among (the member) states into a European Union'. In other words, although the main objective of the SEA was to create a single market and provide for the free movement of labour, goods, and capital among the member states, the Act also contained clear political objectives, which all pointed in the direction of building a federation rather than a loose community of states. Finally, the participants were not only engaged in the 'deepening' of the Community, they were also actively working to widen membership so that eventually almost all European countries would belong to the Union.

As suggested, the federalist rhetoric and relatively minor institutional changes of the SEA did not transform the EC into a federation. However, they did help set the agenda for Maastricht where federalist rhetoric was in some respects translated into fact.

MAASTRICHT: THE BASIS OF A FEDERAL STATE

Both the negotiations and the eventual outcome at Maastricht were extremely complex and this is not the place for the sort of systematic account which has been provided quite adequately by others. Three aspects of the Treaty are of particular concern to us, which can be labelled institutional, rhetorical, and functional. Institutionally, Maastricht continued the incremental process of strengthening the European institutions in relation to national governments. The main changes involved the adoption of 'co-decision-making' by the Council and the Parliament. While the EP was denied the status of full legislature responsible for approving all laws, it was designated as a 'partner' of the Council in the sense that it could block Council positions in a number of designated policy areas. It was also given the power, by simple majority vote, to reject national governments' nominations to the Commission. Together with existing budgetary powers the EP would become, therefore, a sort of second legislature with primarily negative powers in relation to the 'first' legislature, the Council, which would remain the main source of major policy decisions in response to proposals originally emanating from the Commission.

Along with the extension of qualified majority voting in the Council these changes add up to a weakening of the member states in relation to the 'central' institutions of the Union. For although the Council of Ministers remains essentially a meeting of national heads of government and their representatives, the individual members of the Council are now more constrained in terms of their influence on internal decision-making and legislative and appointment powers.[10]

The rhetoric of Maastricht was indisputably federalist in nature. Indeed it was only at the insistence of the British that the European Union was labelled thus rather than being called a federation. This semantic quibbling by John Major is somewhat surprising given that by almost any known definition, a union implies at least as strong a central state as a federation.[11] This aside, attention should be brought to two further rhetorical flourishes in the Treaty. The first concerns the intention to establish a common European citizenship. In fact this amounted to something more than rhetoric as the Treaty mandated that Community citizens had the right to vote in local and EP elections if they were resident in any member state of the Union. Although these changes do go some way towards the creation of a European citizenship, the Treaty fell far short of creating full citizen rights and obligations, including the right to vote in all elections irrespective of nationality, the introduction of supranational EP constituencies, and the formal ratification of citizens' civil rights and liberties.[12] But the point remains that in its rhetoric, at least, the Treaty was clear in its determination eventually to create a European 'nation'.

Second, although the Treaty resolved to 'implement a common foreign and security policy, including the eventual framing of a common defence policy, which might lead in time to a common defence',[13] few meaningful institutional changes occurred. Foreign affairs and defence

[10] For a comprehensive description of these changes, see Richard Corbett, *The Treaty of Maastricht: From Conception to Ratification: A Comprehensive Reference Guide*, London, Longman, 1993, ch. 4.

[11] As Charles Bidwell notes, 'Semantics are otiose when trying to decide on a precise meaning of the word [union] in this context, and the clues are to be found in the tangible policies making up the union', quoted in *Maastricht and the UK*, London, PACE, 1993, 20–1.

[12] See Duff, *Maastricht and Beyond*, 29–30.

[13] Bidwell, *Maastricht and the UK*, 18.

remained very much a matter for intergovernmental co-operation rather then supranational co-ordination and direction.

Together with the provisions of the SEA these changes mark a clear move towards a federal-like political system. On their own, however, they amount to the creation of what might be called a peripheralized federalism. The governments of the component states would remain responsible for most aspects of domestic policy and, crucially, for foreign and defence policy. Maastricht is best known, however, not for these changes but for a fundamental shift in the functional allocation of economic policy from the national to the supranational level. The proposed monetary union would remove what is arguably the most important of government functions from the national level and reserve it exclusively to the supranational level. The proposed European Central Bank (ECB) would, moreover, be largely independent of political influence. As one American commentator puts it: 'the Europeans have created an instrument that would greatly widen the already large democratic gap. The Maastricht agreement would create a powerful body of Platonic guardians, effectively accountable to no one, yet with strong influence on the course of economic affairs.'[14] The negotiators at Maastricht, while not wholly agreed on the timetable for monetary union or the institutional details of the central bank, were determined to make monetary union the centre-piece of the Treaty.[15]

Two further aspects of the Treaty should be noted. First there is the acceptance of the principle of 'subsidiarity'. Article 3b Title II reads:

> The Community shall act within the limit of the powers conferred upon it by this Treaty and of the objectives assigned to it therein. In areas which do not fall within its exclusive competence, the Community shall take action, in accordance with the principle of subsidiarity, only if and insofar as the objectives of the proposed action cannot be sufficiently achieved by the Member States and can therefore, by reason of the scale or effects of the proposed action, be better achieved by the Community.[16]

By accepting that there were areas that were the 'exclusive' competence of the Community, and by assuming that with all other areas there should be a presumption of member state competence, the Treaty was formalizing a delineation of powers between the federal and the state

[14] Richard Cooper, quoted in Barry Eichengreen, *International Monetary Arrangements for the 21st Century*, Washington, Brookings Institution, 1994, 107.

[15] Kenneth Dyson, *Elusive Union: The Process of Economic and Monetary Union in Europe*, London, Longman, 1994, ch. 5.

[16] Quoted in Bidwell, *Maastricht and the UK*, 23.

or regional levels. And as with the Tenth Amendment to the United States Constitution, the Treaty also left great ambiguity as to how this delineation should work out in practice.

The major difference between the two documents is that the US Constitution is both more elegantly and more skilfully written than the Maastricht Treaty. For example, the Tenth Amendment—'The Powers not delegated to the United States by the Constitution, nor prohibited by it to the States, are reserved to the States respectively, or to the people'—says in simple language what the Maastricht Treaty says in convoluted prose without involving the slippery and ultimately elusive concept of subsidiarity.[17]

Second, the Treaty is infused not only with federalist rhetoric but also with specific intentions that the EU is on a path towards ever closer union. In this sense Maastricht should be viewed as an interim or provisional constitution rather than a formal and final statement. Again, the uniqueness of the European experience should be noted. Most federations begin with formal and final constitutions; the EU's transition to federalism has been incremental and is as yet incomplete.

We can conclude, however, that although, after the implementation of Maastricht, the EU would remain an unusual and still evolving political entity, it would also qualify as a species of federal state. Almost all of the conditions for federalism will then have been met, including the assumption of exclusive powers for the federal government, the acceptance of two levels of citizenship, and a supranational institutional framework, which, in some areas at least, provides for Europe-wide policy-making by European politicians and officials rather than what has been called 'intergovernmentalism' or policy-making by *ad hoc* meetings of national representatives. As indicated, by some criteria, European federalism remains incomplete. In the defence and foreign policy sphere no genuine shift in responsibilities has occurred. Mere good intentions have prevailed. Institutionally, the Council of Ministers is far from being a genuinely federal body answerable to a Europe-wide electorate. The powers of the EP are also limited compared with legislatures in most modern federations. Finally, the Court of Justice has

[17] The EU actually accepts this in its own documentation. Consider the following, for example: 'Subsidiarity is a dynamic concept and should be applied in the light of the objectives set out in the Treaty. It allows Community action to be expanded where circumstances so require, and conversely, to be restricted or discontinued where it is no longer justified. 'Conclusions of the Edinburgh Meeting of the Council of Ministers', from Corbett, *The Treaty of Maastricht*, 496.

only limited jurisdiction with no brief available over foreign policy and defence matters. All this accepted, moves towards 'federalizing' all three institutions have occurred and are likely to continue. Even without such moves, the full implementation of Maastricht will witness the complete transfer of monetary policy to a federal institution. We should be in no doubt, therefore, that unusual though it is, what we are dealing with in Europe is an emerging federal state.

FEDERAL THEORY AND EUROPEAN UNION

When attempting to explain the phenomenon of a developing European federation an obvious starting-point is federal theory or that body of work devoted to explaining the emergence and viability of federations. This general subject area attracted a great deal of attention in the twenty years following the end of the Second World War. During this period two distinct phases of state-building occurred, one involving the constitutional arrangements for the defeated Axis powers and the other the constitutional arrangements for former European colonies. In both cases federal political structures were considered the most appropriate systems for a range of countries. In addition, the federal idea received fresh impetus from the post-war debate on the future of Europe. Following two devastating wars in just thirty-five years some political leaders, especially on the Continent of Europe, were convinced that the only way to ensure peace was to cement the countries of Western Europe together in federal system of government. Given this context it is not surprising that most scholars writing on the subject had an essentially sanguine view of federal-like political arrangements. In the former colonies federalism was seen as a means of exploiting the economic and political advantages of the old colonial borders while also preserving a degree of autonomy for distinct ethnic, linguistic, and religious groupings. In the case of Germany, federalism was seen as a means of preventing the re-emergence of a strong central state. Finally, most commentators pointed to the successful examples of federations in the New World. Australia, Canada, and, especially, the United States, were held up as exemplars of countries enjoying democracy and economic growth while at the same time preserving a degree of regional or provincial autonomy.

By the 1960s, therefore, most of the academic scholarship on the subject viewed federalism as a device for achieving particular political or economic ends. Two broad schools of thought emerged around this theme. One school, associated with the work of Karl Deutsch, K. C. Wheare, and R. L. Watts, saw federalism as an appropriate political form should certain pre-conditions organized around the notion of common interest exist. A second school, associated with the work of Thomas M. Franck, conflated the subjective question of the essential desirability of federalism with the objective conditions of the countries involved in the federalizing process. In this sense federalism acquired a distinctive ideological status. 'Federalists', convinced of the intrinsic benefits of federation, could, in the right circumstances, bring about the fact of federation. It would be fair to say that most observers of the current European scene would attempt to explain federalizing trends in Europe in terms of one or both of these perspectives. In other words 'ever closer union' is happening because of a conviction among the interested parties that union is intrinsically beneficial and/or because the countries of the EU share a range of common interests which makes the objective of federation both feasible and desirable. However, a critical examination of both perspectives demonstrates that neither constitutes an adequate explanation of the origins of political unions.

Federalism as Common Interest

Writing in 1957 with specific reference to the feasibility of federations as potential security communities, Karl Deutsch outlined what he called the 'essential' conditions for a federation:

1. mutual compatibility of main values
2. a distinctive way of life
3. expectation of stronger economic ties or gains
4. marked increase in administrative capabilities of at least some participating units
5. superior economic growth on the part of at least some participating units
6. unbroken links of social communication both geographically between territories and sociologically between different social strata
7. a broadening of the political élite
8. mobility of persons at least among the politically relevant strata
9. a multiplicity of ranges of communications and transactions.[18]

[18] Karl Deutsch *et al.*, *Political Community in the North Atlantic Area*, Princeton, Princeton University Press, 1957, 58.

As a number of commentators have pointed out, none of Deutsch's criteria are universal. A. H. Birch applied the list to the new federations of Nigeria, East Africa, and Malaysia. Only 3, 4, 5, and 9 were present in all three cases, although to be fair none of these federations survived in their original forms.[19] K. C. Wheare and R. L. Watts have produced shorter, more commonsensical lists which, they claim, federations may exhibit at their inception. Wheare lists the following:

1. a sense of military insecurity and the need for a common defence
2. a desire to be independent of foreign powers, for which the union is necessary
3. a hope of economic advantage
4. some previous political association
5. geographic neighbourhood
6. similarity of political institutions.[20]

Watts expanded Wheare's criteria to include the following:

7. a need for efficiency
8. community of outlook based on race, religion, language or culture
9. enterprising character of the leadership
10. existence of models
11. influence of the United Kingdom government in constitution making[21]

Again, neither of these lists has universal application (by definition in Watt's case as he is dealing specifically with British Commonwealth countries). Even the most simple of empirical tests confirms that this is so. There are, first, those instances of groups of countries which clearly share a common interest but which have failed to form lasting federations. In Scandinavia, for example, at least three states (Sweden, Norway, and Denmark) have a high degree of cultural, linguistic, religious, political, and economic common interest. Yet political co-operation goes no further than the Nordic Council, which has no constitutional authority. A similar degree of common interest exists among the countries

[19] A. H. Birch, 'Approaches to the Study of Federalism', *Political Studies*, 14/1, 1966, 22–30.

[20] K. C. Wheare, *Federal Government*, Oxford, OUP, 3rd edn., 1956, 37–8.

[21] R. L. Watts, *New Federations: Experiments in the Commonwealth*, Oxford, OUP, 1966, 42.

of Central America, but their one attempt at federation failed with the constituent parts breaking up into separate units in 1839.[22]

Second, there are many instances of groups of countries forming federations where there is little evidence of the existence of common interest criteria (3, 4, 5, and 8 in the list above). The former Soviet Union contained within its boundaries great linguistic, cultural, religious, and economic diversity. At its inception, the United States consisted of at least three quite distinct socio-economic systems—a vast frontier region based on a hunting and trapping economy; the coastal North-east based on smallholding and trade, and the South with its slave-based cash crop economy. Malaysia is a further example of a federation displaying great diversity among the states of its component parts. In sum, although common interest criteria may be present at the formation of federations, there are no hard and fast rules about which particular economic, social, geographic, or political characteristics have to be present. Clearly, countries which come together to form unions are likely to share some features in common—a point we will return to later. But on its own, the common interest approach has little or no explanatory power. In the Europe of the 1990s, for example, only 3, 4, and 5 on the Wheare/Watts list could unambiguously be identified as important and all of these have, in varying degrees, been features of the European scene for several centuries.

Federalism as Ideology

A normative element is, of course, at least implicit in the common interest approach. Because certain benefits will flow from the co-operation of a group of countries sharing certain characteristics, federation or political union is *ipso facto* a good thing. Advocates of co-operation, or federalists, show, therefore, a commitment to the idea of federalism, which in turn may help transform that idea into reality. In his study *Why Federations Fail* Franck formalizes this reasoning by accepting that although common interest may be *useful* for federation and in some cases may be *necessary*, it is certainly not *sufficient* for the maintenance of a successful federation. Ideological commitment to the *idea* of federation, on the other hand, he considers a necessary condition and in some circumstances a sufficient condition. This 'positive political or ideological commitment to the *primary* goal of federation *as an end in*

[22] Common interest can be a powerful non-political force in areas as wide apart as sport and transportation. The West Indies have no difficulty identifying with a common cricket team, for example, and the Scandinavians happily share an airline.

itself' (emphasis in original)[23] can emanate either from élite leadership or from the 'broadly shared values of the people',[24] although in developing societies (which were the subject of his study) a deep commitment to federalism from élites was considered more important than pre-existing popular support for the idea. Although Franck acknowledges that political élites' commitment to federalism was ultimately linked to particular *interests*,[25] he fails to elaborate on the precise relationship between ideology and interest. Instead, the causal chain ends with the beliefs and values of political leaders. This is unfortunate because it leaves unanswered the question of *why* élites are so convinced of the value of federation. It also leaves Franck and other scholars working in the same tradition open to the accusation that all it needs for the creation of a successful federation is a belief in the value of such arrangements. Identification of which interests in the proposed federation are like to gain or lose from the new system and in particular why the representatives of national governments are willing to give up some national independence to a supranational or federal authority is not at the core of his analysis.

Riker makes this point very bluntly in his critique of Carl Friederich's work on federalism:

> A tremendous amount of propagandizing and even political organizing has been based on the mistaken premise that somehow, if people just work hard enough for it, federation will occur. It is perhaps unkind to disturb such naive faith, but the hope of the scientific enterprise is that the more people know, the more effectively they can act. A particularly unfortunate example of this naiveté is to be found in Friedrich (1968),[26] where it said that federalism is a process of federalizing, as if such a thing comes about by some kind of magic without rational human calculation. (This example is doubly unfortunate, if as the author claims in his preface, this is the frequent advice he has offered to real politicians in the European Community).[27]

More recently, a critic of the federalist trends in the European Union has made much the same point by noting that federalist ideologues seem to believe in some 'kind of cartographic mysticism that intuits that certain large areas of the map are crying out to merge as single

[23] Thomas M. Franck (ed.), *Why Federations Fail*, New York, New York University Press, 1968, 173.

[24] Ibid. 174.

[25] Ibid., pp. xiii–xiv.

[26] Friedrich, *Trends of Federalism in Theory and Practice*.

[27] William H. Riker, 'Federalism', in Fred I. Greenstein and Nelson Polsby (eds.), *The Handbook of Political Science*, vol. v: *Government Institutions and Processes*, Reading, Mass., Addison Wesley, 1975, 131.

geopolitical units'.[28] To be fair to Franck in particular, he is not necessarily a federalist ideologue himself. In his study he is merely identifying the importance of the ideological commitment to federalism on the part of political leaders.

As earlier indicated, however, some students of the subject have pointed to the intrinsic advantages of federalism. In the European context, integration theory is infused with such assumptions. Starting with David Mitrany's work in the inter-war period all the way to the neofunctionalists of the 1980s and 1990s, a small army of scholars have argued that ever closer economic and political integration is the best way to avoid the destructive nationalisms which in the past have wrought such havoc among the peoples of Europe.[29] Moreover, functional integration in key economic areas have an internal logic of their own. Once interdependence is established in one area it will spill over into others. Eventually, only supranational political institutional arrangements can accommodate this complex interdependence. This body of work represents much more than mere scholarship given that many of its standard bearers, including Jean Monnet, have been leading figures in the drive for European integration. While this is not the place to reprise the many debates surrounding this literature, it is worth noting that as an explanation of the formation of political unions, integration theory in all its variants is open to a number of trenchant criticisms.

There is, first, the simple historical fact that European integration did not, as the early integrationists predicted, proceed on some linear path towards ever closer union. On the contrary, progress towards integration was erratic and halting. It is true that the proponents of integration theory did not always claim that spillover was automatic—a convergence of interests between states was also necessary to achieve institutional change.[30] But this caveat did nothing to discourage both academic and political proponents of further integration from insisting that there was something inevitable about a convergence of interests among the countries of Europe.[31]

[28] Noel Malcolm, 'The Case Against Europe', *Foreign Affairs*, Mar./Apr. 1995, 53.

[29] For a summary of this literature, see Michael Burgess, *Federalism and European Union: Political Ideas, Influences and Strategies in the European Community 1972–1987*, London, Routledge, 1989, chs. 1 and 2.

[30] For a discussion of this point see Robert O. Keohane and Stanley Hoffmann (eds.), *The New European Community: Decision Making and Institutional Change*, Boulder, Colo., Westview Press, 1991, ch. 1.

[31] See e.g. Andrew Duff, John Pinder, and Roy Pryce (eds.), *Maastricht and Beyond: Building the European Union*, London, Routledge, 1994.

As serious, numerous examples of highly integrated states or groups of states can be found which have not proceeded towards political integration or which have actually disintegrated. Canada and the United States are, for example, closely integrated economically but have witnessed no irresistible drive towards political union. Russia and the Ukraine had achieved a very high level of economic interdependence by the last decades of the Soviet Union, but none the less broke away from one another. Even more telling is the example of the former Czechoslovakia, which was highly integrated both politically and economically and where that part of the country with most to lose from secession (Slovakia) actually led the movement to secede.[32]

Ultimately, the integrationists and their neo-functionalist successors hold such an ideological commitment to integration as an end in itself that they infer spurious causes from perceived outcomes. As will be argued below, the fact of integration has much more to do with the interaction of politically articulated interests than with some quality inherent in the act of integrating.

Federalism as a Rational Bargain: Adapting the Riker Model

The interaction of politically articulated interests is at the heart of the third approach to the origins of federations. At its most elemental this perspective argues that the decision to form federations depends on the costs and benefits to the politicians involved in the process. Two sets of actors contribute to this calculus: politicians representing the national or state governments and politicians (drawn from one or more of the existing national governments) hoping to represent the new supranational (or federal) government. The latter offer the benefits of enlargement and the former concede some independence because they calculate that the benefits of enlargement outweigh the costs. The most prominent advocate of this approach, William Riker, is in little doubt about the nature of these costs and benefits. Taking an essentially Hobbesian approach, he argues that politicians are, above all, concerned with the territorial integrity of their states. Some may wish to form a union in order to advance freedom and democracy and some to encourage larger markets or to enhance economic growth. Empirically, however,

[32] On the political circumstances of the breakup of Czechoslovakia, see Carlos Flores Juberias, 'The Break Up of the Czechoslovak Federation: Political Strategies and Constitutional Choices', Paper Before the ECPR Joint Sessions of Workshops, Bordeaux, 27 April–2 May 1995.

such motivations among collectivities of states do not always lead to federal-like political arrangements and, crucially, do not always lead to the creation of *successful* unions. Instead, the following two conditions must always be present at the inception of successful unions:

1. A desire on the part of politicians who offer the bargain in order to expand their territorial control by peaceful means, either to meet an external military or diplomatic threat or to prepare for diplomatic aggrandizement. But though they desire to expand, they are not able to do so by conquest, because of either military incapacity or ideological distaste. Hence, if they are to satisfy the desire to expand, they must offer concessions to the rulers of constituent units, which is the essence of the federal bargain. The pre-disposition of those who offer the bargain is, then, that federalism is the only feasible means to accomplish a desired expansion without the use of force.

2. The politicians who accept the bargain, giving up some independence for the sake of union, are willing to do so, because of some external military-diplomatic threat or opportunity. Either they desire protection from an external threat or they desire to participate in the potential aggression of the federation. And furthermore the desire for either protection or participation outweighs any desire they may have for independence. The pre-disposition is the cognizance of the pressing need for the military strength or diplomatic maneuverability that comes with a larger and presumably stronger government. (It is not, of course, necessary that their assessment be objectively correct).[33]

Riker accepted a modification to this scheme by A. H. Birch which extended the perceived threat to include *internal* challenges to a political entity. Invoking the examples of Malaysia and Nigeria, Birch argued that some federations come into being as a result of a bargain between politicians eager to avert a threat from some part or parts of the potential union to the rest.[34] Neither Birch nor Riker are able to identify examples of successful federations which do *not* fit their theory.[35]

Riker's work has been subject to a number of criticisms, three of which are of central concern to any attempt to apply the scheme to the European context. There is, first, the alleged vagueness with which he treats the concept of 'threat'. There are three strands to this critique. First, all political systems or states with a defence capability are, by definition, actually or potentially exposed to some non-peaceful challenge by other states with defence capabilities. As military threat is universal, it can always be invoked to explain political change.[36] But

[33] Riker, *Federalism*, 12–13.
[34] A. H. Birch, 'Approaches to the Study of Federalism', *Political Studies*, 14/1, 1966, 32.
[35] Birch, 'Approaches to the Study of Federalism'; Riker, *Federalism*, 115–28.
[36] Preston King, *Federalism and Federation*, London, Croom Helm, 1982, 80–1.

this line of thinking misses the point. Potential threats may indeed be universal, but the world is characterized by a wide variety of political systems. The mere existence of threat may lead to a country's demise (Austria, 1939) and when converted into military action often results in disappearance (Poland, 1939). In other cases, external threats, whether exercised or not, may lead states into adopting a high degree of centralization (China after the Communist revolution, Britain in the Second World War). Or, internal threats may lead hitherto centralized states to devolve powers to regions or provinces (present-day Italy and Spain). In other cases again, something resembling federal arrangements emerge. In other words, the universality of threats to the territorial integrity of states in no way predicts how politicians respond and what the institutional / constitutional results will be. In the case of emerging federations geographic proximity and some common history or interest are likely to be present—although they do not *have* to be. What *has* to exist, however, is a perception among politicians that the costs and benefits for all the interested parties fall in such a way that the bargain is worth striking.

A related problem is that Riker fails to tell us what *level* of threat is likely to lead to political union. Nor does he tell us what weight to ascribe to threats as opposed to other motivations including 'greed, hope or fatigue'.[37] The latter is, in fact, irrelevant if Riker's realist perspective is accepted. For politicians will voluntarily give up political power *only* if they believe that a threat to the existing territory exists and which can be resolved through enlargement. Other values, including hope or greed, simply do not come into it. As for the level of threat, this must always be a matter for empirical investigation. Recall Riker's claim that it is the *perceptions* of politicians involved in the bargain rather than objective reality that is important. If they *believe* that the trade-offs involved fall the right way, they will go ahead with union.

A third criticism of Riker's use of perceived threats centres on his insistence that the threats must be military or diplomatic. The reason for this uncompromising position is, simply, that he could find no empirical evidence to refute it. Given this, he is angered by more traditional federal theorists who take what he calls economistic or ideological positions. The ideologists are convinced that federal political arrangements encourage freedom and democracy. Economistic approaches see a clear relationship between federalism and economic growth. Empirically, however, neither is true. For many decades federal

[37] Ibid. 84–5.

Mexico languished in the economic doldrums while its federal partner to the north experienced rapid economic growth. Federal Mexico, Yugoslavia, and the Soviet Union proscribed, in varying degrees, free political expression, while the United States and Canada encouraged it. As long ago as 1975 Riker railed against these misconceptions specifically in the European context:

> If this theory [on the importance of military and diplomatic threats] is important, as I believe it is, then one of the profound misunderstandings of the last generation is the question of what will engender a European Union of federation or, on another level of discourse, a world federalism. For either to appear there must be some significant threat. And in the absence of a threat large enough to render the federal bargain mutually profitable to the participating governments, there is nothing that will bring such unions as these about, no matter how much people *wish* for them to happen.[38]

For Riker, the formation of political unions is about political power. Sensing dangers and/or opportunities, politicians make rational calculations involving certain trade-offs. After the bargain is struck it may be, of course, that particular desiderata, including economic growth, will follow; but equally they may not. Riker's insistence that the threats must be military or diplomatic is based on two premisses, one theoretical and one empirical. Empirically, he can find no example of an emergent and successful federation where such threats do not play a significant part. Theoretically, political leaders will only exchange power resources if the stakes are high, and nothing is more important than the protection of a state's territorial integrity.

There is nothing in the logic of Riker's scheme to suggest that the threat *has* to be military or diplomatic, however. By the time of his last major contribution on the subject in 1975, he had already conceded that the threat could be internally as well as externally generated.[39] Empirically, the examples of internal threats provided by Birch happened to involve actual or potential military challenges to part or parts of the emerging federations (Nigeria and Malaysia),[40] but there is no reason why the threat, if sufficiently grave, could not come from some other source, political, economic, or social. Certainly if politicians believed that the existing constitutional order was threatened in some way (whether by external or internal forces) and that association with a

[38] Riker, 'Federalism', 130–1.
[39] Ibid. 114–15.
[40] Birch, 'Approaches to the Study of Federalism', 31–2.

larger political unit might remove or avert that threat, then Riker's conditions would be fulfilled. In a sense, Riker concedes this possibility by including *diplomatic* as well as military threats and opportunities. By so doing he is conceding that what politicians are doing when forming federations is bargaining to preserve the national interest—although he does not actually use this term himself. It may that this interest is better served by becoming a secure but smaller part of a larger entity than remaining a weaker and insecure independent state.

Logically, threats to the national interest could be military, diplomatic, economic, social, or whatever. This is a matter for empirical investigation. What is important is not the source of the threat but the political calculation that this threat can be reduced or averted by joining a political union or federation. Writing in the 1960s and the 1970s, it is not surprising that Riker reduced his explanation to military and diplomatic threats alone. He was clearly influenced by the dominant realist perspective on international relations which saw the national interest as a synonym for the successful protection of discrete nation states from external aggression. Since then, research in international relations and history has shifted away from treating the nation state as a unitary actor. The links between domestic politics and the international environment, including international institutions, have been recognized as an important influence on how politicians behave in defence of the national interest.[41] Some scholars have even argued that international co-operation can, in fact, strengthen the nation state by changing the terms on which domestic political interests bargain with national executives.[42] National politicians may, therefore, see some advantage in international co-operation in order to remove or reduce some domestic threat or threats. Riker would, I think, concede this point, but would demand evidence that there was a broad consensus among the national politicians of all the countries involved in union-building that association with a larger political entity would remove a threat which in some way constituted a challenge to the prevailing political order. We will return to this point later.

[41] This perspective has been championed by the journal *International Organization*. See also Robert O. Keohane and Joseph S. Nye, Jr., *Power and Interdependence: World Politics in Transition*, Boston, Little, Brown, 2nd edn. 1989; Peter B. Evans, Harold K. Jacobson, and Robert D. Putnam, *Double Edged Diplomacy: International Bargaining and Domestic Politics*, Berkeley and Los Angeles, University of California Press, 1993.

[42] Andrew Moravcsik, 'Introduction: Integrating International and Domestic Theories of International Bargaining', in Evans, Jacobson, and Putnam, *Double Edged Diplomacy*, 1–42. For an economic historians perspective, see Alan S. Milward, *The European Rescue of the Nation State*, London, Routledge, 1994.

A second and related potential problem with Riker's schema concerns his failure to incorporate mass-élite linkages into the formation of unions. In a sense this failing is entirely understandable. Almost all the unions created before the 1960s were élite driven; often the decisions were taken totally outside any sort of democratic institutional structure (the Communist federations, the post-colonial unions). European union, by way of contrast, has been subject to a complex and varied ratification process. While acknowledging this, the presence of a ratification procedure does not in itself undermine the logic of the Rikerian model. Indeed, as will be discussed in Chapter 4, while the existence of democratic pressures may change the *nature* of the decision-making calculus involved in union formation, they do not remove the *need* for such a calculus. On the contrary they may feed directly into the decision process by changing élites' perceptions of internally generated threats to the political status quo. They may also encourage those politicians intent on striking the federal bargain to present to general publics only the advantages of federalism during the ratification process. In this sense, it may be all too easy to infer from the language of political leaders an ideological commitment to federation.

A final criticism of Riker dwells on the relationship between his scheme and ideology. Riker condemns those who equate federalism with freedom, democracy, or economic well-being as ideologists. His unequivocally positivist position requires such a response: as, empirically, such links are demonstrably false, those who insist on their importance are, by definition, ideologues.[43] Put another way, beliefs and values *as ideology* have no place in his schema. Countries come together to form unions because the security benefits of so doing outweigh the costs, not because of the influence of those who champion what they believe are the inherent moral or economic advantages of a federal form of government. Of course Riker would concede that beliefs are important in the narrow sense that it is the perceptions of politicians involved in the bargain that are important. These perceptions are, in turn, based on interests, or, as Burgess has put it: 'They are "interested parties" precisely because they intend to benefit from a deal which directly and indirectly will entrench their interests, and secure their future, for generations to come.'[44]

[43] Riker, 'Federalism', 130–1.

[44] Michael Burgess, 'Federalism as Political Ideology', in Michael Burgess and Alain-G. Gagnon (eds.), *Comparative Federalism and Federation: Competing Traditions and Future Directions*, London, Harvester Wheatsheaf, 1993, 104.

Does this mean that the great advocates of federalism from the American Founding Fathers to the post-war champions of the European ideal were merely 'interested parties'? Riker's response would be, I think, that proponents of federalism as ideology cannot, on their own, persuade politicians to give up a degree of national independence. The decision to do so must be based on calculations relating to the interactions of political interests. He would not discount *any* role for ideology, however. It is possible, for example, that federalist ideas might help contribute to the creation of a political union which subsequently fails precisely because it results from ideas rather than calculations relating to the interests of the component states. Such has been the case with a number of failed federations including the East African and the West Indian.[45] In addition, the political discourse involved both in union formation and over the practicalities of working out the precise relationship between the states and the states and the federal government may well be couched in the language of political ideals. Such was certainly the case during the early years of the United States,[46] and, as will be discussed at length in the next chapter, during the formative years of the European Community.

Once this last point is conceded, it does, of course, leave open the possibility that the perceptions of politicians involved in the federal project will be coloured by federalist discourse; or that their purportedly rational calculations are bounded by the language of political debate. In Pocock's famous phrase: 'Men cannot do what they have no means of saying they have done; and what they do must in part be what they can say and conceive that it is.'[47] While this general point must be accepted, it in no way undermines Riker's basic methodology. At all times he is intent on identifying reasons, based on national interest, to explain why it is that politicians are prepared to enter into larger political units. He is concerned with political action rather than with political debate. As we will discover in the European context, the rhetoric of the European federalist ideal was much stronger during the immediate post-war years, when little was achieved in terms of building a political union, than during the 1980s and the 1990s, when political union came close to being realized.

[45] See Franck, *Why Federations Fail*, chs. 1 and 3.

[46] Beer, *To Make a Nation*, pts. 2 and 3; Stanley Elkins and Eric McKitrick, *The Age of Federalism: The Early American Republic, 1788–1800*, New York, OUP, 1993, chs. I–V.

[47] Quoted in Elkins and McKitrick, *The Age of Federalism*, 13.

CONCLUSIONS: EXPLAINING POLITICAL UNIONS—A FRAMEWORK FOR ANALYSIS

The purpose of this chapter has been twofold. First, to establish that a post-Maastricht Europe would indeed be a species of federal state; and, second, to elaborate a theory on the origins of federation which meets the basic tests of reliability and validity. We have already demonstrated that the common interest and ideological explanations have only limited applicability. The rational choice perspective is more attractive partly because of its focus on the perceptions of politicians and the subsequent decisions to form or not to form a political union. In this sense it confirms that union formation is unambiguously a *political* decision. An adaptation of Riker's theory also establishes that politicians will take the crucial decision to associate with a larger political entity if they believe that by so doing some threat to the national interest will be removed or reduced. This adaptation requires what might be called a 'strong' definition of the national interest. Because national governments are sacrificing some significant degree of independence by joining a union, the threat to the national interest must be considerable. For Riker it had to involve the threat of potentially destructive military or diplomatic activity. But in a much more complex international system, the threat could come from other sources, including domestic political interests. What, precisely, the threat is, must always be a matter for empirical investigation. At the highest level of generality what politicians are engaged in is a defence of their perception of the national interest. In this sense, they have made the calculation that the political benefits of enlargement outweigh the costs of continuing to go it alone.

A reworking of Riker's scheme as adapted by A. H. Birch in 1966 would, therefore, read like this (changes in italics):

> A necessary condition for the establishment of a federation is that the political leaders of all the territories should believe that union would either:
> (*a*) help to protect one or more of the territories from an internal or external threat, whether actual or potential, to the security *or stability* of the established regime, or:
> (*b*) enable them to benefit from the improved diplomatic, military *or political* position that the larger unit could be expected to enjoy; although it is not necessary that the considerations influencing the leaders of the various territories should be identical.[48]

[48] Birch, 'Approaches to the Study of Federalism', 32.

What is the relevance of this model in the European context? There are two dimensions to this question. First, how might it explain the erratic and halting progress towards European integration in the 1950–86 period; and, second, how useful is it as an explanation of the much more dramatic progress towards union since 1986? Chapter 3 will deal with the first part of this question and Chapter 4 with the second.

3

Understanding European Union I: 1945–1982

AFTERMATH OF WAR

As Alan Milward has noted, it is difficult to overestimate the traumatizing effect of the Second World War. In just two years between 1938 and 1940 'three [of the twenty-six European nation states] had been annexed, ten occupied by hostile powers, one occupied against its wishes by friendly powers, and four partially occupied and divided by hostile powers. Two others had been reduced to a satellite status which would eventually result in their occupation.'[1] By early 1940 recognition that a number of national governments had singularly failed to carry out the most basic obligation to their citizens—the defence of the territorial integrity of the state—led to a rapid surge in the popularity of the idea of an Anglo-Franco federation. Almost all the leading British politicians of the day, including Churchill, Attlee, Chamberlain, Halifax, Bevin, and Eden supported the idea, as did most of the British national press. Although Churchill's offer of an 'indissoluble union' between the two countries was overtaken by the French capitulation to Germany, the sudden abandonment of Britain's traditional view on the inviolability of national sovereignty demonstrates nicely the role that an external threat can play in provoking support for federal political arrangements.[2] Writing in 1940, R. Gordon Mackay's prognosis for a

[1] Alan S. Milward, *The European Rescue of the Nation State*, London, Routledge, 1994, 4.

[2] For a discussion of this period, see Andrea Bosco, 'What is Federalism: Towards a General Theory of Federalism', Paper before the 2nd ECSA World Conference on Federalism, Subsidiarity and Democracy in the European Union, Brussels 5–6 May 1994. The most influential contemporary texts were William Beveridge, *Peace by Federation*, London, Royal Institute of International Affairs, World Order Papers, No. 3, 1940; William Curry, *The Case for Federal Union*, Harmondsworth, Penguin, 1939; Ivor Jennings, *A Federation for Western Europe*, Cambridge, CUP, 1940; R. W. G. Mackay, *Federal Europe*, London, Michael Joseph, 1940; Kenneth Wheare, *What Federal Government Is*, London, OUP, 1941.

post-war political settlement was typical of the period: 'The minimum, however, is a union of Great Britain, France and Germany. With that union war amongst the European states is ended for all time. Without it, war in Europe will continue.'[3]

By the end of the war, however, the landscape of international politics had been transformed. What had started as a regional European conflict had developed into a global war, with, in 1945, three world powers dominating the international scene. By the late 1940s the dominant of these powers, the United States and the Soviet Union, had developed clear policies towards Europe and European reconstruction. The Soviets were intent on consolidating their grip on Eastern Europe and in spreading Communist influence to the rest of the Continent. The Americans were quite happy to conflate their national interests with those of the democratic Western European states in the belief that, with American support, these countries would become an essential bulwark against Soviet expansionism. The more prosperous and economically interdependent were the states of Western Europe, the better. As successful capitalist democracies they could take on their share of military defence as well as become important trading partners with the United States.

Britain's position was somewhat different. As a victorious power with its global sphere of influence virtually intact, the British were keen to advance the cause of European integration but only on British terms. Unlike 1940, when they and the French faced Germany alone, the British believed they had a special relationship with the United States and, with the British Empire and Commonwealth, could continue to play the role of world power. It is in this light that the much vaunted British initiatives on European integration and co-operation in the immediate post-war years should be understood. Hence, Winston Churchill's call for a 'United States of Europe' in September 1946 was motivated more by a desire to cement France and Germany together in some sort of military and economic pact rather than subsume the sovereignty of the individual European nation states under some new supranational authority.[4] Churchill was not, of course, in government at the time and the official position of the British government was more circumspect on the question of European unity. It is summed up well in a speech by the Foreign Secretary, Ernest Bevin, on 22 January 1948, in which he identified the British government's view as supporting 'the closer

[3] Mackay, *Federal Europe*, 23–4.

[4] For a discussion see Derek W. Urwin, *The Community of Europe: A History of European Integration Since 1945*, London, Longman, 1991, 30–5.

consolidation and economic development [of Europe] and eventually for the spiritual unity of Europe as a whole'.[5] Britain's position in this new Europe was never spelt out, but there is considerable evidence that the British saw European unity more in terms of binding treaties and economic co-operation rather than the construction of a European federation.[6]

The insistence of the British to put ties with the Commonwealth and the United States before European union, although much criticized in recent years,[7] was entirely rational if judged in terms of national interest and, especially, national defence. The Empire and Commonwealth countries provided a valuable supply of cheap and essential primary products and were a reliable market for British manufactured products. Europe remained economically devastated and in the East, at least, politically unstable. Even more important was the American perception of Britain's role in the new Europe. Economically, the Americans were intent not only on supporting British recovery (much as they were with the other West European countries), but also on elevating the pound sterling to junior partner status with the dollar as the currencies of international exchange. No other European country was expected to play an equivalent role. Put another way, the international economic order created at Bretton Woods was expected to be underpinned by both the American and the British economies. Free trade and fixed exchange rates would in turn be the basis of economic growth and a guarantor against political instability.[8] This vital role would have been compromised by close political and economic membership of a wider European union.

Militarily, too, the British enjoyed a special relationship with the Americans. The two countries shared military intelligence, including the latest research in nuclear science. And following the creation of NATO in 1949 it was widely expected that the lead alliance members

[5] Cited in David Weigall and Peter Stirk (eds.), *The Origins and Development of the European Community*, Leicester, Leicester University Press, 1992, Document 3.6. See also his references in this book.

[6] Urwin, *The Community of Europe*, 32.

[7] For a summary see David Sanders, *Losing an Empire, Finding a Role: British Foreign Policy Since 1945*, London, Macmillan, 1990, chs. 2 and 7.

[8] For a good summary of this point see Paul McCracken *et al.*, *Towards Full Employment and Price Stability*, Paris, OECD, 1977, Peter J. Katzenstein (ed.), *Between Power and Plenty*, Madison Wisc., University of Wisconsin Press, 1978, ch. 1; Sanders, *Losing an Empire*, ch. 7.

would be the Americans and the British.[9] Of the major Continental powers, one, Germany, was divided and occupied and expected to play no immediate military role. Like the British, the French placed a high priority on continuing and strengthening links with their overseas territories. The French were also intent on establishing themselves as the major Continental power responsible not only for containing Germany, but doing so independently of the United States.

It is in this context that the tentative moves towards European co-operation in the immediate post-war years should be assessed. The first initiative, the creation of the Council of Europe in 1949 grew out of the 1948 Treaty of Brussels which established a fifty-year pact 'for collaboration in economic, social and cultural matters, and for collective self defence'.[10] Negotiations at the subsequent Hague Conference revealed the conflicting positions of the participants—positions which were to remain largely unchanged for several decades to come. One group of countries represented by the Benelux States (who had already attempted to form a customs union immediately after the war) and Italy favoured a federal-like institutional structure, including a European Assembly with executive powers. Britain, Ireland, and the Scandinavian countries wanted no change in national sovereignty, preferring instead the creation of a forum for intergovernmental co-operation. Finally, the French also accepted the idea of a European assembly but viewed the whole integration process as a means of establishing control over a potentially resurgent Germany.[11]

The eventual compromise involved the creation of a Consultative Assembly representing the ten states of the Council of Europe. Ironically, in view of the British semantic quibbling at the time of the Treaty of Maastricht, the original name for the new organization, the European Union, was dropped following British objections. This first attempt at political integration in no way challenged national sovereignty. The institutional structure effectively guaranteed this as each state was given one vote and one veto on all Council decisions. As Derek Urwin has noted:

> Despite the resounding phraseology, the creation of the Council of Europe had not in any degree diminished national sovereignty as represented by the

[9] See in particular, John Bayliss, *Anglo-American Defence Relations, 1939–1984*, London, Macmillan, 2nd edn., 1984.

[10] Quoted in Urwin, *The Community of Europe*, 32.

[11] See the discussion in David Arter, *The Politics of European Integration in the Twentieth Century*, Aldershot, Dartmouth, 1993, chs. 4 and 5 and sources cited.

ministers. In the last resort the aims of the Council were to be achieved by 'discussion of questions of common concern and by agreements and common action in economic, social, scientific, legal and administrative matters and in the maintenance and further realisation of human rights and fundamental freedoms'.[12]

Perhaps the major achievement of the Council in the following years was its support for human rights, including the role it played in the creation of the European Convention for the Protection of Human Rights and Fundamental Freedoms in 1950. This apart, the Council has been little more than a talking shop.

Clearly, the conditions for a federal bargain were absent in the 1945–50 period. Certainly a military and diplomatic threat existed. As early as 1946 it was apparent that the Soviet Union planned to establish a military and political hegemony over Eastern Europe. By the time Harry Truman declared his doctrine on the need to contain Communist expansionism in 1947, most Western European political leaders were convinced of the seriousness of the Soviet threat—a perception that was strengthened by the blockade of Berlin in 1948. In addition, all the interested parties accepted that the future prosperity of Europe depended in part on German economic recovery, but this had to be achieved without the risk of a resurgence of German militarism. On the face of it, a federal Europe might have provided the necessary security on both scores.

However, the two powers who would be most crucial in striking any bargain, Britain and France, had little to gain from a Europe-wide federation. The French were primarily concerned with ensuring that any future settlement of the German question was achieved on their terms. This could have involved some sort of political union, but only one in which the Franco-German relationship dominated. Britain's three spheres of influence approach effectively ruled out full participation in a European union. The British were happy to encourage co-operation among European governments, but no more than that. Finally, all the major Western powers were signatories to the NATO Treaty in 1949. Effective defence against the Soviet Union was provided by old-fashioned diplomacy with supporting military guarantees, rather than by experimenting with federal institutional arrangements.

[12] Urwin, *The Community of Europe*, 35.

ALMOST A UNION?: THE EUROPEAN DEFENCE AND POLITICAL COMMUNITIES

The initial negotiations on European union took place in the absence of German participation. It was not until 1949 that the two new German states were created and almost immediately proposals for economic co-operation between the new Federal Republic of Germany and France were forthcoming. Almost parallel to these developments (which will be discussed in the next section) came proposals for European-wide defence and political communities. Two related events precipitated these moves. First, the outbreak of the Korean War in 1950, following as it did the Soviet's first testing of the atomic bomb, greatly intensified the Cold War. If the Soviet-backed North Korean Communists could invade South Korea, then surely the probability of an invasion of West Germany from the East was increased? Moreover, the sheer number of Soviet conventional forces in Eastern Europe required a NATO response that was beyond the capacity of the United States alone. A major European effort was required.

Second, such an effort would be greatly aided by German participation. The problem was, therefore, how to rearm the Germans while keeping its army under political control. Opposition to rearmament was particularly strong in France and the first proposal for putting ten German divisions under NATO control was quickly rejected. What the French proposed in its place was the creation of a European army under the control of a federal-style institutional structure. On 24 October 1950 the French Prime Minister, René Pleven, presented proposals for a common European defence to the French National Assembly. The so-called Pleven Plan placed the new European army under the control of a supranational European Minister of Defence. Although at the time the EDC was seen as a natural extension of the Council of Europe and of the nascent European Coal and Steel Community (ECSC),[13] it was far more radical than either. It would have created an integrated European army under one command. All the German military effort would be confined to the European army; other participants could continue to

[13] See the discussion in Arter, *The Politics of European Integration*, ch. 5; also Ernest B. Haas, *The Uniting of Europe: Political, Social and Economic Forces, 1950–1957*, Stanford, Calif., Stanford University Press, 1968; Alan S. Milward, *The Reconstruction of Western Europe, 1945–1952*, London, Unwin, 1984.

organize part of their armed forces under national command. Because the new army would be genuinely European in nature it raised the difficult question of political control. Between the original Pleven proposals in 1950 and the eventual demise of the EDC idea in 1954, most of the debate on the question was centred on this issue.

The British were fully aware that a common defence budget to finance the army could only be properly controlled by a democratically elected body; in effect it was impossible to administer a common army in the absence of a European government. As such they were immediately and unambiguously hostile to membership—even if they accepted that it might be appropriate for the Continental states.[14] In France there was continuing opposition, especially from the left, to the very idea of German rearmament whatever the nature of the administrative details. And in Germany the Social Democrats saw the future in terms of a totally demilitarized German state.

None the less an EDC pre-treaty agreement was signed by the member states of the ECSC (France, Italy, Germany, and the Benelux countries) in May 1952. After much discussion, mainly on the question of political control, a draft treaty was formulated in Strasburg on 10 March 1953. Known as the European Political Community (EPC) the new organization displayed all the features of an embryonic federation including an Executive Council, a Council of Ministers, a Court of Justice, and a popularly elected European assembly. Although it is easy to exaggerate the federal nature of the treaty (for example, the proposed Executive Council was essentially an intergovernmental authority with wide veto powers), the EPC did represent the most ambitious plan for European union to date. Moreover, the most enthusiastic federalists of the time, and especially the Dutch and the Belgians, saw EDC and EPC as part of a general process of integration which would also embrace economic matters.

In the event, the agreement came to nothing, for the following year the French National Assembly failed to ratify the treaty by refusing to debate it. The failure of the EDC can be attributed to three main causes. There was, first, the continuing hostility of the British. During 1953 and 1954 serious attempts were made to water down the federalist elements in the treaty in the hope that the British would then accept the idea. But even had the French Assembly accepted the treaty it is unlikely that the

[14] The British Foreign Secretary, Ernest Bevin, could not countenance British forces being under a European-wide command. See Alan Bullock, *Ernest Bevin: Foreign Secretary, 1945–1951*, London, Heinemann, 1983, 787.

British Parliament would have—although they may have favoured some association with the EDC. Second, international conditions generally changed during 1953 and 1954 in ways which reduced the immediate pressure for united European action. Stalin died in 1953 and his successors took on a more accommodating style in their relations with the West. Also in 1953 the Korean War was ended with a treaty endorsing the inviolability of the 38th Parallel. Finally, the Soviets' acquisition of the hydrogen bomb established what was seen at the time as an uneasy stalemate between the superpowers, thus reducing the strategic importance of conventional forces.

As important as any of these events were changes in French domestic politics. In December 1952 the French government under Antoine Pinay fell, following his threat to bring the EDC treaty before the National Assembly. Opposition to the idea of a European army came both from the right—the Gaullists were vehemently opposed—and from the left—the Communists were, by definition, hostile to the idea.[15] The crisis over ratification finally came to a head in response to events in Indo-China. Following the débâcle at Dien Bien Phu, Pierre Mendes France became Prime Minister on a platform of economic revival. Given the cost of the war in Indo-China, he was all too aware that France had to settle with the North Vietnamese. In the context of the national humiliation in South East Asia it would have been doubly difficult for Mendes France to endorse another—although quite different—challenge to French sovereignty which the proposed European army implied. So in spite of the fact that the other Continental powers had already ratified the treaty (or in Italy's case, were about to) Mendes France was quite happy to see it die. He was helped in this by the fact that the increasingly powerful French left, while very enthusiastic about European union, continued to be suspicious about any attempt to rearm Germany.[16]

Although largely forgotten with the passage of time, the EDC initiative was easily the most radical plan in the direction of European union in the immediate post-war period and, arguably, until the proposals for the Single European Act in the 1980s. There is no question that the plan was precipitated by increased fears of a Soviet threat and by the need to meet this threat in part through the deployment of a politically

[15] François Duchene, *Jean Monnet: The First Statesman of Interdependence*, New York, Norton, 1994, 253–5.

[16] For a discussion of this period, see Duchene, *Jean Monnet*, ch. 7; also Simon Serfaty, *France, de Gaulle and Europe: The Policy of the Fourth and Fifth Republics Towards the Continent*, Baltimore, Johns Hopkins Press, 1968.

subordinate German army. Considerable contemporary evidence exists to indicate that the demise of EDC and EPC was seen as a defeat both for the European movement and for a united defence against the Soviets. The Americans were incensed at what they saw as European indecision and duplicity. The US Secretary of State, John Foster Dulles, made this point in no uncertain terms:

> The French rejection of the European Defence Community is a saddening event. France thus turns away from her own historic proposal made nearly four years ago. That proposal sought a unification of the military strength of continental Europe into a single European Army so as to end the era of recurrent European wars, the last two of which became world wars. . . . the United States stands ready to support the many in Western Europe who despite their valiant efforts are left in grave anxiety. We need not feel that the European idea is dead merely because, in one of the six countries, a present majority seems against one of its manifestations. There is still much on which to build, and those foundations should not be shaken by any abrupt or any ill considered action of their own. . . .
>
> It is a tragedy that in one country nationalism, abetted by communism, has asserted itself so as to endanger the whole of Europe.[17]

Dulles was almost certainly exaggerating the consequences of defeat—which did, of course, imply a greater American presence in Western Europe. The effect on the federal idea should not be underestimated, however. François Duchene notes, for example, that following the rejection, 'the word *federal* was preserved as the political equivalent of Latin for the rare religious occasion. . . . The idea of Europe in some sense above the nations was no longer stated in the open.'[18] With the problem of German rearmament unresolved, the British suggested that the 1948 Treaty of Brussels could become the vehicle for European defence co-operation. This eventually resulted in the creation of the Western European Union (WEU) in 1954 which established a joint command for selected British, French, and Benelux divisions. In 1955 Italian and German forces were admitted to the Union. The French were willing to accept this arrangement largely because of the British commitment to station substantial forces in Western Germany. In no sense was the WEU a federal structure, however. WEU troops operated under NATO command, and although any military response was

[17] Press conference, 31 Aug. 1954. Quoted in Weigall and Stirk, *Origins and Development of the European Community*, Document 5.10.

[18] Duchene, *Jean Monnet*, 256.

designed as a integrated action, no institutional machinery for supranational decision-making was established.[19]

In effect, the WEU was a simple political device to sell the idea of a German army to the French while at the same time providing a forum for intergovernmental co-operation on defence matters. It quickly passed from the centre of the political stage during the 1950s. It continued to function, but only in the shadow of NATO and, eventually, of the European Community. The existence of NATO and the United States' commitment to European defence were enough to persuade most European governments that an adequate force to counter any Soviet threat existed. Put another way, the conditions for the construction of federal bargain were absent. They came close to emerging when a federal army might have guaranteed the subservience of a new German force to the European cause while at the same time providing a bulwark against Soviet expansionism. Even then, British preoccupation with quite distinct spheres of influence would have prevented full British participation in a European federal government.

Interestingly, the whole debate over the EDC was couched almost entirely in the language of *realpolitik.* The common interest among the peoples of Western Europe was a need to contain Germany, and ward off the Soviets. Similarities and differences of language, culture, geography, and even economy were peripheral to the central debate. In other words, the events of 1950–5 can be accommodated quite nicely by Riker's theory of federalism. The conditions for a federal bargain were present in embryonic form only. As events unfolded the pressure for a federal solution weakened, leading eventually to intergovernmental rather than supranational institutional arrangements.

ALTERNATIVE ROUTES: FUNCTIONAL INTEGRATION 1950–1960

It is common among writers on European integration to view the 1945–60 period as a continuum characterized by linear progress towards integration.[20] In the narrowest sense this perception is correct, for by the

[19] See Arnold Zurcher, *The Struggle to Unite Europe*, Westport, Conn., Greenwood, 1958, 129–31.

[20] See e.g. Roy Pryce (ed.), *The Dynamics of European Union*, London, Croom Helm, 1987; William Wallace (ed.), *The Dynamics of European Integration*, London, Pinter/Royal Institute of International Affairs, 1990.

end of the period, functional economic integration had become the defining characteristic of European co-operation. In terms of the construction of a political union, however, the high-water mark occurred in the early 1950s when proposals for EDC and EPC came close to being realized. Between 1954 and 1980 political union was simply not on the agenda and after 1960 even progress towards functional integration was erratic and halting.

All the evidence suggests that the founding fathers of the European movement expected something more than this; that their initial attempts to build economic and military co-operation would indeed develop into a federal-like arrangements. Few dispute that of the leading advocates of European integration, Schuman, Spaak, Spinelli, and Monnet, it was Monnet who was the main driving force behind the movement. It is clear both from Monnet's memoirs and from contemporary research that Monnet's ultimate aim was the creation of a united Europe.[21] But it is also the case that Monnet was a gradualist, who viewed increasing economic interdependence as the means towards the federal end. For all his federalist rhetoric, he was convinced that political union could only come when the time was right.[22] In this sense, Monnet, rather than being a federalist visionary, was a practical politician who was only too aware that co-operation between sovereign states could only be achieved if their interests coincided.

It is in this light that the early efforts at economic integration should be judged. Above all, the creation of the European Coal and Steel Community in 1951 and the European Economic Community (EEC) in 1957 represented *politically* motivated bargains between the French and the Germans designed to strengthen both countries' national positions. Milward notes that research on French post-war diplomacy 'made it obvious that integration was an attempt to restore France as a major national force by creating an integrated area in Western Europe which France would dominate politically and economically. The German Federal Republic began to be depicted as a country which espoused the cause of European integration precisely in order to establish itself as the future German nation-state.'[23] Already by the 1940s, German prosperity was regarded as an essential condition for the successful

[21] For a summary, see Martin Holland, *European Integration: From Community to Union*, London, Pinter, 1994, 6–9, and sources cited.

[22] Duchene, *Jean Monnet*, ch. 7.

[23] Milward, *The European Rescue of the Nation State*, 17.

reconstruction of Europe. Functional integration might not only bring economic benefits—although most economists considered that these would be small[24]—it would also cement the six countries together politically, thus reducing the chances of future conflict.

Functional integration, first in iron, coal, and steel, and later in atomic energy and agriculture, introduced elements of common control and required, therefore, the creation of supranational institutions. What eventually transpired, both in the case of the ECSC and the EEC, was a set of institutions which in no way could be described as federalist in structure and function. 'Supranational' or 'intergovernmental' would be more accurate appellations. There are two ways in which this point can be demonstrated. There is, first, the extent to which the decisions of the new institutions were subject to national control. Second, there is the question of the range of policy areas over which national governments ceded control to supranational institutions. Let us deal with each of these in turn.

The 1951 Treaty of Paris which established the ECSC created a nine-member High Authority. In practice three members were drawn from the three largest states (Germany, France, and Italy) and three from the Benelux countries. The High Authority was given a wide brief over fiscal matters (its income was drawn from a levy imposed on the steel and coal producers) and over production. The objective was to create a single market by progressively removing restrictive practices and barriers between countries. Although High Authority decisions could be reached by majority vote, most of the key decisions, for example on restricting output during times of surplus or on allocating supply during periods of shortage, were subject to approval by a Council of Ministers drawn from the national governments. Although the original intention was to institute qualified majority voting in the Council, the issue was eventually fudged with the Treaty allowing for the possibility of unanimous voting over key decisions.[25] Gestures were also made in the direction of legislative control via the creation of a seventy-eight-member Common Assembly which, although constitutionally given ultimate control, had its powers limited to censure and the collective dismissal of the High Authority—a power it never, in fact, exercised. Finally, the Treaty established a nine-member Court of Justice which had powers

[24] Ibid., ch. 4, and sources cited.

[25] See Arter, *The Politics of European Integration*, ch. 5.

of judicial review over the decisions of the High Authority.[26] The only truly federal element in the Treaty was the High Authority's control over its own income (the levy on producers), although this was much less important than the broad policy-decisions relating to over- or underproduction. The triumph of intergovernmentalism was amply demonstrated in 1959 when a crisis of overproduction led to impasse in the Council of Ministers, with the Italians, Germans, and the Dutch refusing to accede to French demands for quotas and import controls. In the event, the impasse lasted until 1964, by which time the reputation of the ECSC as a European institution had been badly damaged.[27]

Superficially, the ECSC did represent a step towards federal political structures. In reality, however, intergovernmentalism prevailed. The ECSC did, of course, exercise authority over just two areas of economic production—albeit important ones. These efforts should, therefore, be kept in perspective. In terms of effects on the real economy and the lives of ordinary citizens, the ECSC was, for example, clearly no more important than the operation of imperial preference between Britain and its Empire and Commonwealth implemented following the Ottowa conference of 1932.[28] Among the peoples of Europe, only in Belgium did it have an important impact on national politics and even here as Milward has noted, 'There was never any question that the ECSC would be able to make Belgium do anything it did not want to do. It presented no threat to the independence of national policy formulation.'[29] Among other European publics the ECSC hardly loomed large in politics. A 1955 poll in *Sondages* revealed that 26 per cent of a French sample were unaware of the organization's existence.[30]

The other attempt to create a functionally integrated industrial sector, in atomic energy, was precipitated by the Suez crisis in 1956. In 1957 the six countries signed the European Atomic Energy Community (Euratom) Treaty with the intention of forging a single effort on the provision of atomic energy as an alternative to imported energy supplies. However, the French were well advanced in this sector compared with Germany and Italy, and, fearing French dominance, the three

[26] On the structure of functioning of the ECSC, see L. Lister, *Europe's Coal and Steel Community*, New York, Wiley, 1960; also Milward, *The Reconstruction of Western Europe*; Urwin, *The Community of Europe*, ch. 4.

[27] Ibid. 54–5.

[28] For a discussion of imperial preference, see Bernard Porter, *The Lion's Share: A Short History of British Imperialism*, London, Longman, 1984, ch. 7.

[29] Milward, *The European Rescue of the Nation State*, 117.

[30] Cited in Arter, *The Politics of European Integration*, 127.

countries soon decided on their own building programmes dictated by individual national needs and interests. Also in 1957 the six countries signed the Treaty of Rome, establishing the European Economic Community. Millions of words have been written on the genesis and early functioning of the EEC and yet another summary is hardly necessary. For our purposes the vital question remains: to what extent was the EEC federalist in institutional structure and in its control over specific policy areas?

Institutionally, the new organization was actually less federalist than either the failed EDC/EPC proposal and the up and functioning ECSC. In fact, the institutional structure was almost an exact copy of the ECSC arrangements. A supranational executive was created in the body of a nine-member commission with two members drawn from the larger states and one each from the smaller. Although nominated by member states, the commissioners were specifically required to represent Community rather than national interests. The Commission was charged with two main roles—making sure that EEC policy was properly implemented, and producing proposals for presentation to a parallel body, the Council of Ministers. Council members were representatives of the national governments and ultimate authority lay with the Council rather than the Commission. Following the confusion over voting rights in the ECSC, the Treaty of Rome laid down very specific voting rights for Council members. For all intents and purposes these rules instituted a national veto on all important EEC decisions. Simple majority decisions were allowed in only a small number of procedural areas. Qualified majority voting was permitted for some other, mainly minor, matters. For all important decisions, unanimity was required. These arrangements were scheduled to last only until 1966 when the qualified and simple majority principle was to be extended.

A Parliamentary Assembly was created in place of the ECSC assembly with very limited powers of censure over the EEC budget. It was not directly elected and was viewed at the time as the embryo of a later genuinely European legislature. Finally, the European Court of Justice was given the job of interpreting Community law and acting as the court of last resort on Community matters.

Functionally, no area was designated as being within the sole competence of the Community. The purpose of the EEC was to create a customs union or common market in goods and services among the member states. How, precisely, this was to operate would become clear only with the passing of time. In the event, agriculture came to dominate among the EEC's responsibilities. All six member states could benefit from a common agricultural policy based on the provision of price supports for domestic producers together with a common external tariff against imports.[31] In the three largest states politically powerful and numerous small farmers would all benefit from the subsidies and protection which the Common Agricultural Policy (CAP) promised. By securing highly protected agricultural sectors the member states were actually strengthening national sovereignty. In the aftermath of years of acute shortages, securing some stability in agricultural output was assigned a high priority. Later, as the importance of agriculture in relation to manufacturing declined, the CAP became a useful device for placating small farmers without incurring the political costs of doing so entirely within the ambit of domestic politics.

We can conclude, then, that as originally organized, the EEC was more in the mould of a mutually beneficial alliance than a federal state. Indeed, writing in 1964, Riker describes the EEC as a 'close alliance' conceptually distinct from a peripheralized or weak federation such as characterized Switzerland before 1798.[32] To be sure, institutionally, the embryo of federal arrangements were present and it is almost certainly the case that proponents of a politically united Europe had some influence on these arrangements as well as on the federalist rhetorical flourishes with which the Treaty of Rome was infused.[33] The actual reality of the Treaty, however, was intergovernmentalism, not federalism. Put another way, the main participants were able to strike a bargain, which, through the creation of a supranational organization, provided benefits for all, while in no way undermining national independence. The absence of the British from this deal was in no way surprising, not because of dread of association with a federalist project, which, as we have established, the EEC was not, but because of their continuing links with the Commonwealth and their historically established choice to exclude themselves from the dominant Franco-German dialogue.

Given the intergovernmental nature of this bargain, it is not surprising that changes in the domestic politics of the member states, some of which were engendered by outside events, would have serious repercussions for the functioning and organization of the EEC. Such was exactly the case over the ensuing twenty years as the next section will show.

[31] Milward, *The European Rescue of the Nation State*, ch. 5.

[32] Riker, 'Federalism', in Fred I. Greenstein and Nelson Polsby (eds.), *The Handbook of Political Science*, vol. v: *Government Institutions and Processess*, Reading, Mass., Addison Wesley, 1975, Table I. p. 101.

[33] See Pryce (ed.), *The Dynamics of European Union*.

THE REASSERTION OF THE NATION STATE, 1960–1970

Among historians there is a general consensus that the EEC suffered a series of crises during the 1960s and that by the end of the decade little progress had been made in the direction of further integration. General agreement also exists on the longer term effects of these crises—it was not until the 1980s that the momentum of the 1950s was re-established.[34] Most commentators attribute the blame for this failure to the personage of General de Gaulle. While, in terms of the specifics of EEC decision-making, this is undoubtedly true, deeper reasons for the failure can be identified, especially after the departure of de Gaulle in 1969. Very broadly, the underlying forces at work during the 1960s related to changing perceptions of the national interest, which were essentially country specific in nature. During the 1970s changes were precipitated not by discrete events in individual countries but by a general reaction to broader structural changes in the world economy.

At least since the 1940s de Gaulle had a vision of Europe which was markedly more nationalistic than the Christian Democratic view, which had been dominant in both France and Germany during the 1950s. Like many other French politicians de Gaulle placed the highest priority on containing an economically resurgent West Germany, but he believed that this could be accomplished through French diplomatic hegemony over Continental Europe, rather than through supranational institutions. He was also convinced that France had a unique role to play as a power able to assert some independence from the Anglo-American dominated NATO and was thus well placed to open a dialogue with the Soviets. For de Gaulle the federalist arrangements implicit in a strengthened EEC involved only costs to the French national interest and no benefits. Put another way, de Gaulle believed that world politics had developed in such a way that French interests would be best served through the ascendancy of the French nation state rather than through European political union. By the 1960s it was clear that West Germany posed no military threat to France. Too close an association with NATO, on the other hand, might drag France unwittingly into an American conflict with the Soviet Union. France's role, therefore, should be to distance itself from the USA—and her closest ally Britain—while attempting to

[34] See Holland, *European Integration*, 33–8; Arter, *The Politics of European Integration*, 145–53; Urwin, *The Community of Europe*, ch. 8; Ernest Wistricht, *The United States of Europe*, London, Routledge, 1994, 33–6.

become the dominant diplomatic and military power on the Continent of Europe.

The three key events in EEC politics during the 1960s—the Fouchet Plan, the rejection of British membership, and the 1965 crisis in agricultural policy—were all directly related to this French world-view. In response to calls among European federalists led by Jean Monnet for an acceleration of integration, de Gaulle produced an alternative plan named after Christian Fouchet, the French Ambassador to Denmark, who had headed an EEC endorsed committee charged with exploring possibilities for greater political co-operation. Reporting in 1961, Fouchet proposed the creation of 'a union of states' with an unambiguously intergovernmental institutional structure. The new organization would be dominated by regular meetings of government heads or foreign ministers, who would proceed with unanimously agreed decisions. A permanent secretariat, based in Paris, would consist of national government nominees and a European Assembly would be made up of nominees of national legislatures. This structure was, in fact, not unlike the United Nations; the purpose would be to bring the member states (the Six) together to discuss mutual problems and to act on the basis of unanimous decisions.

Other member states, and especially Holland, Germany, and Italy, saw the scheme as a thinly veiled attempt to undermine both the EEC and NATO and elevate France to the key diplomatic position in Europe. The plan was eventually rejected in 1962.[35] De Gaulle's intention was not, of course, to create a European federation dominated by France. It was, rather, to establish a diplomatic counterweight to NATO and thus divert attention and energy away from further integration within the institutional context of the EEC. De Gaulle's views on federation were aptly summed up in his press conference following the rejection of the Fouchet Plan:

> These are ideas [on European federation] that might appeal to certain minds but I entirely fail to see how they could be put into practice, even with six signatures at the foot of a document. Can we imagine France, Germany, Italy the Netherlands, Belgium, Luxemburg being prepared on a matter of importance to them in the national or international sphere, to do something that appeared wrong to them because the others had ordered them to do so? Would the peoples of France, of Germany, of Italy, of the Netherlands, of Belgium or of

[35] For a discussion, see J.-P. Duroselle, 'General de Gaulle's Europe and Jean Monnet's Europe', in C. Cosgrove and K. Twitchett (eds.), *The New International Actors: The UN and the EEC*, London, Macmillan, 1970, 187–200.

Luxemburg ever dream of submitting to laws passed by foreign parliamentarians if such laws ran counter to their deepest convictions? . . . At present there is and can be no Europe other than a Europe of the states—except, of course, for myths, fictions and pageants.[36]

Note that de Gaulle is referring to the non-viability of federation 'at the present'. He is, in other words, recognizing that the conditions for a federal bargain were absent in the early 1960s. In his view France *at that time* had little to gain and much to lose by ceding national independence to a supranational authority.

The motives behind de Gaulle's rejection of British membership first in 1963 and second in 1967 were somewhat different. Britain applied for membership not because of any desire to join a federation or political union, but because of a shift in Britain's trade away from the Commonwealth and towards Europe. Long a proponent of free trade, and the driving force behind the creation of the European Free Trade Association (EFTA) in 1960, Britain and some of her closest economic partners in Europe (Portugal, Norway, Sweden, and Denmark) were keen to take advantage of the Europe-wide customs union promised by the Treaty of Rome.[37] De Gaulle's successive vetoes on British membership were more to do with a fear that, via British participation, American influence over France would be extended. As he put it in a press conference following the first veto:

It must be agreed that the entry first of Great Britain, and of [other] states, will completely change the series of adjustments, agreements, compensations and regulations already established between the Six. We would then have to envisage the construction of another Common Market which . . . would without any doubt no longer resemble the one the Six have built. Moreover, the Community, growing in that way, would be confronted with all the problems of the economic relations with a crowd of other states, and first of all with the United States . . . in the end there would be a colossal Atlantic Community under American domination . . .[38]

De Gaulle was quite wrong about the nature of the Anglo-American relationship. Co-operation in defence matters was one thing (the Prime Minister, Harold Macmillan, had earlier opted for American rather than

[36] First part of quote in Weigal and Stirk, *The Origins and Development of the European Community*, Document 7.11, p. 133. Second part cited in Holland, *European Integration*, 34.

[37] Sanders, *Losing an Empire*, ch. 5.

[38] Quoted in Urwin, *The Community of Europe*, 125.

French nuclear weaponry), but with the gradual demise of the sterling area in the 1960s Britain's role as junior partner with the Americans as the providers of international liquidity was becoming increasingly irrelevant. As events turned out, British membership in the 1970s in no way increased American influence in Europe.

The French President was, in any case, no great supporter of deepening the relationship among the Six through a strengthening of EEC institutions. He may have talked of the common interests among the Six—'they are adjacent, they interpenetrate, they are an extension of each other',[39] but all his actions pointed to a weakening of the supranational role of the EC. This became very clear during 1965 and 1966 when the French resisted all attempts to give greater powers to the European Parliament, to provide the Commission with a source of finance independent of contributions from distinct national treasuries, and to finalize the details for the implementation of a Common Agricultural Policy. French obduracy came to a head when two of these issues coincided—the funding arrangements for the CAP. At a Council meeting on 15 June 1965 the French walked out and boycotted all Council meetings for seven months thereafter.

The crisis was resolved only after the French presidential election when de Gaulle was taken to a second round after failing to win an absolute majority in the first. His second-round opponent, socialist François Mitterrand, was firmly endorsed by Jean Monnet and won a surprisingly high 45 per cent of the vote to de Gaulle's 55 per cent. This less than resounding victory was closely linked to the negotiations over CAP with French farmers, in particular, unhappy with their government's stand. It was not the CAP *per se* which concerned de Gaulle but the principle that, up to that point, any member state could cast a veto in the Council of Ministers. Under the Treaty of Rome's timetable, a shift to majority voting should have occurred by 1966 and it was this change that the French were resisting. The eventual settlement, known as the Luxemburg compromise, was, in fact, a victory for the French. In future, national vetoes could be applied to any issue which was considered to affect a member's 'vital interests'. Majority voting could apply on other matters. However, as it was up to individual members to decide what these 'vital interests' were, the unanimity rule was effectively upheld.

[39] From a press conference on 14 Jan. 1963. Cited in Urwin, *The Community of Europe*, 123.

The 1965/6 crisis had a number of consequences. The status of the French as European leader was undermined, de Gaulle's own standing in France was damaged, and, most important of all, the move to supranationalism was stopped dead in its tracks. As Urwin has put it, 'In short, the crisis resolved some of the ambiguity in the Treaty of Rome between supranationalism and intergovernmentalism. The effect of the crisis and its resolution through the Luxemburg compromise was that the future development of the EEC would be much more as an intergovernmental union of independent states.'[40]

It would be wrong to infer from these events that the other member states were championing the cause of supranationalism, let alone federalism. They were not. Some, and most notably Belgium and Luxemburg, may well have been prepared to go down that path. Most were happy with the incremental move to supranationalism implicit in the Treaty of Rome. This would have included the institution of majority voting in the Council, but of course the Council's jurisdiction was limited to a narrow range of policy areas, of which, at the time, agricultural support was the most important. We should remember, however, that the major objective of the Treaty of Rome was the reduction and eventual elimination of tariff barriers between the member states. This was to be achieved in tandem with a competition policy designed to ensure that cartels and other restrictive practices were eliminated, so assuring a level playing field for inter-member trade. The creation of such a customs union in no way challenged national sovereignty—which is one reason why the British were increasingly keen to join.

In other words, even if the French had acceded to the timetable for majority voting in the Council, the CAP had been up and running in full, and a genuine common market had been established by the end of the decade, few commentators would have labelled the European Community (or EC, renamed thus in 1967) anything other than an unusually close alliance of sovereign states. In Rikerian terms, conditions amenable to some sort of federal bargain actually receded during the 1960s. German recidivism looked less likely than ever; the threat from the East was also less acute. NATO and the Warsaw Pact countries had reached an uneasy *modus vivendi* with the last destabilizing event dating back to the Cuban Missile Crisis in 1962. Even the indigenous West European Communist parties, which in the 1940s and 1950s were deferential to policy directives laid down by the Soviets, had begun to assert

[40] Ibid. 115.

their independence from Moscow. In the Italian case the party had been fully converted to parliamentary democracy.[41]

Symptomatic of these changes was the passing of the old post-war Christian Democratic generation of politicians who were often replaced either with more nationalistic leaders (de Gaulle), or more pragmatic and opportunistic politicians (Ludwig Erhard in Germany). Given these circumstances any further advance in the direction of political union looked highly unlikely. By the end of the 1970s the circumstances did, if anything, look even less auspicious, although, as we will see, structural changes in the world economy had, by the early 1980s, laid the foundations for major changes in the functioning and organization of the European Community.

ECONOMIC DISLOCATION AND INTERGOVERNMENTALISM, 1970–1982

In a now famous editorial written to mark the twenty-fifth anniversary of the Treaty of Rome in March 1982, *The Economist* characterized the EC as 'Born March 25th 1957, Moribund, March 25th 1982. *capax imperii nisi imperasset* (It seemed capable of being a power, until it tried to be one)'.[42] *The Economist* was referring in the main to the failure of the member states to agree on their contributions to the organization, which in turn were used overwhelmingly to fund the increasingly expensive Common Agricultural Policy. The EC was not moribund in 1982, however. Far from it, for by that year the organization had been enlarged to include Ireland, Denmark, Greece, and the UK, with full Spanish and Portuguese membership scheduled to be completed by 1986. Apart from the CAP, which was fully operational by the early 1970s, most member states had agreed to a European Monetary System (EMS) in 1979 designed to provide some exchange rate stability among the countries of Europe. Politically, the EC had been strengthened too. Also in 1979 the first direct elections to the European Parliament were held, and in 1974 a European Council had been established to provide regular meetings among heads of governments and thus create a focus of political leadership in what was an increasingly cumbersome institutional structure.

[41] See Donald Sassoon, *The Strategy of the Italian Communist Party from the Resistance to the Historic Compromise*, London, Pinter, 1981.

[42] *The Economist*, 20 Mar. 1982, 8.

In many respects these changes represented a fulfilment of the dashed ambitions of the 1960s. With the departure of de Gaulle in 1969, the road to enlargement and in particular British membership was unblocked. Moreover, the ambivalence of the British Labour governments of the 1960s was replaced in 1970 with the unbridled enthusiasm of the new Conservative Prime Minister, Edward Heath. The CAP soon became acceptable to the politically influential small farmers of France, Italy, and Germany given the sharp fall in world agricultural prices in the late 1960s. As a result, EC farm prices were held artificially high through subsidies and the creation of large surpluses. This was, of course, to become the hallmark of the CAP for twenty years thereafter.

The introduction of the European Council was, however, an endorsement of Gaullist ideas. De Gaulle had always believed in a 'Europe des Patries' where the leaders of equal nation states would meet on a regular basis to discuss common interests and problems. By the mid-1970s the European Council had become just this with regularly scheduled meetings and a rotating presidency with a six-month tenure. Although the precise constitutional relationship between the European Council and other EC institutions was never spelt out, it was clear by the late 1970s that the European Council had taken on the main leadership role in the EC.

Given these developments, why was *The Economist* so damning in its judgement of the EC in 1982? As indicated, much of the immediate criticism was directed at an increasingly wasteful CAP. But the critique ran much deeper than this, for during the decade of the 1970s world economic and political conditions changed in ways that, on the face of it, made the prospect of a European federation less rather than more likely.

Economic Developments

During the 1950s and 1960s debates on the future of Europe took place in the context of relative economic certainties. Most countries enjoyed a combination of full employment, relatively low inflation, and steady economic growth. National finances were also quite healthy. Finally, the whole system of international trade was underpinned by the dollar whose value was fixed in relation to gold and all the leading currencies. By the early 1980s all of these certainties had been challenged. The traditional relationship between unemployment and inflation as predicted by the Philips' curve had broken down (Fig. 3.1); economic

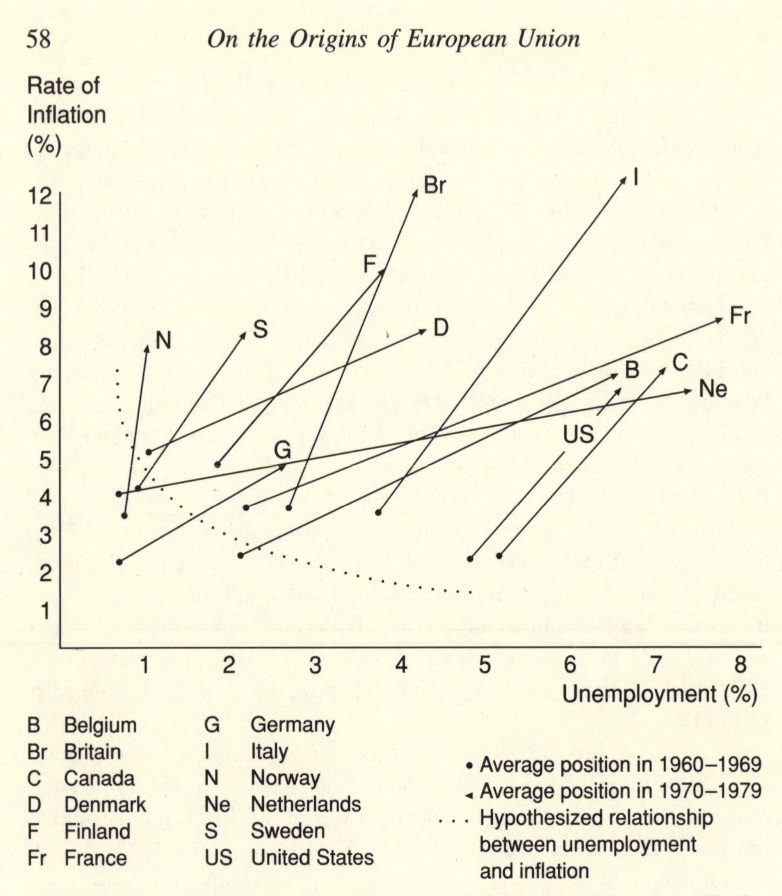

Source: OECD, *Main Economic Indicators*, 1960–1979. Reproduced from James E. Alt and K. Alec Chrystal, Political Economics, Berkeley and Los Angeles, University of California Press, 1983, Fig. 5.2.

FIG. 3.1. Inflation and unemployment in the 1960s and 1970s

growth had slowed in all the leading economies (Table 3.1), and governments everywhere were finding it increasingly difficult to balance their national budgets (Fig. 3.2).

The reasons for this transformation are well known and need not be repeated in detail here.[43] The immediate cause of the breakdown of the

[43] For a comprehensive account see Paul McCracken *et al.*, *Towards Full Employment and Price Stability* (The McCracken Report), OECD, Paris, 1977, ch. 1.

TABLE 3.1. Average annual growth of GDP in selected countries, 1950–1980

	1950–60	1960–70	1970–80
Belgium	2.0	4.1	3.2
France	3.5	4.6	3.0
FRG	6.6	3.5	2.4
Italy	4.9	4.6	2.1
Netherlands	3.3	4.1	2.3
(Av. ECSC/EEC)[a]	(4.08)	(4.2)	(2.6)
Denmark	2.5	3.9	2.2
Ireland	1.8	3.8	2.3
Britain	2.3	2.3	2.0
Austria	5.7	3.9	3.8

[a] Excluding Luxemburg.

Source: Mancur Olson, *The Rise and Decline of Nations: Economic Growth, Stagflation and Social Rigidities*, Cambridge Mass., Harvard University Press, 1982, 6.

Bretton Woods system of fixed exchange rates in 1971 was the inability of the United States to maintain the value of the dollar given its increasingly serious balance of payments problems. The 1950s dollar shortage had been replaced by the late 1960s by an unmanageable dollar surplus, thus undermining the role of the dollar as the key reserve currency.[44] The eventual move to floating exchange rates is now widely regarded as having inflationary effects.[45] Later in the decade the oil crisis precipitated by the OPEC member states' response to the Yom Kippur War was even more inflationary and forced a number of governments into adopting Draconian austerity measures. Eventually, as will be developed later, these events led to a dramatic reappraisal of the fundamentals of economic policy.

As far as the EC was concerned, the dislocations of the 1970s had two major effects. First, they elevated the question of monetary cooperation to near the top of the Community's agenda. Second, they led

[44] On the problems associated with this transformation, see Robert O. Keohane, *After Hegemony: Cooperation and Discord in the World Political Economy*, Princeton, University of Princeton Press, 1984.

[45] For a review see Peter Garber, 'The Collapse of the Bretton Woods Fixed Exchange Rate System', in Michael D. Bordo and Barry Eichengreen (eds.), *A Retrospective on the Bretton Woods System*, Chicago, University of Chicago Press, 1993, 461–94.

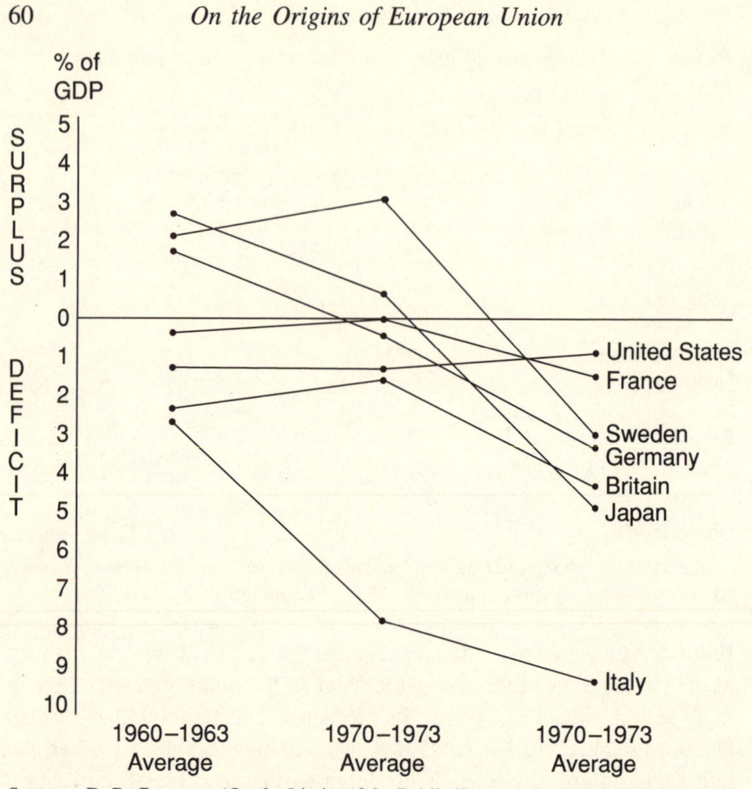

Sources: D. R. Cameron, 'On the Limits of the Public Economy', presented to the annual meeting of the American Political Science Association, New York, Sept. 1980, for earlier years; OECD, Economic Outlook, July 1981 and July 1982. Reproduced from Alt and Chrystal, Political Economics, Fig. 9.5.

FIG. 3.2. Budget surplus deficit in selected countries, 1960–1981

to a considerable divergence in the relative economic performance of the member states, so apparently reducing the prospects for further economic and political integration. Co-operation on monetary matters had been under discussion at least since the 1940s. Painfully aware that the economic mistakes of the 1930s contributed to war, the founding fathers of European integration saw monetary union as an obvious way of cementing the countries of Europe together.[46] Early experiments with a payments union had been necessary, given the failure of the European economies to move as rapidly towards currency convertibility as the

[46] See Kenneth Dyson, *Elusive Union: The Process of Economic and Monetary Union in Europe*, London, Longman, 1994, ch. 3.

Bretton Woods timetable demanded. By the early 1960s, however, the rapid improvement in the trading performance of the Six eased the dollar shortage and accelerated the move to convertibility. By the late 1960s the Six began to consider more permanent arrangements, including complete monetary union.

In 1969 EC leaders met at the Hague with the specific intention of accelerating moves towards greater integration. The major outcome of the Hague Summit was the objective of achieving full monetary union by 1980. A commission was duly established to study how best to achieve European Monetary Union (EMU). The resulting Werner Report called for 'the total and irreversible convertibility of currencies, the elimination of fluctuation in exchange rates, the irrevocable fixing of parity rates and the complete liberation of movements of capital'.[47] Ideally, these changes would culminate in the adoption of a single currency. Reporting in 1970 before the collapse of the Bretton Woods system, the report's authors were, of course, assuming that the whole international monetary system would be underpinned by the dollar. It was also assumed that intra-EC parities would stabilize (there had, in fact, been just two revaluations in the Community (both of the Deutschmark, one accompanied by the guilder), and one devaluation (of the French franc) during the 1960s). As it turned out, the highly volatile conditions of the 1970s produced the very opposite to the Werner recommendations—increased currency fluctuations, only very halting moves towards capital liberalization, and, in the early period at least, a breakdown in co-operation among member states on this issue. As can be seen from Table 3.2, which traces the major changes during the period of the 'Snake', attempts to co-ordinate the values of the EC and associated currencies were doomed to failure during the 1970s.

In response to the oil crisis, economies began to diverge seriously. Some, and most notably Germany, experienced relatively modest increases in inflation and unemployment, while others (Britain) saw large increases in inflation and others still suffered particularly high levels of unemployment (France) (Fig. 3.1). Given such circumstances, which were a function not only of the underlying strength of the respective economies, but also a measure of how sensitive and vulnerable these economies were to an external shock,[48] it is in no way surprising that monetary co-ordination proved impossible.

[47] Quoted in ibid. 80.

[48] For a discussion of vulnerability and sensitivity, see Robert O. Keohane and Joseph S. Nye, *Power and Interdependence: World Politics in Transition*, Boston, Little Brown, 1977. Also the discussion in Chapter 8 below.

TABLE 3.2. Chronology of the Snake

1972	(*Apr.*) Birth of the 'Snake', the exchange rate agreement between Belgium, France, Germany, Italy, Luxemburg, and the Netherlands.
	(*May*) Denmark, the UK, and Norway joined.
	(*June*) The UK and Denmark withdrew.
	(*Oct.*) Denmark rejoined.
1973	(*Feb.*) Italy withdrew.
	(*Mar.*) Sweden joined.
	(*June*) Revaluation of the Deutschmark.
	(*Sept.*) Revaluation of the Dutch guilder.
	(*Nov.*) Revaluation of the Danish krone.
1974	(*Jan.*) France withdrew.
1975	(*July*) France rejoined.
1976	(*Mar.*) France dropped out definitively.
	(*Oct.*) The Frankfurt realignment: the Deutschmark was revalued and the Scandinavian currencies were devalued.
1977	(*Apr.*) The Scandinavian currencies were devalued.
	(*Aug.*) Sweden withdrew and the other Scandinavian currencies were devalued.
1978	(*Feb.*) Devaluation of the Norwegian krone.
	(*Oct.*) Revaluation, against the Danish krone of the Deutschmark (4%), the Dutch guilder, and the Belgian Franc (2%).
	(*Dec.*) Norway withdrew.
1979	(*Mar.*) End of the Snake and start of the European Monetary System.

Source: Tommaso Paoa-Schioppa, *The Road to Monetary Union in Europe: The Emperor, the Kings and the Genies*, Oxford, OUP, 1994, App. 2.

These traumas also exacerbated ideological conflicts both within and between political parties. On the right, free market solutions to economic problems gained in influence, while on the left debate was focused on the extent to which government policy should fall back on economic nationalism and protectionism as a means of combating much higher levels of unemployment. We will discuss how these debates were resolved in different countries in the next chapter, but for now it is important to stress where the EC was located in this debate. Prior to the 1970s it was possible to discern an EC or 'Commission' policy line on economics. Very broadly, the EC represented free trade, a common market in goods and services, and a free market competition policy. In the context of full employment and low inflation such policies remained essentially uncontroversial. During the 1970s, however, the EC policy line clearly favoured open market solutions to economic problems, including the complete liberalization of capital movements and the eventual adoption of a European monetary area. The EC policy line was, therefore, much closer to the national political parties of the centre/right than of the left. As will be stressed in the next chapter, the EC/centre/right position was eventually to become the *only* viable policy position—a fact which was to have enormous impact on the decision to opt for a single currency in the 1990s.

In this context it is not surprising that further proposals for monetary co-operation were forthcoming during the late 1970s. These were to culminate in the European Monetary System which, in 1979, laid down fluctuation margins of 6 per cent for the Italian lira and 2.25 per cent for the other currencies (all the EC members bar Britain which elected not to join). As with the Snake, the early history of the ERM of the EMS was not a happy one. Between 1979 and 1983 there were seven major realignments in the system, most involving the revaluation of the Deutschmark and the devaluation of most of the other currencies.[49] Indeed by the 1980s it was becoming increasingly obvious that most individual EC governments could not pursue policies of full employment and retain the value of their currencies. Again, we will return to this point in the next chapter.

It is important to emphasize that these attempts at monetary co-ordination were not at the time seen as threats to national sovereignty. Both the Snake and the EMS represented an effort to return to the relative stability of the old Bretton Woods system. The EC and its institutional framework was a convenient device for expediting this objective. And although the more ardent of the European federalists continued to talk of the need for a single currency in the context of political union, the underlying economic conditions were moving against rather than towards such an outcome.

Political Developments

On the political front, events were scarcely more encouraging. Both in terms of internal politics and in terms of their response to wider world events, the interests of the countries of the EC appeared to diverge

[49] For a full chronology, see Tommaso Paoa-Schioppa, *The Road to Monetary Union in Europe*, 250–1.

rather than converge during this period. Internally, changes of government in two of the larger states, Britain and France, led to policies which were seriously out of tune with the EC position. In 1974 the Heath government was replaced by a Labour administration pledged to put the very idea of EC membership before the electorate in the form of a referendum. Although the result produced a majority for remaining in the EC, few Labour politicians showed a great enthusiasm for the organization. Indeed after Labour's defeat by the Conservatives in 1979, the party became officially committed to complete withdrawal. Neither was the new Conservative government led by Margaret Thatcher particularly supportive of the EC project, as was shown in Britain's decision not to join the EMS in 1979. Very soon after coming to power, the Thatcher government began a long and often bitter campaign to reduce the British contribution to the EC budget. This issue dominated the internal politics of the EC during the early 1980s.

More importantly, the victory of the Socialists in France under François Mitterrand in 1981 signalled a major change in economic policy in the direction of a greatly enhanced role for government in the economy. This involved an extension of the state sector via nationalization, including, in 1981, the nationalization of banking.[50] It also involved elevating a reduction in unemployment to the top of the political agenda. This would be achieved via increased state spending and, if necessary, protectionist trade policies.[51] Mitterrand remained committed to the EC and to monetary co-operation, but this commitment was increasingly at odds with his new domestic economic strategy. In effect, the French had adopted an economic policy which was directly at odds with the new EC orthodoxy of exchange control abolition, competition, and open markets. As it turned out, the French government's position was not sustainable. Between 1981 and March 1983 successive devaluations of the franc reduced the value of the French currency by almost 30 per cent in relation to the Deutschmark.[52] Eventually, the French government was forced into a major 'U' turn in economic policy involving the abandonment of a prominent role for the state and the adoption of free market economics. These events are particularly significant because, along with Germany, France had always been considered one of just two key players in EC politics. Indeed, the post-war

[50] For an extensive review, see Peter Hall, *Governing the Economy: The Politics of State Intervention in Britain and France*, New York, 1986, Chapter 8.

[51] Ibid. 202–10.

[52] Quoted in Dyson, *Elusive Union*, 115.

history of European integration was essentially about the Franco-German relationship. During the peak of Gaullist nationalism (1963–8) this relationship was seriously undermined, and it was again during France's flirtation with economic nationalism during the early 1980s.

In the wider political context, the 1970s and early 1980s produced few, if any, advances in political co-operation among the member states. We have already noted the widely varying economic reactions to the 1973/4 oil crises. Other events, including the Falklands War in 1982 and the European response to increasingly tense US–Soviet relations after 1979, resulted in discord rather than harmony among the member states. While the Soviet invasion of Afghanistan did provoke a uniform response—condemnation followed by selective sanctions—a united stand *vis-à-vis* the Soviets did not continue into the 1980s, when serious differences between the British and other EC states emerged. Similarly, the initial EC response to the invasion of the Falkland Islands was unanimous condemnation. Later, however, Ireland and Italy withdrew from an EC-wide package of sanctions against Argentina. European Political Co-operation (EPC) was, then, just that: i.e. an attempt to co-operate on foreign policy and defence matters rather than produce a position binding on all the member states. David Sanders has put this point well:

> The main reason for this dearth of genuinely European foreign policy was simple. It is extraordinarily difficult for any group of nation states, no matter how ingenious the procedural arrangements which it has established, to achieve agreement on complex matters of external policy when individual members of that group continue jealously to guard their own national sovereignty and national interests. Notwithstanding the sentiments underlying both the Treaty of Rome and EPC, this was precisely the position inside the European Community throughout the 1970s and 1980s.[53]

CONCLUSIONS

Had this book been written in 1982 or 1983, there would have been no reason to dissent from Riker's characterization of the EC as a 'close alliance'. Certainly, the Community had been successfully enlarged; certainly it was becoming involved in a much wider range of policy concerns beyond agriculture. It had even developed a distinctive position

[53] Sanders, *Losing an Empire*, 163.

on markets and competition which was increasingly in tune with those of Western governments generally. But it had not evolved into an organization which was remotely federalist in structure or function. An embryonic federalist institutional apparatus including a popularly elected Parliament was in place, but in no major area of government activity, bar agricultural supports and trade and competition policy, had national governments ceded independence to the EC.

Indeed, the Continental states had come much closer to this position with the proposals for EDC in the early 1950s. After then the EC developed into a customs union of independent states with an admittedly unique and unusually intrusive institutional structure. It is also the case that both within EC institutions and without, federalist officials and politicians continued to work for the creation of a genuine political union. However, as of 1983 the conditions for a federal bargain looked as far away as ever. What, then, happened during the ensuing eight years to transform this situation and apparently convince almost all the member states that a federal bargain was indeed worth striking?

4

Understanding European Union II: 1983–1992

INTRODUCTION

Until the passage of the Single European Act (SEA) in 1986 the process of European integration attracted relatively little attention among more theoretically oriented social scientists. As the last chapter suggested, there was, in fact, rather little to explain. Traditional realist and neo-realist approaches, taking the nation state as the basic unit of analysis, looked adequate given the discord and national assertiveness which characterized the 1970–83 period. At the same time, integration and functionalist theories became increasingly discredited as the predicted march towards ever closer union, whether it be from institutional or from functional 'spillover', failed to materialize.[1] The acceptance of the SEA marked a significant change in the way the EC operated, however, so inspiring new theories on the nature of European integration. The formal acceptance of a Treaty on European Union represented another, and much more significant, development, which demanded further explanation. In this context, the present chapter has two main purposes: it will, first, review the more influential of the explanations invoked to explain the SEA and Maastricht; and, second, it will provide an alternative explanation based on an adaptation of Riker's theory of federalism.

THEORETICAL PERSPECTIVES ON THE SEA AND MAASTRICHT

Most of the contributions to the debate on the origins of the Single European Act and of Maastricht emphasize not only the interaction of

[1] For a review of this literature, see Robert O. Keohane and Stanley Hoffman, 'Institutional Change in Europe in the 1980s', in Robert O. Keohane and Stanley Hoffmann (eds.), *The New European Community: Decision Making and Institutional Change*, Boulder Colo., Westview Press, 1991, 1–39.

domestic political actors and interests with the supranational institutions of the EC, but also the broader international economic context in which these interactions took place. As we saw in the last chapter, the 1970s had produced a transformation in the international economy which, for the most part, led to a divergence in the economic performance of the EC member states and to a breakdown in consensus on how governments could best deal with the twin evils of inflation and unemployment. It is hardly surprising, therefore, that all of the most quoted accounts of the SEA and Maastricht assign great importance to this international context. Indeed, it would not be stretching causality too far to argue that both initiatives were directly in response to events in the international sphere.

Linking EC change to the international economy was a new development. Prior to the 1980s most explanations of European integration emphasized the centrality of the Franco-German relationship—either with regard to defence or economic questions. Later, the debates on enlargement, the CAP, and individual member contributions were also essentially intra-Community in nature. When, during the 1970s, the international economic environment deteriorated, it led not to solutions underpinned by EC actions but to a downgrading of the institution in relation to the economic roles played by national governments.

Not until the creation of the European Monetary System (EMS) in 1979, did (most of) the member states begin to co-operate meaningfully in response to international change, and, as was pointed out in the last chapter, the early years of EMS operations were less than successful. Why was it, then, that by the mid-1980s solutions based on co-operation and supranationalism had replaced the essentially national responses of the 1970s? Very generally, scholars have approached this question from two broad perspectives: *macro* approaches, which address the problem via broad changes in the international system; and *micro* approaches, which dwell on the response of individual actors and institutions to economic and political developments. Let us look at each of these in turn.

Macro Perspectives

Over the last twenty years, theorizing within the broad tradition of international relations has grown in both quantity and complexity, and any attempt to apply all the competing theories to the European case would in itself generate enough material to fill at least one book. Most of the relevant approaches are concerned with the link between international co-operation and the decline of the United States as an economic and political hegemon.[2] Some of the earliest work in this area by Gilpin and Kindleberger dwelt on the uncertainty and instability in the international system which results from the decline of hegemonic powers such as Britain in the 1930s or the United States in the 1970s. While in the position of hegemonic power, it was in the interest of the United States to impose order and co-operation on the international system via the Bretton Woods regime of fixed exchange rates. Once in decline, however, the erstwhile hegemon, now in competition with other successful states, will have little incentive to continue the regime.[3] Increased co-operation in the 1980s among the European powers could only be explained by the rise of a new hegemon, Germany, which would become the lead nation in moves towards the creation of a new regime. However, as will be demonstrated in a later section, Germany is not hegemonic and was not unambiguously the lead nation either with respect to the SEA or Maastricht.

A more recent and highly influential literature links the behaviour of states and political actors to the increased uncertainties characteristic of the post Bretton Woods era. Hence international 'regimes' (such as GATT, the EC) or a set of convenient 'ideas' can perform useful functions in an age when the danger of a return to international anarchy is always present. International regimes can instil particular beliefs and values on members, which can engender co-operation and reduce cheating.[4] Members are prepared to go along with regime norms because the benefits of doing so outweigh the costs—better to have your competitor conform to standardized rules of behaviour than, as in the 1930s, to indulge in beggar-thy-neighbour policies which leads eventually to

[2] For an excellent review of this literature in the European context, see Helen Milner, 'The Domestic Political Economy of International Economic Co-operation: A Comparison of the NAFTA Accord and the Maastricht Treaty', Paper before the 22nd Joint Sessions of Workshops of the European Consortium for Political Research, Madrid, 1994. Available from the ECPR Central Services, University of Essex, England.

[3] Robert Gilpin, *US Power and the Multinational Corporation*, New York, Basic Books, 1975; see also his *The Political Economy of International Relations*, Princeton, Princeton University Press, 1987; Charles Kindleberger, *The World in Depression, 1929–1939*, Berkeley and Los Angeles, University of California Press, 1973.

[4] This approach is particularly associated with the work of Robert Keohane. See *After Hegemony: Cooperation and Discord in the World Political Economy*, Princeton, Princeton University Press, 1984.

reduced welfare for all. Moreover, once established, regimes acquire an impetus of their own; they can, in other words, act independently of nation states and become the source of new policies and ideas.

A refinement on this theme is provided by Peter Haas, who argues that, in their search for order and certainty, policy makers will fall back on the advice of 'transnational epistemic communities', or 'a network of professionals with recognised expertise and competence in a particular policy domain and an authoritative claim to policy relevant knowledge within that domain or issue area'.[5] On the face of it, both approaches look relevant to the EC of the 1980s. The EC does approximate to Keohane's definition of an international regime; economists and other experts were indeed generating ideas about the macroeconomy and exchange rate stability, which were taken up by politicians and officials. More generally, the function of the EC regime during the 1980s was to provide for common rules of behaviour in economic affairs which would help prevent a return to the relative chaos of the 1970s.

Although useful—and we will return to the role of ideas later—the regime approach has only limited explanatory power when applied to the European context. It can, of course, apply to a constellation of regimes throughout the world including NAFTA, GATT, and various co-operative economic efforts in East and South Asia. Although co-operation may have increased in all these cases, in no case has co-operation proceeded as dramatically as in Europe. At this stage it is important to make a distinction between the SEA and the Maastricht Treaty. Writing in 1991, Keohane and Hoffmann attempted, largely successfully, to apply regime theory to the negotiations leading to the adoption of the SEA. They conclude that the SEA was adopted because of a 'convergence of preferences' among the major European governments in economic matters.[6] Following the failure of the old regulatory policies, the move to market economies, the French abandonment of economic nationalism after 1983, the expansion of EC membership, and continuing problems in the world economy, the member states found their interests converging in ways which facilitated the striking of a series of interstate bargains.[7]

These were, however, interstate bargains rather than a federal bar-

[5] Quoted in Milner, 'The Domestic Political Economy', 7. See also Peter Haas (ed.), 'Knowledge, Power, and International Policy Coordination', Special Issue of *International Organization*, 46/1, 1992.

[6] Keohane and Hoffmann, 'Institutional Change in Europe', 23–5.

[7] Ibid. 25.

gain between individual states and a new supranational authority. This becomes obvious when it is realized just how little national independence was ceded to EC institutions on the adoption of the SEA. The major thrust of the SEA was the intention to create a single market in goods, capital, and labour by 1992. In this sense the objective was to fulfil the original ideals of the Treaty of Rome. Britain, long the reluctant European, was one of the more enthusiastic signatories, which was altogether predictable, given the incumbent Conservative's commitment to free market ideas. Although the SEA included further declarations of intent in such areas as research and technology, the reduction of regional inequalities, the improvement of working conditions, and the raising of health standards, these provisions were not central to the Act, and no timetable for the systematic transfer of responsibility for these areas from national governments to Brussels was established. Most importantly, monetary co-operation was excluded from the Act, even 'though some of the participating states, including France, favoured advances in this area'.[8]

As far as institutional arrangements were concerned, the SEA did represent some movement towards the federal model, although these were not fundamental in nature. Unanimity in the Council of Ministers remained for the admission of new members and the adoption of general policy principles. Once policies in principle had been adopted, however, the details of implementation could be expedited via qualified majority voting. Of the 76 votes allocated to what by 1986 had become twelve members, 54 would be sufficient for a decision, so a strong element of the concurrent, rather than the simple majority, principle remained. In effect, three or four members with a common interest or position could block a Council decision. Changes affecting the European Parliament (EP) were largely cosmetic in nature and fell far short of the hopes of European federalists. Following the adoption of the SEA, the EP had the right to reject or amend any Council decision arrived at by qualified majority vote. Moreover, the Council could, in turn, reject an EP amendment only through a unanimous vote. Although this change involved elements of co-decision-making, it hardly elevated the EP to the status of a genuine European legislature.

Finally the SEA codified European Political Co-operation (EPC) and declared the intention that the European states should jointly formulate

[8] See Andrew Moravcsik. 'Negotiating the Single European Act', in Keohane and Hoffmann, *The New European Community*, 41–84.

a foreign policy and co-operate on defence and security matters. Again, this represented a step towards federal-like arrangements, but fell far short of the adoption of a single foreign or defence policy. If individual states wanted to go their own way, they could.

While the institutional changes did represent a real break from the stasis characteristic of the 1970s and early 1980s, no commentator at the time or since has described them as federalist in nature. SEA was, above all, a reaffirmation of the principle of a unitary, open market among the countries of Europe. In terms of the classification of international regimes or institutions, it was much closer to the genus 'customs union' than to the genus 'federation'. It is, therefore, perfectly plausible for regime theorists to apply the same, slightly adapted, framework to the SEA, GATT, NAFTA, and other efforts at international co-operation. Maastricht, however, is another matter. The Treaty on European Union was just that—an effort to create a new, federal state, involving the removal of the most fundamental of the nation state's domestic functions—macroeconomic policy—and its transfer to the supranational or federal level. There is, simply, no precedent for this in the history of international institutions. None of the systems or regimes created since the Second World War has evolved into a new federation, and none was expected to. Indeed, it is doubtful whether any of the many varieties of international relations theories are conceptually equipped to deal with the unique European case. For whatever the complexities of the domestic/international linkages, or the role of inter- or supranational actors, ultimately in international relations research, the nation state remains the basic unit of analysis.[9] Perhaps it is for this reason that scholars of international relations have tended to neglect the question of why countries come together to form unions and why, in some cases, federations fall apart.

Micro Perspectives

Keohane and Hoffmann's approach, along with those of a number of other scholars, is particularly useful, however, because it highlights the importance of domestic political actors and interests in the bargaining process. At its most elemental, this perspective links the interests of

[9] See e.g. David A. Baldwin, 'Neoliberalism, Neorealism and World Politics', in David A. Baldwin (ed.), *Neorealism and Neoliberalism: The Contemporary Debate*, New York, Columbia University Press, 1993, 3–28.

national politicians to international institutions. If the interests of a number of countries converge, national politicians are likely to exploit existing international bodies to advance these interests in mutually advantageous ways. National politicians may, in turn, be under pressure from domestic interest groups or electorates to opt for a particular supranational policy choice. Variations on this theme are numerous, with some contributions emphasizing the role of domestic interest groups, others domestic political institutions and others still, the preferences of national politicians and officials.[10]

By focusing on the behaviour of individual actors and interests, these studies are micro rather than macro in approach. The actual decisions of policy makers are at the core of the analysis. Not surprisingly, given the number of actors and the range of issues involved, negotiations over the adoption of the EMS, the SEA, and Maastricht were highly complex in nature. None of the studies is able to come to simple conclusions drawn from a single theoretical perspective. The conclusions of one of the most thorough researchers of the decision-making processes in both the EMS and EMU is typical:

> The characteristics of the policy process . . . make the development of a single theory to account for the EMU outcome extremely hazardous. The diversity of the actors involved; the different dimensions of bargaining and their complex interaction; the variations in the relative importance of the bargaining relations over time; and iteration of bargaining and its inseparability from a broad policy package that could not be entirely separated from other EC policy areas; the accumulation of these factors inhibits the simultaneous achievement of parsimony in theorizing and sensitivity and comprehensiveness in understanding.[11]

In another study, Wayne Sandholz comes to a similar conclusion. Having reviewed three possible explanations for EMU—spillover from the SEA,

[10] For a review, see Milner, 'The Domestic Political Economy'; Wayne Sandholz and John Zysman stress the role of domestic interests groups; see their '1992: Recasting the European Bargain', *World Politics*, 42, 1989, 1–30; Kenneth Dyson stresses the role of officials and politicians, *Elusive Union: The Process of Economic and Monetary Union in Europe*, London, Longman, 1994; Andrew Moravcsik emphasizes the role of domestic politics, 'Negotiating the Single European Act'.

[11] Kenneth Dyson, Kevin Feathersone, and George Michalopolous, 'The Politics of EMU: The Maastricht Treaty and the Relevance of Bargaining Models', Paper before the annual meeting of the American Political Science Association, New York, 1994, 13. This is also the broad conclusion of Dyson's major study of EMU and EMS, *Elusive Union*, ch. 9. Other important studies include, Milner, 'The Domestic Political Economy'; Moravcsik, 'Negotiating the Single European Act'; Sandholz and Zysman, '1992: Recasting the European Bargain'; Wayne Sandholz, 'Choosing Union: Monetary Politics and Maastricht', *International Organization*, 47, 1993, 1–39.

internal politics of the EMS, and the need on the part of governments to convince economic actors of the seriousness of their commitment to maintain low inflation regimes—he concludes that: 'This analysis has demonstrated the futility of trying to collapse the distinct perspectives into one. Perhaps our explanatory goals are best served by specifying the analytic strengths—and limitations—of approaches that work better in combination than alone.'[12]

Most of these studies recognize the centrality of bargaining in defence or promotion of particular interests when describing the decision-making processes at work in European integration. In this sense they are sensitive to the fact that what national actors are engaged in is a weighing of the costs and benefits involved in participation in supranational institutions. They also recognize that EC-level actors can have an important role to play independently of national representatives. What is missing in this sometimes impressive body of work is an appreciation that the decisions taken at Maastricht, and especially the decision to create a single currency under the control of a European central bank, was conceptually quite distinct from earlier initiatives over the EMS and the SEA. To repeat the point, Maastricht represented a challenge to the very idea of the nation state. Put at its most dramatic, what national politicians and officials were engaged in at Maastricht was the effective dismantling of one of the two major pillars of nationhood (the other being national defence). They must, therefore, have calculated that the costs of non-participation were, potentially, higher than the sacrifice of a fundamental facet of national independence—control over macroeconomic policy.

In this sense, Maastricht was very much closer to the deliberations at Philadelphia in 1787 or to the negotiations over the creation of federal states in the post-colonial era, than to the decision to establish the SEA or, for that matter, NAFTA or the GATT[13] agreements. This conclusion raises two obvious questions: what was it that drove politicians to take such a momentous decision? And why is it that the sometimes very careful research into the bargaining at Maastricht has so far failed to come up with a convincing answer? In answering the first question, considerable light will be thrown on the second.

[12] Wayne Sandholz, 'Choosing Union', 39.

[13] Yet scholars working in the international relations tradition have made no clear conceptual distinction between EU and other supranational initiatives. See references at Milner, 'The Domestic Political Economy', Sandholz, 'Choosing Union'; Keohane and Hoffmann (eds.), *The New European Community*.

MAASTRICHT: EXPLAINING THE EUROPEAN FEDERAL BARGAIN

Recall that in Riker's theory on the emergence of federal states it is necessary that national politicians be convinced that entering into a larger political entity will avert some internal or external military or diplomatic threat to the integrity of those component states seeking a solution through enlargement or provide an opportunity for diplomatic aggrandizement. However, as was argued in Chapter 2, there could be no logical objection to extending Riker's reasoning to include threats and opportunities other than those originating in military or diplomatic concerns. As it happened, Riker could find no case of an emerging and successful federation which did not fit his criteria. But if by association with a larger political entity national politicians could avert some actual or potential threat to the constitutional order, and if a consensus existed that this threat could not be averted by national action alone, then surely Riker's conditions would be fulfilled? If this is so, the following have to be established in the European case:

1. That among the signatories to the Treaty on European Union, perception of such a threat existed and that it was only in the late 1980s and early 1990s that enlargement through monetary union was perceived as a means of averting this threat. Recall also that, for Riker, the nature of the threat or opportunity does not have to be the same for all parties. It could be quite different from country to country or from individual to individual. It is enough that the threats and opportunities, whatever their roots, are perceived as sufficiently serious by all the concerned parties.

2. That the conditions for European union during this period were unique. In other words, the perception of the non-military threat and the solution to it through union only applied in the European case. Elsewhere, and in particular in comparable industrial countries, the conditions had to be different because nowhere else was there an attempt to create a political union.

This book's main claim is that, for most of the participating countries, the threat came from a near universal perception among political élites that the pursuit of any economic policy bar one which guaranteed low inflation in the context of open national and international markets, was not only untenable but would, in the worst possible case, lead to serious and potentially regime-threatening political consequences. Only

European monetary union would provide a guarantee of low inflation. For Germany, the motives were different, for although they may have been related to a low inflation philosophy, they may, alternatively, have been linked to an opportunity for diplomatic aggrandizement. The rest of this chapter will be divided into two parts. Part one will outline what can only be described as an intellectual revolution in economic policy, which transformed the policy options available to political parties and governments during the 1980s. Part two will synthesize a large body of research on the move towards monetary union during the period and will attempt to disaggregate the motives of different actors using a modified Rikerian framework.

1. The Transformation of Economic Policy, 1976–1990

As was noted in Chapter 3, the 1970s was a period of considerable economic dislocation throughout the industrialized world. Reporting in 1977, the McCracken Report, commissioned by the Organization for Economic Co-operation and Development (OECD), warned that unless the OECD member states managed to control inflation there was no hope of a return to a period of steady economic growth and full employment. The report was also unambiguous in its recommendation that the only way to achieve low inflation in an increasingly open international environment was through fundamental changes in the domestic economic policies pursued by most member states.[14] What this meant was cuts in public expenditure, the pursuit of free market policies, increased taxation in the short term to reduce national budget deficits, and greater discipline in dealing with the demands of organized interests, and in particular, the labour unions. As far as exchange rates were concerned, the report endorsed the existing regime of floating rates, mitigated only by 'active intervention' by governments in the exchange rate markets designed to stabilize parities. Significantly, some of the economists contributing to the report believed that in the case of smaller countries there was a need to 'peg [currencies] formally or informally, to that of a major country with a satisfactory price performance'.[15]

Although attacked at the time as representing an ideologically biased position,[16] the recommendations of the McCracken Report were widely

[14] Paul McCracken *et al.*, *Towards Full Employment and Price Stability*, Paris, OECD, 1977, Summary, pp. 11–33.

[15] Ibid. 32.

[16] Robert O. Keohane, 'Neo-Orthodox Economics, Inflation and the Role of the State: Political Implications of the McCracken Report', *World Politics*, 27, 1977.

quoted and almost certainly influenced governments' policies in the longer term. Concurrent with McCracken came a number of warnings that continuing high levels of inflation constituted a threat to the very fabric of democratic society itself. Some of the most convincing of these analyses predicted that in democratic systems characterized by powerful organized interests, vote-maximizing politicians, and high levels of public expenditure, there was a tendency for each successive political-business cycle to be completed at a higher level of inflation. One of the most influential exponents of this view, Samuel Brittan, expressed it thus:

> If we combine the short-term political cycle with the long-term deterioration between unemployment and inflation, we reach the following account. Each stimulus takes the economy to a fresh inflationary height; and the subsequent check to demand raises the unemployment rate while administering only a limited and temporary check to the inflation rate, which resumes its upward drift once governments have become sufficiently worried about unemployment to restimulate demand.[17]

Brittan labelled this process a 'doomsday machine' where Keynesian stimulation increases 'output and employment in the short run, but only prices in the long run'[18]—a process which monetarist economists had rather more formally labelled 'the expectations augmented Phillip's curve'.[19] In an open international trading environment, excessive inflation in one country is likely to lead to devaluation, which in itself will be inflationary for an import-dependent economy. In effect, democracy was causing inflation. And history had taught us that ever higher levels of inflation were incompatible with the maintenance of a stable social structure and democratic political institutions.[20] By the late 1970s this general analysis had grown in influence especially in Britain and the United States.[21] Continuing high levels of inflation were simply not

[17] Samuel Brittan, 'Inflation and Democracy', in Fred Hirsch and John H. Goldthorpe (eds.), *The Political Economy of Inflation*, Oxford, Martin Robertson, 1978, 173.

[18] Ibid. 181.

[19] See Milton Friedman, 'Inflation and Unemployment', *Journal of Political Economy*, 85, 1977.

[20] For a review see Charles S. Maier, 'The Politics of Inflation in the Twentieth Century', in Hirsch and Goldthorpe, *The Political Economy of Inflation*, 37–72.

[21] In the United States 'overload' was considered to have adverse social as well as economic and political consequences. See the special edition of the *Public Interest*, 41, 1975, contributions by Daniel Bell and Samuel Huntington; also Aaron Wildavsky, 'Government and the People', *Commentary*, August 1973, 25–32. For a British perspective see Anthony King, 'Overload: Problems of Governing in the 1970s', *Political Studies*, 23, 1975, 162–74; Samuel Britain, 'The Economic Contradictions of Democracy', *British Journal of Political Science*, 5, 1975, 129–59.

sustainable in a democratic society; history had taught that unless appropriate action was taken, inflation could become a major contributing factor, if not the major cause, of a drift towards authoritarianism or fascism.[22]

Very generally, the suggested solutions to this apparent impasse took one of two forms. On the left, the proffered solution was to use government intervention to regulate the activities of open markets including, if necessary, the adoption of protectionist measures and exchange controls to defend currencies.[23] On the right, the solutions were precisely the opposite: reduce the role of government as a regulator and provider of selective benefits to powerful groups; let unemployment rise to its 'natural' level; use monetary tools to combat inflation. As far as exchange rate instability was concerned, monetarist economists and others on the right were convinced that with the appropriate reduction in the role of governments and the abolition of exchange controls, currencies would find their proper value and fluctuate in relation to the objective performance of domestic economies.[24]

In retrospect, what is interesting about the first solution is that its adherents, along with many others not associated with the left, assumed that governments would always be impelled to maintain low levels of unemployment. Indeed the whole model, organized around the idea of the economic contradictions of democracy, took this as a basic assumption—in Europe, at least, no government would allow itself to go into a general election in the context of high and/or rising unemployment.[25] Under the Bretton Woods international monetary regime, high levels of employment had been achieved in all the leading industrial countries and especially in Europe. The assumption was that even amid the dislocations of the 1970s publics would continue to demand full employment. As it turned out, it was not low unemployment but low inflation which became the dominant value in economic policy. In other words it was policies of the right rather than of the left which prevailed during the 1980s.

In historical perspective this is a remarkable development because it

[22] See Hirsch and Goldthorpe, *The Political Economy of Inflation*, ch. 2; also Michael Jefferson *et al.*, *Inflation*, London, John Calder, 1977.

[23] So influential was this movement on the British left that it became, if only briefly, official Labour Party policy during the mid-1970s. See *The Labour Party Programme 1973*, London, the Labour Party, 1973.

[24] See e.g. A. A. Walters, *Britain's Economic Renaissance: Margaret Thatcher's Reforms, 1979–1984*, Oxford, OUP, 1984; also his *Sterling in Danger: The Economic Consequences of Pegged Exchange Rates*, London, Fontana Collins, 1990.

[25] This view was formalized by Edward Tufte in his *Political Control of the Economy*, Princeton, Princeton University Press, 1978.

marks a convergence in the economic policies of the major political parties of the right and of the left which has no precedent this century. Moreover, it became increasingly obvious during the decade of the 1980s that low inflation could only be achieved as part of a general economic strategy involving limiting government expenditures and the deregulation of labour and capital markets. Deregulation applied not just to domestic markets but also to capital movements as, starting with Germany in 1974, country after country reduced or abolished exchange controls. In this sense the new orthodoxy of the 1980s was more complete than that prevalent during the Bretton Woods era. Then, political parties offered a variety of economic alternatives to electorates ranging from free market choices all the way through to highly interventionist protectionist and corporatist strategies.[26] While governments were clearly constrained by the international environment during this period, the existence of exchange controls allowed governments to make relatively modest adjustments in domestic economic policy in response to outside pressures on their currencies.[27]

Ideologically, parties of the left in particular saw no necessary contradiction in pursuing policies of economic nationalism while at the same time remaining full members of a system of international monetary co-operation policed by the International Monetary Fund and underwritten by a strong dollar. By the 1980s, in contrast, one after another parties of the left were forced into abandoning protectionism and economic nationalism as simply irreconcilable with the realities of the international system. Undoubtedly the most notable case of a leftist government undergoing such a conversion was that of the French Socialists in 1983/4. Having initially favoured policies of economic nationalism and reflation, the French were forced to abandon this strategy in favour of deflation and monetary orthodoxy following serious runs on the franc which culminated in two devaluations in 1982 and 1983.[28] Earlier a British Labour government had been forced into an almost equally dramatic about face, following a near collapse of the pound

[26] Until quite recently it was common for political scientists to distinguish state societal relations in different countries according to the extent of corporatist arrangements. For a general review see Gerhard Lehmbruch and Philippe C. Schmitter (eds.), *Patterns of Corporate Policy-Making*, London, Sage, 1982. As recently as 1983 scholars were writing in ways which implied a degree of choice in state/society relations, John Zysman, *Governments, Markets and Growth: Financial Systems and the Politics of Industrial Change*, Ithaca, NY, Cornell University Press, 1983.

[27] For a discussion, see Barry Eichengreen, *International Monetary Arrangements for the 21st Century*, Washington, Brookings Institution, 1994, 49–54.

[28] See Peter Hall, *Governing the Economy: The Politics of State Intervention in Britain and France*, Oxford, Polity, 1986, chs. 8; Sandholz, 'Choosing Union', 6–7.

sterling on the international exchanges in 1976. During its subsequent period in opposition, the British Labour Party reverted to policies favouring interventionism and economic nationalism, but was eventually converted to the new orthodoxy during the late 1980s and 1990s.[29] Although it is not possible to discern a similar transformation in the context of Italy's complex and volatile coalition politics, the Italian Communists gradually warmed towards the EC and the EMS during the late 1970s and the 1980s.[30] Generally, the Italian governments of the 1980s moved towards the new orthodoxy, gradually extending independence to the Bank of Italy and removing exchange controls.[31] Political parties in most of the other EC countries, whether of the left or the right, have also moved towards macroeconomic discipline, with the new orthodoxy becoming declared government policy in Belgium, the Netherlands, Ireland, Spain, and Denmark.[32] By 1990 even Greece and Portugal, with their endemically high rates of inflation, were officially committed to moving towards the EC norm.

As can be seen from Fig. 4.1, the consequences on prices both among the 'core' EC states and in Italy, Spain, and Britain, were profound. Having begun the decade of the 1980s with widely diverging inflation rates, almost all of the member states had achieved low inflation by the end of the decade. Although the precise relationship between unemployment and inflation remains a point of controversy in economic theory, few economists would argue that, at least in the short term, no relationship at all exists.[33] If this is so, the very high levels of unemployment that persisted throughout the 1980s (Table 4.1) can at least in part be attributed to the low inflation (or deflationary) policies of that decade.

What is remarkable about these figures is that both governments of

[29] On Labour during the 1970s, see Hall, *Governing the Economy*, chs. 3 and 4; on the transformation of the party while in opposition see Andrew Gamble, 'The Labour Party and Economic Policy Making', in Martin J. Smith and Joanna Sear (eds.), *The Changing Labour Party*, London Routledge, 1992, 61–74; Eric Shaw, *The Labour Party Since 1979*, London, Routledge, 1994, ch. 2.

[30] See Giacomo Luciano and Guiseppe Sacco, 'The PCI and the International Economic Crisis', in Simon Serfaty and Lawrence Gray (eds.), *The Italian Communist Party: Yesterday, Today and Tomorrow*, London, Aldwych Press, 1980, 191–210.

[31] See Gerald A. Epstein and Juliet B. Schor, 'Divorce of the Bank of Italy and the Treasury', in Peter Lange and Marino Regina (eds.), *State, Market and Social Regulation: New Perspectives on Italy*, Cambridge, CUP, 1989, 147–64.

[32] See Sandholz, 'Choosing Union', 9–11.

[33] For a discussion of the relationship in the context of monetary union, see Ali M. El-Agraa, *The Economics of the European Community*, London, Harvester Wheatsheaf, 4th edn., 1994, 109–18. For a good popular account of the relationship and of the recent rejection of the monetarist position, see Paul Krugman, *Peddling Prosperity: Economic Sense and Nonsense in an Age of Diminished Expectations*, New York, Norton, 1994, chs. 1 and 8.

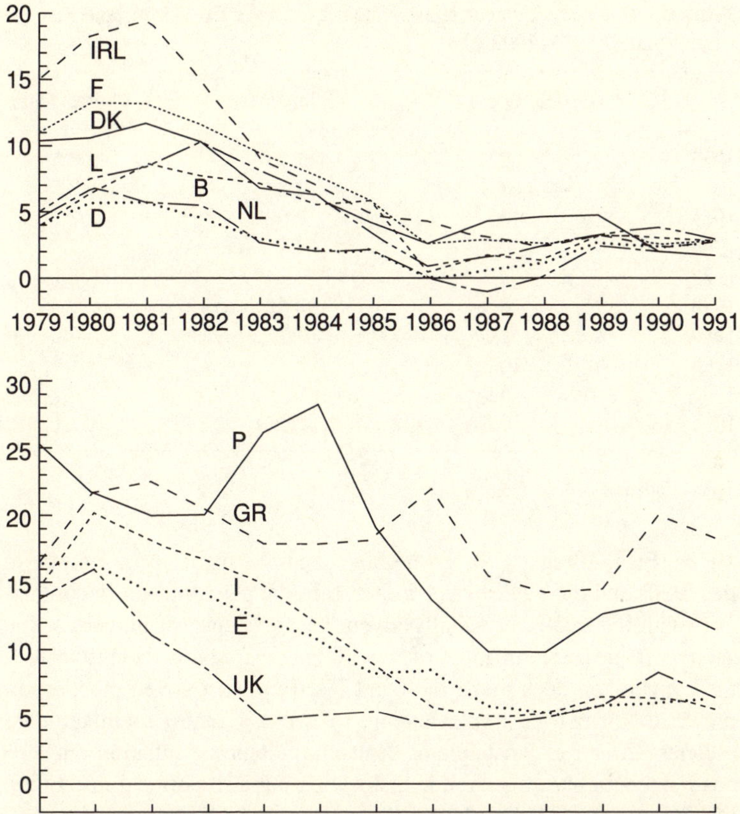

Source: reproduced from Loukas Tsoukalis, *The New European Economy*, Oxford, OUP, 1993, Fig. 7.1.

FIG. 4.1. (a) Price deflator private consumption in EC-7, 1979–1991
(b) Price deflator private consumption in EC-5, 1979–1991

the right and of the left were prepared to bear the political costs of such high unemployment levels. Put another way, low inflation had become so entrenched as a policy objective that it completely overwhelmed other priorities, including full employment, which had been a dominant value (arguably *the* dominant value) in governments' economic policies as recently as the 1970s. Only in Europe was it deemed necessary to tolerate such high levels of unemployment in order to tame inflation (Table 4.1). An even more dramatic comparison can be drawn between Europe and the USA since 1989 and their relative positions in the

TABLE 4.1. Unemployment rates (annual averages), EC, Japan, and the United States, 1975–1992

	Europe 12	Japan	United States
1975	2.9	1.9	8.5
1981	7.8	2.2	7.6
1985	10.6	2.6	7.2
1986	10.7	2.8	7.0
1987	9.7	2.8	6.1
1988	8.9	2.5	5.4
1989	8.3	2.3	5.2
1990	10.8	2.1	5.4
1991	8.9	2.2	6.7
1992	9.8	2.2	7.1

Souce: *Eurostat*.

1930s (Figs. 4.2 and 4.3). To be fair, unemployment in the Europe of the 1980s and the 1990s was a rather different phenomenon in comparison with the 1930s, especially given the prevalence of modern social safety-net measures in most of the EC member states. None the less, the comparison does make the point that European governments were prepared to go to extreme lengths to avoid a return to inflationary policies. Countries incapable of controlling domestic inflation ran serious risks not only of economic dislocation but also political instability. Examples from around the world, and in particular Latin America, seemed to testify to this.[34] Much closer to home, worries about political stability in one of the member states, Greece, were widely perceived to be linked to that country's apparent inability to manage its macroeconomic policies in a responsible manner.[35] And a potential member state, Turkey, had already witnessed the erosion of its fragile democratic institutions amid raging inflation and the near collapse of its currency.[36]

[34] See Hirsch and Goldthorpe, *The Political Economy of Inflation*, ch. 2.

[35] See G. Yannopoulos, *Greece and the European Economic Community: Integration and Convergence*, London, Macmillan, 1986.

[36] Between 1988 and 1991 Turkish inflation averaged 66 per cent per annum, and the economy is known for its volatility. For a discussion of the problems Turkey has experienced making a transition to democracy and its relations with the EU, see William Hale, 'Turkey: A Crucial but Problematic Applicant', in John Redmond (ed.), *Prospective Europeans: New Members for the European Union*, London, Harvester Wheatsheaf, 1994, 113–32.

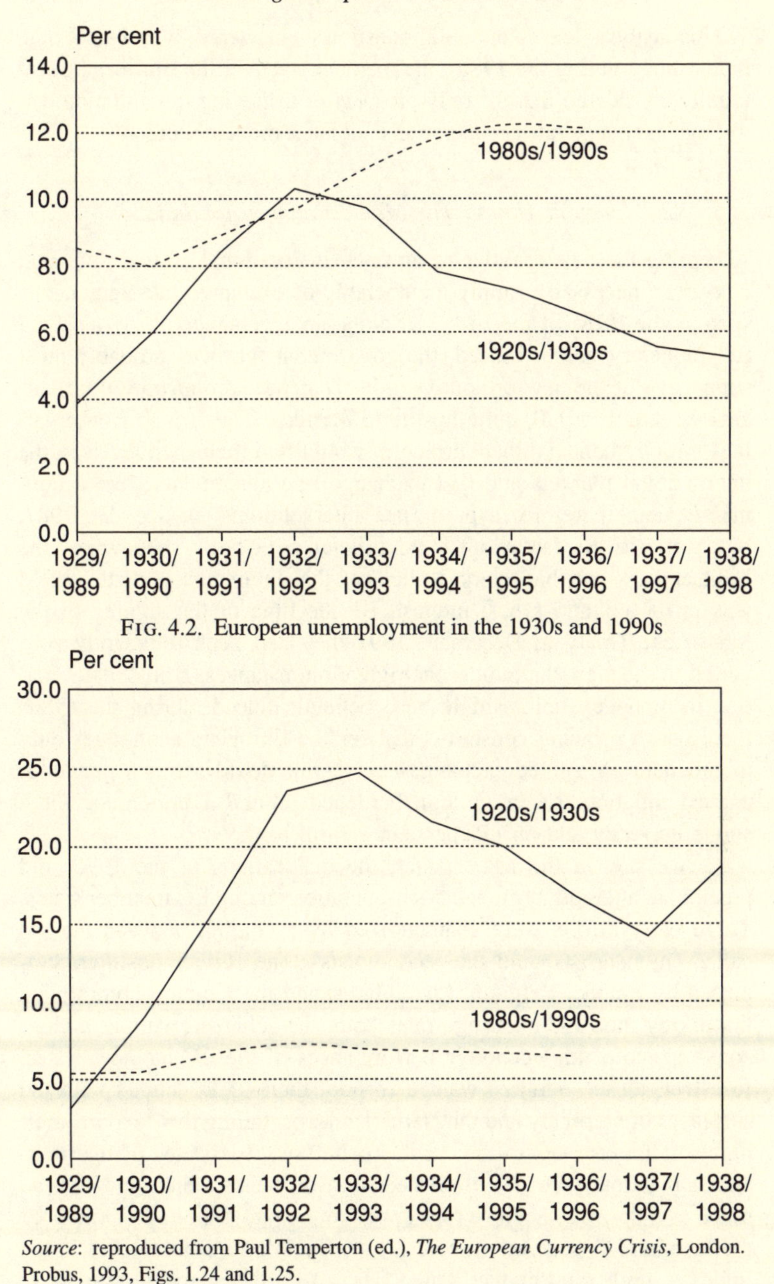

FIG. 4.2. European unemployment in the 1930s and 1990s

Source: reproduced from Paul Temperton (ed.), *The European Currency Crisis*, London. Probus, 1993, Figs. 1.24 and 1.25.

FIG. 4.3. US unemployment in the 1930s and 1990s

This analysis leaves one vital question unanswered: why was it that, increasingly during the 1980s, the member states of the European Community considered that the only prospect of achieving low inflation was through exchange rate co-operation and, later, monetary union?

2. *Monetary Union: The Magic Panacea for Inflation?*

Accepting the new realities of an open international system does not, of course, necessarily imply membership of exchange rate agreements such as the ERM of the EMS, let alone an acceptance of the need for full monetary union. Indeed, the government that was probably most supportive of the new orthodoxy—the Thatcher administration in Britain—was, until 1990, quite hostile to the idea. The British Conservatives initially believed that currencies would find their own levels in the international markets and that exchange rate agreements were a non-market, and therefore inappropriate interventionist device. By 1987, however, the British adopted an official policy of 'shadowing' the Deutschmark and had come to believe that membership of the ERM was in the country's best interest. By the time of the signing of the Maastricht Treaty in December 1991 they had been reluctantly converted to the view that, under the right circumstances, British participation in monetary union might be beneficial. Indeed, during the 1980s there was a growing consensus that for the European economies only membership in a fixed exchange rate regime could act as a guarantor against inflation. Later, opinion hardened around a preference for a single currency and an independent central bank.

As we saw in the last chapter, the dislocations of the 1970s did precipitate attempts at monetary co-operation among EC member states. These early efforts were characterized by a conflict between the so-called 'monetarists' and the 'economists'. The former position, supported by France, Belgium, Luxemburg, and the Commission, argued that fixing intra-EC exchange rates could be achieved without a close convergence of the economic performances of the EC member states. In effect, these countries wanted to pool their trade deficits with the surpluses of Germany and the Netherlands, or, failing this 'export' their higher inflation rates to the surplus countries. Advocates of the monetarist position were not motivated by a desire to reduce inflation so much as a desire to achieve further economic integration. Supporters of the 'economist' position, in contrast, insisted that a convergence in the inflation, trade, and budget deficit rates of all the member states were required before currencies could be fixed in relation to one another. In other words, the Germans and the Dutch wanted the other member states to comply with the strictest standards of macroeconomic management.[37] This debate occurred during 1969 and 1970 when the EC states were seeking to co-ordinate their exchange rates in the context of the relative certainties of the Bretton Woods system, and the recommendations of the high-level group commissioned at the 1969 Hague Summit to resolve the problem (the Werner Committee, which proposed a ten-year transition period for effective monetary union) were quickly overtaken by the collapse of the global fixed exchange rate regime.

In contrast to the debate in 1969 and 1970, the debate in the late 1970s was dominated by the spectre of inflation. As we saw in the last chapter, the 1970s had seen a wide divergence in the economic performance of the member states, and the first attempts to deal with the volatile post-Bretton Woods world via the currency 'snake' had ended in abject failure (Chapter 3, pp. 61–62). What eventually transpired in the form of the European Monetary System (EMS) in 1979 was the effective acceptance of the original German/Dutch 'monetarist' position of 1970. As Tsoukalis has put it, 'The EMS was considered as an important instrument in the fight against inflation, and its creation meant an implicit acceptance of German policy priorities by the other EC countries. The experience of the 1970s was seen as validating the uncompromising anti-inflationary stance combined with the strong currency option adopted by the Federal Republic.'[38] Among academic economists there is considerable disagreement both as to the precise economic effects of the EMS and as to whether or not it can be deemed a success. In one respect—longevity—it has been successful and until the traumatic events of 1992 and 1993 when the system very nearly collapsed, the consensus of opinion was that it had become a very useful device for fighting inflation by pegging some of the weaker EC currencies (including the pound sterling after 1990) to the Deutschmark.[39] The critical question was whether the EMS was disinflationary as its supporters argued, or whether it was deflationary as its detractors claimed. On balance, most commentators accept that for some of its members

[37] For a discussion, see Dyson, *Elusive Union*, ch. 3; Loukas Tsoukalis, *The New European Economy: The Politics and Economics of Integration*, Oxford, OUP, 1993, ch. 7.

[38] Ibid. 184.

[39] For a generally sanguine view, see ibid., ch. 7. For negative views see Paul Temperton (ed.), *The European Currency Crisis*, Cambridge, Probus, 1993, contributions by Paul Temperton, Alan Walters, and Tim Congdon; Also Barry Eichengreen, *International Monetary Arrangements*.

and in particular France (after 1983), Italy, and Belgium it was deflationary. Some academic economists also point to the continuing gap between the unemployment levels of the EMS members and those of other OECD countries as evidence of the deflationary effects of the system, especially during the period of greatest stability in the EMS from 1987 to 1992, when there was just one major realignment of the EMS in the ERM (involving the Italian lira). This gap holds even accounting for the alleged greater rigidities in the labour and capital markets of many EMS countries compared with the United States and Britain.[40] As Paul Krugman notes: 'The reality of the EMS was that it was a useful way for governments to justify hard choices, while obscuring the harshness of the consequences of those choices. The European experience, like that of the United States, was that controlling inflation required a prolonged, extremely painful recession . . . European governments chose to cloak the reality of their policy in the mystique of international finance rather than admit it openly.'[41]

Whether membership of the EMS was deflationary or not did not, of course, alter the fact that *all* the major industrial countries were pursuing anti-inflationary policies during the 1980s. During this decade, however, authorities in all the more vulnerable—often the smaller—economies of Western Europe gradually came around to the view that a formal link to the EMS was necessary if inflation was to be contained in the longer term. Between 1989 and June 1992, four countries, Norway, Finland, Sweden, and Cyprus, announced they would formally link to the European Currency Unit (ECU or the basket of currencies which made up the EMS). Spain joined the EMS in 1989 and the UK in 1990. It is against this backdrop that the negotiations at Maastricht, which culminated in firm plans for complete monetary union, should be understood.

Progress towards monetary union was very rapid indeed after 1988. In fact it took just two years and eight months from the publication of the Delors Report on Economic and Monetary Union in 1989 and the final drafting of the Maastricht Treaty in December 1991 for the plans and timetable to be concluded. Although, under the leadership of Jacques Delors, the Commission had become a strong advocate of monetary

[40] For a full discussion, see Paul De Grauwe, *The Economics of Monetary Integration*, Oxford, OUP, 1994.

[41] Paul Krugman, *Peddling Prosperity: Economic Sense and Nonsense in the Age of Diminished Expectations*, New York, Norton, 1994.

union,[42] it is unlikely that events would have moved as fast as they did in the absence of three key developments which greatly strengthened the case for the adoption of a single currency.

1. As earlier suggested, by the late 1980s the Exchange Rate Mechanism of the EMS was widely regarded as a success. Following an early period of instability, the system settled down after 1986 with only one major realignment in 1987 and one minor one between 1987 and Maastricht (Table 4.2). If most EMS members could achieve currency stability within the very narrow band of no more than 2.25 per cent fluctuations, then the feasibility of fixed and irrevocable parities inherent in monetary union was surely enhanced.

2. In June 1988, in accordance with the aims of the Single European Act, the Council of Ministers approved a move to a complete liberalization of capital movements within the EC. The 1st of July 1990 was fixed as the date for achieving this objective, although special provisions were made for Spain, Greece, Portugal, and Ireland, all of whom were allowed a longer transitional period. All the other countries had achieved liberalization by 1990 with the Italians being the last to abolish all controls in April 1990. Both Britain and Germany had long before removed controls, but even in the late 1980s, the French and the Italians continued to use them as an instrument of exchange rate policy. As Dyson notes, without such controls the Italians and French were 'persuaded that urgent and probably radical action was needed to strengthen the EMS'.[43]

3. Between 1987 and 1992 almost all the member states experienced a resurgence of inflation (see Table 4.1). Although, in most countries, the increase was relatively modest, it did served to emphasize the need for some sort of external discipline to guarantee lower inflation in the longer term. In Britain, the price increase was a direct result of an overreaction to the stock market crash of October 1987. Fearing a return to recession, the Conservative government reduced interest rates and expanded the money supply, thus creating upward pressure on prices. In France, official reaction to the 1987 ERM crisis, when the franc came under unsustainable pressure, was anger that, although the French had done everything in accordance with the rules in pursuing a

[42] For accounts of Delors' role see Charles Grant, *Delors: Inside the House that Jacques Built*, London, Brealey, 1994; George Ross, *Jacques Delors and European Integration*, Oxford, Polity, 1995.

[43] Dyson, *Elusive Union*, 121.

TABLE 4.2. EMS realignments: changes in central rates (% change: minus sign denotes a devaluation)

Currency	24 Sept. 1979	30 Nov. 1979	23 Mar. 1981	5 Oct. 1981	22 Feb. 1982	14 June 1982	21 Mar. 1983	22 July 1985	7 Apr. 1986	4 Aug. 1986	12 Jan. 1987	8 Jan.[a] 1990
Deutschmark	2.0			5.5		4.25	5.5	2.0	3.0		3.0	
French franc				–3.0		–5.75	–2.5	2.0	–3.0			
Netherlands guilder				5.5		4.25	3.5	2.0	3.0		3.0	
Belgian and Luxembourg franc					–8.5		1.5	2.0	1.0		2.0	
Italian lira			–6.0	–3.0		–2.75	–2.5	–6.2				–3.0
Danish krone	–2.9	–4.8			–3.0		2.5	2.0	1.0			
Irish punt							–3.5	2.0		–8.0		
Spanish peseta[b]												
Pound sterling[c]												
Portuguese escudo[d]												

[a] On this date the Italian lira moved from fluctuation bands of ±6% around its central rate to narrow fluctuation bands of ±2.25%.

[b] The peseta joined the ERM on 19 June 1989 with a fluctuation band of ±6% around its central rates.

[c] The pound entered the ERM on 8 Oct. 1990 with a fluctuation band of ±6% around its central rates.

[d] The escudo entered the ERM on 6 April 1992 with a fluctuation band of ±6% around its central rates.

Source: *Eurostat*, quoted in Loukas Tsoukalis, *The New European Economy*, Oxford, OUP, 1993, Table 2.

policy of disinflation, the markets could still launch speculative attacks leading to devaluation and therefore inflation. These events strengthened French resolve to move to a genuinely unassailable system of fixed exchange rates. Only EMU would assure this.[44] In Spain inflation was supposed to fall from 8 per cent in 1986 to 3 per cent in 1989. After initial success it rose again to 6 per cent in 1990 thus fuelling higher wage demands. In the case of Italy, it was large government budget deficits that were blamed for the upturn in inflation. Officials in both countries became convinced that the discipline of EMU would force those macroeconomic changes necessary to control inflation.[45] In all these cases a strengthened EMS, possibly in the form of EMU, brought clear domestic political benefits by transferring the responsibility for controlling inflation to a supranational authority. The German case was slightly different, for although, in the wake of reunification, German inflation rose above the EC average in the early 1990s, a strengthened EMS or EMU offered no more discipline than that provided by the Bundesbank. In fact, the German monetary authorities' response to inflation was swift and severe with sharp rises in interest rates and reductions in the money supply. We will return to German motivations for agreeing to EMU later.

We can conclude, then, that with the notable exception of the Germans, all the leading member states of the EC had an incentive to transfer responsibility for controlling domestic inflation to a supranational authority. Moreover, since the collapse of the Bretton Woods regime in 1971–3, these same countries had been through a series of national traumas relating to a failure to control inflation. Alternative strategies to harness inflation based on economic nationalism were widely discredited, both intellectually and politically. For most politicians and officials, whether in or out of government, monetary union was the only true long-term guarantee of price stability. Studies of the actual negotiations leading up to the Maastricht Treaty confirm this general point, if sometimes only by implication. The proceedings were greatly influenced not only by elected politicians but also by central bankers who, almost by definition, were converts to price stability. Other actors, who may have had an interest in other economic values, including rapid economic growth and low unemployment, played no part in the proceedings. As Dyson, Featherstone, and Michapolous note: 'The EMU

[44] Dyson, *Elusive Union*, 211–12.

[45] See Robert Minikin, *The ERM Explained*, London, Kogan Page, 1993, 41–5.

process, in short, was dominated by political leaders and their officials and by central bankers. It was a relatively enclosed environment. Our research has found no evidence of any significant policy impact in the EMU process on the part of either domestic or European private interest groups, whether at domestic or EU levels.'[46] Much of the negotiating time was, indeed, devoted to exchanges between bankers and politicians with the latter alerting elected officials to the political and economic consequences of monetary union.[47]

Research has also revealed a number of different motives on the part of the participating countries. For example, asymmetries in the EMS with most members forced to adhere to the strictest standards of macroeconomic discipline as represented by the German Bundesbank almost certainly convinced the more inflation-prone countries that a single currency would lead to more balanced arrangements. The French and Italian currency crises of 1985 and 6, when both countries were forced to devalue in relation to the Deutschmark, had resulted in serious domestic political repercussions, which both countries were keen to avoid in the future.[48] A desire to iron out the asymmetries in the EMS must, however, have been secondary to the overriding aim of controlling inflation. If the asymmetries had been that serious—and as earlier argued the EMS did have deflationary effects on the French and Italian economies—why did not these countries simply leave the EMS? In fact, leaving the EMS was simply not on the agenda because to do so would be to signal to the foreign exchange markets that the country concerned had given up the struggle for macroeconomic discipline and therefore was not prepared to maintain price stability.

The motives of the British and the Germans in their stance towards EMU are rather more difficult to fathom. A priori we should have expected the British to be strong EMU backers and the Germans, EMU detractors. In fact, the opposite was the case. British behaviour is rather easier to understand than the German. Long the reluctant Europeans, British negotiators at Maastricht were under considerable intra-Conservative Party pressure not to agree to a single currency. They did,

[46] Kenneth Dyson, Kevin Featherstone, and George Michalopoulis, 'The Politics of EMU: The Maastricht Treaty and the Relevance of Bargaining Models', Paper before the annual meeting of the American Political Science Association, New York, 1994, 3.

[47] Tsoukalis, *The New European Economy*, 209–10.

[48] Dyson *et al.*, 'The Politics of EMU', 17; see also Andrew Moravcsik, 'Preferences and Power in the European Community: A Liberal Intergovernmentalist Approach', *Journal of Common Market Studies*, 31, 1993.

however, propose the adoption of the 'hard ecu' policed by a European Monetary Fund. By pooling the resources of European central banks, the hard Ecu would be traded in its own right on the foreign exchanges. This proposal, which was not unlike the original plans for the use of Special Drawing Rights under the old Bretton Woods system, would undoubtedly have provided a stronger currency area than that provided by the EMS. The British promised that if it worked it could be a precursor to a single currency.[49] To go one step further and accept EMU was not acceptable to the British because this implied political union—something which the Conservative Party had always resisted. Note, however, that what was eventually negotiated at Maastricht was a British opt out from Stage Three—the adoption of a single currency. In other words, EMU was not unambiguously ruled out. The British always argued that if the conditions were right British participation in EMU was a possibility and they did agree to proceed with Stages One and Two. Moreover, British Conservative governments continued with this policy position all the way through 1995. It should also be noted that the other two main British political parties remained strong supporters of British participation throughout.

Econometric models demonstrate that Germany has little incentive to join with higher inflation countries in European monetary union. De Grauwe, for example, notes that 'Germany has nothing to gain (in terms of inflation and unemployment) from joining a union with high-inflation countries. Even if it insists, and succeeds, in obtaining a European central bank which is a copy of the Bundesbank, Germany still does not gain anything. It will face the same inflation equilibrium. All the gains are for the high inflation countries.'[50] If this is so it suggests that German motives were other than economic. Certainly the initial enthusiasm of the Foreign Minister, Hans Dieter Genscher, for EMU was dampened by Bundesbank caution.[51] But the Germans went ahead anyway with the strong support not only of Genscher but also Chancellor Helmut Kohl.

[49] For a discussion see Dyson, *Elusive Union*, 141–2.

[50] De Grauwe, *The Economics of Monetary Integration*, 160. See also R. Barro and D. Gordon, 'Rules, Discretion and Reputation in a Model of Monetary Policy', *Journal of Monetary Economics*, 12, 1983, 101–21.

[51] Sandholz, 'Choosing Union', 31; Tim Dickson, 'Genscher Call for Closer European Monetary Links', *Financial Times*, 21 Jan. 1988, 2; Karl Otto Pohl, 'Prospects of the European Monetary Union, in James Buchanan (ed.), *Europe's Constitutional Future*, London, Institute of Economic Affairs, 1990, 43–52.

There are two possible explanations for German behaviour. The first, proposed by Dyson, is that broader political considerations were at work in the German case. In sum:

> for Kohl and the German foreign policy establishment, the costs of non-agreement on measures to promote European union were potentially high, the more so with German unification. The calculation that motivated Kohl was that distrust of German power would generate anti-German alliances that, in the long term, would deeply damage German interests.[52]

A slightly more formal way of putting this argument is that monetary union would, for the first time in the post-war era, allow the Germans to play a major foreign policy role. Trade-offs across issue areas could be organized to please everybody. The Italians, French, and others would benefit from integration with the low inflation German monetary regime, and the Germans, in return, could, via political integration in the EU, play a role in world affairs commensurate with their economic and political status. Such considerations had, of course, long been prominent in the minds of the post-war generations of German politicians, but were they sufficiently strong to convince the Germans that the much cherished independence of their central bank could be sacrificed in the name of European union? It seems unlikely that all the advantages of German fiscal rectitude would be given up in return for some vague, longer-term ambition to avoid the emergence of anti-German alliances. A more convincing explanation of German motives is that they believed that EMU *on their terms* would involve little or no economic sacrifice but reap all the political advantages of European union. German terms would, of course, be an insistence that only countries that met their standards of macroeconomic discipline would join the single currency area. As it turned out this is precisely what the Germans insisted on in the negotiations over the Maastricht convergence criteria.[53] An examination of the criteria for Stage Three of EMU would, taking historical averages, have excluded all but Germany, Holland, and Luxemburg—although in the wake of unification not even Germany met the criteria in 1991 and 1992.[54]

[52] Dyson *et al.*, 'The Politics of EMU', 15.

[53] Sandholz, 'Choosing Union', 16–20; Dyson, *Elusive Union*, 282–92.

[54] The criteria were: (1) A rate of inflation in the consumer price index no more than one and one half percentage points higher than the average of the three states with the best performance in price stability; (2) interest rates on long term government bonds no more than two percentage points higher than the average of the three countries with the lowest rates; (3) a central government budget deficit no greater than three per cent of

A cynical interpretation of German motives could be, then, that they never expected countries such as Italy, Spain, or Britain to meet the criteria, in which case EMU would be confined to a small German-dominated core of countries including Holland, Luxemburg, Austria (once admitted to the union), and possibly Belgium and France. Economist Paul De Grauwe has put this point more formally: '[The Maastricht convergence criteria] have been introduced in the Maastricht Treaty to overcome the German reluctance to form a monetary union. Put differently, the convergence requirements ensure that the monetary club will remain small, and, in so doing, make a monetary union more attractive to Germany.'[55] If this is so, the Germans were engaged in a very limited federal bargain, where they would be the dominant component state. For the smaller German satellite states, EMU was merely the codification of what had for some years been the status quo. Politicians and officials from the more inflation-prone states may have had different perceptions and may, indeed, have believed that they were striking a much more ambitious federal bargain which would facilitate price levels nearer those of the best performers in the union. In Rikerian terms, therefore, the Germans saw, in accepting monetary union on their terms, the opportunity for major diplomatic gains, with few of the economic costs that almost certainly would have been involved in any close association with high inflation states such as Britain, Italy, and Spain.

A burgeoning literature in applied economics confirms that any claim that the countries of the EC member states make up what economists call an 'optimal currency area' is essentially contestable. Sometimes widely differing economic performances together with rigidities across national labour markets suggest that a single currency might reduce rather than enhance welfare for member states.[56] We will return to this point in Part II. Even the claimed reductions in transaction costs much quoted by politicians and industrialists, are, according to expert economic opinion, very difficult to measure.[57] The negotiations at Maastricht

gross domestic product (GDP); (4) a public debt of no more than 60 per cent of GDP; a national currency that has remained within the narrow (2.25 per cent) fluctuation margins of the ERM for the previous two years and has not been devalued against any other member state currency over the same period. By Stage Three, all participating countries should have established central bank independence.

[55] De Grauwe, *The Economics of Monetary Integration*, 176.

[56] Ibid., ch. 6; Barry Eichengreen and Jeffrey Friedan, 'The Political Economy of European Monetary Unification', *Economics and Politics*, 5, 1993, 85–104; Barry Eichengreen, 'Is Europe an Optimum Currency Area?', CEPR Discussion Paper, 478, 1990.

[57] De Grauwe, *The Economics of Monetary Integration*, 94, and sources cited.

were not greatly influenced by arcane economic research, however. Instead they were dominated by a broad consensus that a return to the high levels of price inflation characteristic of the 1970s must be avoided. The political costs of not doing so were, simply, too high. For many of the negotiators at Maastricht, the spectre of national economies—and therefore polities—falling into an inflation-induced spiral of decline was the most powerful of incentives to remove macroeconomic policy from national control. Most of the bargaining was devoted to how best to achieve this objective, given different national perspectives and interests. Ultimately this process was not the product of powerful industrial or labour interests, but of politicians and officials intent on finding a solution to domestic inflation. Monetary union offered the best chance for achieving price stability in the context of an open and increasingly capricious international monetary system.

Alternative strategies, including a return to protectionism and manipulating national economies for electoral advantage, had by the late 1980s either become discredited or were simply not practical options. Politicians from countries with independent central banks were by definition more circumscribed in their attempts to manipulate the economy, and throughout the 1980s country after country acted to strengthen central bank independence.[58] The Maastricht timetable did, of course, require member states to have established full central bank independence as a condition for moving into Stage Three of monetary union. This is not to argue that politicians suddenly ceased to see the electoral advantages of pre-election booms,[59] it is merely to state that by the 1980s, politicians from the right and the left had become increasingly aware of the longer-term costs of such manipulations. So much so, in fact, that many had initiated reductions in their own freedom of movement by strengthening the independence of their central banks.

The anti-inflationary position was so widely accepted that the economic costs of EMU were absent from the agenda during the key intergovernmental conference leading up to Maastricht. As Tsoukalis

[58] Economists increasingly agree that independent central banks produce lower rates of inflation. See G. Demopoulos, G. Katsimbris, and S. Miller, 'Monetary Policy and Central Bank Financing of Government Budget Deficits: A Cross Country Comparison', *European Economic Review*, 31, 1987, 1023–50; A. Cuckierman, *Central Bank Strategy, Credibility and Independence: Theory and Evidence*, Cambridge, Mass., MIT Press, 1992; A. Alesina and L. Summers, 'Central Bank Independence and Macroeconomic Performance: Some Comparative Evidence', *Journal of Money, Credit and Banking*, 25, 1993.

[59] On this theme generally, see James E. Alt and K. Alec Chrystal, *Political Economics*, Berkeley and Los Angeles, University of California Press, 1983.

emphasizes: 'During the intergovernmental conference, the economic and political desirability of EMU was not seriously put in question. This matter was supposed to have been already settled.'[60] Put rather more formally, if politicians come together intent on concluding a federal bargain, a consensus on the basic purpose of the bargain will exist. Most of what is actually discussed during negotiations on the institutional shape of the new federation will be technical, as it was, indeed, at Philadelphia in 1787. None of the Founding Fathers questioned the need for federation; their concern was for the consequences of alternative institutional forms.[61] As Riker notes: 'Once [the decision to form a union] is made, the decision on the procedure of expansion is purely technical. Since the normative question is usually settled by unconscious consensus, the salient question at the beginning of federalism is typically the technical one.'[62] Research attempting to disaggregate the motives of individuals involved in the decision-making process at Maastricht is likely, therefore, to throw (probably interesting) light on these technical questions. It will not necessarily tell us why the representatives of the member states felt impelled to come together to make the momentous decision to form a union in the first place.

MAASTRICHT IN HISTORICAL AND COMPARATIVE PERSPECTIVE

An adapted Rikerian framework has the advantage of helping to explain not only the timing of European Union, but also the uniqueness of the European political response to changes in the international economic environment. Neither the United States nor Japan has any incentive to join with neighbouring or nearby states to form a currency union. The American domestic market is so large that fluctuations in the value of the dollar have not (at least historically) greatly limited the ability of US governments to manage macroeconomic policy.[63] American presidents may still believe that they can use fiscal and other

[60] Tsoukalis, *The New European Economy*, 166.

[61] For a stimulating account, see Stanley Elkins and Eric McKitrick, *The Age of Federalism: The Early American Republic, 1788–1800*, New York, OUP, 1993.

[62] William H. Riker, 'Federalism', in Fred I. Greenstein and Nelson S. Polsby, *The Handbook of Political Science*, vol. v: *Government Institutions and Processes*, Reading, Mass., Addison Wesley, 1975, 138.

[63] Herbert Stein, *Presidential Economics: The Making of Economic Policy From Roosevelt to Reagan and Beyond*, New York, Simon and Schuster, 1984.

TABLE 4.3. Foreign trade (imports and exports) as a percentage of GDP, Germany, Japan, and the USA, 1992

USA	16.9
Japan	16.4
Germany	52.4 (of which traded with EC countries, 53%)

Source: *Statistical Abstract of the United States, 1994*, Washington, Department of Commerce, 1994, computed from Tables 1366 and 1400.

means to manipulate the economy for electoral advantage. More generally, the US economy can continue to operate at levels compatible with relatively low unemployment. As in the first half of 1995, the international markets may decree that the US dollar is a poor investment in relation to the yen or the Deutschmark, but the resulting depreciation of the dollar does not force the American authorities into Draconian austerity measures. Close monetary association with either Mexico or Canada is simply not necessary. It would bring high economic and political costs, with few benefits. In this sense, studies comparing moves towards union in Europe with those towards economic co-operation in North America must always be quite limited conceptually. Along with other customs unions, the North America Free Trade Agreement (NAFTA) represents a very limited inter-state agreement rather than a federal bargain.[64]

Japan, too has little incentive to join with her neighbours in a political or economic union. The Japanese economy is both large and resilient and thus has long been insulated from the negative inflationary effects of speculation on the foreign exchange markets. Even if the yen were to depreciate rapidly, the Japanese domestic market is sufficiently large to provide some protection from imported inflation. As judged by dependence on international trade, the Japanese economy is actually more self-sufficient even than the American (Table 4.3). Neither Germany nor any European country is in an analogous situation. Germany's imports and exports amount to more than 50 per cent of that country's GDP (Table 4.3). In terms of the overall size of GDP, the German economy was approximately 25 per cent of the EU total in 1990 (less, following the expansion of the Union to fifteen members). In the same year the US economy was around 84 per cent of the NAFTA area, and the Japanese economy 80 per cent of the East Asian

[64] Milner, 'The Domestic Political Economy', and sources cited.

area.[65] Among industrialized countries, only in Europe did the costs and benefits fall the right way for close monetary co-operation. These figures demonstrate the greater potential vulnerability of the German economy to imported inflation and may provide an additional reason why the German authorities have supported monetary union on terms which would reduce inflation rates among its major trading partners down to historical German levels.

Discussion of the European federal bargain in this chapter has so far been confined exclusively to the question of monetary union. What, then, is the significance of the other provisions of the Maastricht agreement, some of which aroused great controversy at the time? Interestingly, most of the provisions of the Treaty were quite unrelated to the question of EMU. A relatively precise timetable was established for EMU and the move to a single currency was specifically labelled 'irreversible'.[66] Moreover the European Central Bank (ECB) was removed from political control. As an independent central bank it was designated as part of the institutional structure of the EU, but was not subject to direct control by the Parliament, the Council, or the Commission. As Richard Cooper has put it: 'the Europeans have created an instrument that would greatly widen the already large democratic gap. The Maastricht agreement would create a powerful body of Platonic guardians to look after monetary affairs, effectively accountable to no one, yet with strong influence on the course of economic affairs.'[67] The other provisions of the Treaty relating to democratic institution-building, including the strengthening of the Parliament, the creation of common citizenship, the adoption of the Social Chapter on conditions of employment and related matters, and the rhetorical flourishes in the direction of greater defence and foreign policy co-operation, had no direct

[65] Figures from the World Bank, *World Development Report*, and Eurostat's *Basic Statistics of the EC.*

[66] Stage One had begun on 1 July 1990 and was designed to improve co-operation and co-ordination between member states in monetary and economic affairs, partly through meetings of the Committee of Governors of the central banks. Stage Two was scheduled to begin on 1 January 1994 and involved the creation of the European Monetary Institute (EMI) as a precursor of the European Central Bank. By this date all capital movements would be liberalized. Stage Three would start on 1 January 1997 or 1 January 1999 at the latest, when the ECB would begin operations with a single currency. Participating states would have to have meet the convergence criteria by this date. Under Protocol 11 the British would participate in Stages One and Two, but had an 'opt-out' for Stage Three. In effect, the British reserved the right to put Stage Three before the British Parliament for approval at the appropriate time. For a full discussion, see Dyson, *Elusive Union*, ch. 5.

[67] Quoted in Eichengreen, *International Monetary Arrangements for the 21st Century*.

link with EMU. As was stressed in Chapter 2, without EMU, a post-Maastricht EU would at best have qualified as a 'peripheralized' union. Put at its bluntest, such matters as the extension of qualified majority voting in the Council and the institution of co-decision-making powers between the EP and the Council, while clearly strengthening supranationalism, did not amount to serious constraints on the freedom of movement of national governments except in certain, quite limited, policy areas.

For although the EU had greatly expanded its competence in a number of areas during the 1970s and the 1980s, this mostly applied to regulatory as opposed to distributive or redistributive policy.[68] A quick audit of what member state governments do would reveal little or no EU competence in social security and welfare, health care, elementary and secondary education, levels and quality of defence spending; most aspects of land use planning, law enforcement, and intergovernmental relations (within member states). Indeed, just over 1 per cent of the collective GDP of member states is allocated to the EU budget. In other words, the strengthening of central EC institutions as occurred at Maastricht, although notable, hardly transformed the organization, given the very limited competence of the EC in a range of vital policy areas. This is not to belittle the EU role in such areas as competition policy, agriculture, and environmental protection. It is merely to assert that this role is peripheral in relation to those functions of national governments which are considered most central to the link between the state and the citizen.

Monetary union would, of course, be another matter and might indeed force a greatly enhanced role for EU institutions in a range of other policy areas. (We will return to this point in Part II.) In other words, without monetary union, which was to be facilitated by an independent, essentially non-democratic, institutional structure, the provisions of the Treaty did not amount to a quantum leap in EC competence. Federalist rhetoric, especially as applied to such notions as citizenship and nationhood, may have given the opposite impression, but the cold reality of Maastricht is that without EMU, it represented a modest advance in the direction of supranationalism rather than the first act in the creation of a federal state.

[68] See Mark A. Pollock, 'Creeping Competence: The Expanding Agenda of the European Community', *Journal of Public Policy*, 14, Apr.–June 1994, 95–145.

CONCLUSIONS

When countries come together voluntarily to form federations they do so for good practical, political reasons. In the European case, a group of proximate countries with a history of increasing co-operation in the context of the EC found it convenient to go one step further and form a political union because of the perceived advantages that union would bring in the shape of supranationally imposed macroeconomic discipline.

Following the traumas of the 1970s and the early 1980s, politicians in most of the member states became increasingly aware that high rates of inflation were incompatible not only with economic stability, but, in the longer term, also with social and political stability. Alternative policies based on economic nationalism had been discredited; the policy preferences of major political parties of the right and of the left converged around the need for monetary orthodoxy, and monetary union seemed to provide the best potential guarantee of this. It is enough that the main negotiating parties at Maastricht *believed* that this was so—it may be, of course, that an independent European central bank would not, in fact, effectively perform this role.[69] Low inflation was not just a desired economic objective in the same way that high economic growth and full employment were; it was, rather, viewed as the essential precondition for general economic and political well-being. Without it the very fabric of the social structure was threatened. In this sense, the decisions taken at Maastricht were not, in Riker's terms, 'economistic' or based on the view that political union must always bring economic benefits. They were, instead, *political* decisions designed to remove the destabilizing threat of inflation. There would, for sure, be political costs involved in transferring macroeconomic policy to a European Central Bank—costs we will return to in Part II. But the calculation must have been that these were worth bearing in relation to the benefits stemming from price stability. Only in Europe were the conditions right for the striking of such a bargain. By the late 1980s, following the limited success of the EMS, which demonstrated that European countries could co-operate over monetary matters, the liberalization of capital

[69] Although the relationship between central bank independence and inflation is complex the balance of opinion is that independent central banks produce lower inflation (see the references at n. 58). However in the European case all the national central banks would be independent by the time of full EMU, so the effects of a Europe-wide central bank are particularly difficult to judge.

movements, and an upturn in prices in most countries, EMU was the logical next step.

This analysis does not deny the importance of the role played by federalist ideologues such as Jacques Delors—their imprint is evident in both the rhetoric and the substance of the Treaty. It is merely to claim that, on their own, the federalists would have achieved little. They had, after all, been actively seeking federal solutions to Europe's problems at least since 1945, but with relatively little success. To repeat the point, it was the proposals for monetary union that, once implemented, would precipitate a fundamental shift in power relations between the component states of the union and supranational or federal authorities. All the rest was, by comparison, merely window-dressing.

A final and vital point about the negotiations at Maastricht is that, as far as EMU was concerned, discussion of the *costs* of union was focused on how quickly and to what extent countries could meet the convergence criteria, rather than on the economic and ultimately the political consequences implicit in a single currency. We will return to this question in Part II. First, however, we should address the events of 1992 and 1993 when the foreign exchange markets produced what looked like a fatal challenge to the ERM of the EMS. How do these events fit into our theoretical framework?

5

Aftermath, 1992 and 1993

INTRODUCTION

Writing in 1994, the respected American economist Paul Krugman passed judgement on the Maastricht Treaty. He noted that:

a group of highly dignified, serious people, sitting at their baize covered tables with their bottles of mineral water, created an agreement that sounded good but on closer examination was sheer nonsense . . . by early 1993 political and economic stresses had made the solemnity of Maastricht seem almost comic. If there is a lesson here, it is that serious and dignified men and women in impressive international meetings may have absolutely no idea what they are talking about.[1]

Krugman's dismay was rooted in the belief shared by many economists that the convergence criteria for monetary union agreed at Maastricht, and especially the required two-year period of exchange rate stability, was simply not tenable given the ways in which international currency markets operate in the absence of exchange controls.[2] Generally, students of international monetary regimes agree that in the longer run systems of fixed exchange rates fall apart. Paul De Grauwe, for example, says of the EMS: 'after 1987, when the system evolved into a truly fixed exchange rate regime, it was unable to cope with the problems that have plagued every fixed exchange rate arrangement of the past. Its downfall therefore did not come as a surprise and had been predicted by many economists.'[3] Barry Eichengreen makes an even bolder statement with regard to the EMS:

[1] Paul Krugman, *Peddling Prosperity: Economic Sense and Nonsense in the Age of Diminished Expectations*, New York, Norton, 1994, 191, 192.

[2] For a comprehensive review, see Barry Eichengreen, *International Monetary Arrangements for the 21st Century*, Washington, Brookings Institution, 1994, chs. 6–9; also his 'The Endogeneity of Exchange Rate Regimes', in Peter B. Kenen (ed.), *Understanding Interdependence: The Macroeconomics of the Open Economy*, Princeton, Princeton University Press, 1995; Paul Krugman, 'Target Zones and Exchange Rate Dynamics', *Quarterly Journal of Economics*, 51, 1991, 669–82.

[3] Paul De Grauwe, *The Economics of Monetary Integration*, Oxford, OUP, 1994, 144.

> Aside from small countries lacking a history of monetary sovereignty, monetary unions of separate nations have almost never been observed. From this perspective, recent setbacks to efforts to establish a European monetary union should come as no surprise. If, for the reasons detailed . . . compromise arrangements like the pegged but adjustable exchange rates of the EMS will no longer be feasible, and for the reasons discussed . . . monetary union without political unification is not on the cards, the only viable option is some form of floating exchange rates.[4]

Officials in the Commission and in the governments of many of the EU member states took a quite different view. They argued that the events of 1992 and 1993 when the ERM came close to collapse reflected the failure of authorities in Italy, Spain, and the UK to contain inflation and maintain external trade balances.[5] Others still blamed German reunification, which forced high and politically unsustainable interest rate levels throughout the ERM area.[6] Generally the official line in the mid-1990s is that with the shock of German unification now over and inflation largely under control in those states remaining in the ERM, the system has once more settled down, and rather than demonstrating the non-viability of the ERM, the events of 1992 and 1993 actually provide guidance on how the member states can proceed more efficiently towards the ultimate goal of monetary union.[7]

Yet from August 1993 those currencies remaining within the ERM could fluctuate up to 15 per cent either side of the central rates—hardly a system of fixed exchange rates—and during the 1992 and 1993 crises governments in a range of countries went to extreme lengths to defend their ERM parities, most of which ended in abject failure. In spite of the very high costs incurred by national treasuries during this period, not to mention the political fallout following failure to defend EMS parities, governments in almost all of the EU countries continue to support the idea of monetary union. It is the major argument of this chapter that the EMS crises of the early 1990s demonstrate the extent

[4] Eichengreen, *International Monetary Arrangements*, 95.

[5] Ibid. 99. Some academic economists put the blame at the feet of politicians, see the references in ibid. 99. Central bankers, too, generally reject the view that EMS, or a fixed exchange rate regime, is inherently superior to floating rates. A sample of central bankers' views is provided by Paul Temperton (ed.), *The European Currency Crisis: What Chance Now for a Single European Currency?*, London, Probus, 1993, 159–287.

[6] See the discussion in De Grauwe, *The Economics of Monetary Integration*, ch. 6.

[7] A good example of this view is Christopher Johnson, 'Fiscal and Monetary Policy in Economic and Monetary Union', in Andrew Duff, John Pinder, and Roy Pryce (eds.), *Maastricht and Beyond: Building the European Union*, London, Routledge, 1994, 71–83.

of the *political* commitment to the system, and, by implication, to the timetable for EMU. Put another way, given the absolute importance of EMU to the federal bargain concluded at Maastricht, politicians had a substantial political investment in exchange rate stability. Without monetary union the low inflation benefits of the federal bargain would ebb away. The chapter will be divided into two parts. Part one will point out some of the potential anomalies in the EMS. Part two will consist of brief case-studies of those countries most affected by the crises and will concentrate on the political and economic context in which key decisions to cope with the crisis occurred. The focus will be on the Nordic countries, the UK, Italy, Spain, and France. Special attention will be paid to the Nordic countries (Finland, Norway, and Sweden) where, it will be argued, the advantages of striking a federal bargain with the EU became the conventional wisdom during this period.

THE EMS AND THE CRISES OF 1992 AND 1993

Underpinning the EMS—and indeed EMU—was an economic philosophy which convinced policy makers that fixed exchange rates would bring benefits (stable prices) with very few costs (a short-term increase in unemployment). In the longer term unemployment would fall through wage and price flexibility. In other words, fixed exchange rates were analogous to macroeconomic discipline in domestic economies. The market would sort out cost differentials between countries just as it does within individual economies. So, with exchange rates fixed between (say) Germany and Italy, Italian firms would, in order to compete, reduce their prices and costs to that point where demand for their products increased. This would not, as the Keynesians argued, be a long and painful process involving deindustrialization in some regions and countries. Instead, the market's 'gales of creative destruction' would lead to a relatively quick adjustment. As important, all the alternative policies from economic nationalism to devaluation held out the prospects of increased inflation, and as we discussed in Chapter 4, inflation had to be avoided at all costs.[8] So influential was this general philosophy that it led country after country either to join the EMS, or in the case

[8] For a lucid analysis and critique of this position, see Krugman, *Peddling Prosperity*, ch. 7.

of the British from 1987 to 1990 and the Nordic countries until the 1992 crisis, to 'shadow' the Deutschmark on the foreign exchanges.

The Maastricht convergence criteria were predicated on the same assumptions. By obliging countries to achieve exchange rate stability for two years prior to EMU and requiring a convergence of inflation and interest rates as well as government deficits and debt, the framers were assuming that the 'market sorting out' would already have occurred prior to the adoption of a single currency. Any short-term costs involved in a fixed exchange rate regime would already have been borne by those countries with historically high levels of inflation. While intuitively feasible, a number of economists have noted that the insistence on this particular set of convergence criteria made little economic sense. As Krugman points out, the two-year currency stability involved the perverse logic that: 'only a country that showed that it was very good at living with an independent currency would be allowed to abolish it'.[9] Related is the fact that the two-year period of currency stability 'without severe tensions', had to be achieved while countries retained control of their own monetary policies. If, therefore, in the absence of exchange controls, a run on (say) the Italian lira occurred, the Italian authorities would be obliged to intervene in the foreign exchanges and to raise domestic interest rates to levels sufficient to deter further speculation. But the political costs of doing so, in the form of higher unemployment and deflation, would be very high, and eventually might force the Italians into a devaluation or, more serious, an abandonment of the EMS.

This is precisely what happened to a number of countries in 1992 and 1993 (Table 5.1). What is interesting about this sequence of events is not that so many countries eventually capitulated to the markets, but that they did so only after incurring very considerable political and economic costs. It is also significant that in many of the countries involved it was politicians of the left rather than of the right who were prepared to make such sacrifices in the name of exchange rate stability.

While economists have attributed these events to a number of causes, including German unification, a lack of competitiveness in Italy, Spain, and the UK, and high levels of inflation in the more vulnerable countries, most are puzzled that officials in so many countries refused to realign their currencies (or devalue) until *after* very high costs had been incurred. Most have a residual category which they label 'political' but

[9] Krugman, *Peddling Prosperity*, 191.

TABLE 5.1. Chronology of the ERM crisis, 1992–1993

8 Sept. 1992	Finland floats the markka
13 Sept.	Italy devalues the lira by 7%
16 Sept.	UK withdraws from the ERM
16 Sept.	Italy suspends intervention agreement in the ERM
16 Sept.	Spain devalues the peseta by 5%
19 Nov.	Sweden floats the krona
22 Nov.	Spain and Portugal devalue by 6%
10 Dec.	Norway floats the krone
30 Jan. 1993	Ireland devalues the punt by 10%
13 May	Spain devalues the peseta by 8%
13 May	Portugal devalues the escudo by 6.5%
2 Aug.	All ERM currencies move the bands of ±15% around unchanged central rates. Separate agreement between Germany and Holland to maintain 2.25% bands

Source: adapted from Paul Temperton, *The European Currency Crisis*, Fig. 6.1.

take the argument no further because they consider the 'political' beyond their professional competence. This applies both to economists considered to be on the ideological right and those associated with more centrist positions. Alan Walters calls the 'calcification' of exchange rates a 'macho' phenomenon which is at heart 'political and bureaucratic' rather than economic in origin.[10] Paul Temperton talks of the need for policy makers to maintain 'credibility' of the counter-inflationary policies required by Maastricht.[11] Paul Krugman argues that 'European policy makers had convinced themselves that fixed exchange rates were always a good thing, and had committed their own political credibility to maintaining a rigid EMS and moving on to EMU'.[12] Barry Eichengreen makes the same point: authorities in a number of countries fought to support their currencies because of the political commitment to Maastricht.[13] The extent of this commitment can be measured by a brief review of the sequence of events affecting the weaker members of the EMS.

[10] Alan Walters, 'Why the ERM Cannot be Reformed', in Temperton, *The European Currency Crisis*, 57–8. See also his *Sterling in Danger: The Economic Consequences of Pegged Exchange Rates*, London, Fontana Collins, Institute of Economic Affairs, 1990.

[11] Temperton, *The European Currency Crisis*, 15–16.

[12] Krugman, *Peddling Prosperity*, 193.

[13] Eichengreen, *International Monetary Arrangements*, 99–100.

THE POLITICAL ECONOMY OF THE CURRENCY CRISES

The United Kingdom

When Britain joined the ERM of the EMS in October 1990 sterling was permitted to fluctuate in 6 per cent bands in relation to its 1990 value. The decision to join had been highly controversial within the Conservative Party. The Prime Minister, Margaret Thatcher, had long resisted membership, believing as she did that the markets were the best determinant of a currency's value. Britain had, however, been 'shadowing' the Deutschmark from March 1987 to March 1988, and had maintained its value in relation to the German currency (at around three to the pound) quite successfully ever since. Eventually, the Prime Minister was persuaded by her Chancellor, Nigel Lawson, and by a potential revolt in her cabinet, that Britain must join the ERM.[14] And while the British maintained their right to opt out of full EMU, they were committed to Stages One and Two of the transition to monetary union. Moreover, until June 1992, when the Danes rejected Maastricht in a national referendum, sterling's performance in the ERM had been quite satisfactory. Interest rates had been steadily reduced in 1991 and 1992 in the face of a deepening recession, without damaging the pound on the foreign exchanges. By mid-1992 the broad consensus among bankers and politicians from all political parties was that British membership had been a success.

Although the immediate effects of German unification for the ERM were relatively benign—indeed the Deutschmark initially sank below its parity within the system—German interest rates were raised to high levels to combat inflation and they stayed high for several years after unification. Meanwhile, the Americans, unhindered by any fixed exchange rate regime and experiencing a recession during an election year, had reduced their interest rates quite dramatically. The resulting yawning gap between American and German interest rates weakened the dollar and strengthened the Deutschmark on the foreign exchange markets. Currencies linked to the Deutschmark but known to be more vulnerable to inflation and competitiveness pressures were the next target of the exchanges, and the pound was one of the first to feel the

[14] For a discussion, see Roy Pryce, 'The Treaty Negotiations', in Andrew Duff, John Pinder, and Roy Pryce, *Maastricht and Beyond*, London, Routledge, 1994, 36–40.

full effects of the markets in the summer of 1992, eventually falling out of its 6 per cent band. In September the Bank of England spent nearly £20 billion on the exchanges in support of the pound—close to half of total British foreign reserves.[15] After a desperate attempt to stem the flow with a 5 per cent increase in interests rates in less than twenty-four hours, the government finally capitulated and left the ERM on 16 September.

While, in the British case, clear sacrifices were made to defend the currency—and public opinion data shows that the crisis did more to damage the reputation of the Major government than any event down to April 1994[16]—the crisis was reasonably short term and led in the end not to a realignment within the ERM but to a departure from the system. This reflects the weaker political commitment of the British to the whole EMU project. It should be noted, however, that British politicians and officials, including the politically damaged Chancellor Norman Lamont, refused to rule out the possibility of rejoining the EMS.[17] So even the reluctant Europeans retained some faith that ERM membership would ensure currency stability in the longer term. By implication, at least, full participation in EMU remained a possibility, and as we noted in the last chapter, the British Conservative chancellors and prime ministers have consistently refused to state that British participation in EMU must be ruled out completely. Of course both the other main British political parties, Labour and the Liberal Democrats, remained enthusiastic supporters of British membership of the EMS throughout.

Moreover, considerable evidence exists to suggest that had the British weathered the September storm on the foreign exchanges the government would have been prepared to make considerable longer-term sacrifices to maintain the pound at 2.95 DM. According to contemporary accounts, John Major was ready to defend Britain's membership of the ERM and the resulting historically low rates of inflation at the Conservative Party conference in October 1992. He was also prepared to continue with a deflationary fiscal stance in the face of fierce opposition from representatives of British industry.[18] As Barry Eichengreen

[15] 'A Ghastly Game of Dominoes', *The Economist*, 19 Sept. 1992, 115–16.

[16] For a summary, see John Curtice, 'Failures That Will Outlast a Change of Face', *Independent*, 6 Apr. 1994, 14.

[17] The Governor of the Bank of England at the time of the crisis, Robin Leigh Pemberton, has also expressed his support for British membership of the EMS, Robin Leigh Pemberton, 'A UK Perspective', in Temperton, *The European Currency Crisis*, 287–96.

[18] 'Major is Committed to Keeping Strong Pound', *Financial Times*, 3 Aug. 1992, 1.

notes: 'Absent the attack, ERM countries—for example Britain—would have been willing to maintain the policies of austerity required to defend their ERM pegs indefinitely, enduring the costs of unemployment in return for the benefits of exchange rate stability.'[19]

Italy

The first signs of pressure on the lira were discernible in May 1992 amid deterioration in Italy's public finances. By July the lira was widely regarded as the 'sick currency of Europe'.[20] However, in spite of budget reforms, and an agreement worked out by Italy's centre-left coalition government to end Italy's long-standing practice of linking wage increases to the inflation rate, the lira dropped to its ERM floor in August. In early September interest rates were raised to 15 per cent, the highest since 1985, provoking cries of protest from industrial interests.[21] By 9 September the Socialist Premier, Giuliano Amato, had called for emergency powers from Parliament to rule by decree in the event of an economic emergency. These included the right to revoke previously approved expenditures and to raise taxes without parliamentary approval once a 'neutral party'—widely understood to be the Bank of Italy—had declared that such an emergency existed.[22] In other words, normal democratic procedures as they applied to key economic policy, at least, would be suspended on the advice of the central bank. Far from being placated by these measures and by a further threat to increase interest rates, the markets put more and this time irresistible pressure on the lira, culminating in a 7 per cent devaluation on 16 September.

Devaluation was not, however, enough to satisfy the markets and in spite of continual denials, the Italian authorities announced on 16 September that its membership of the ERM would be temporarily suspended. In effect, this signalled to the markets that the lira would thereafter float free on the exchanges. The Italian crisis of September 1992 was much more serious than the British. Italian governments had long had a strong commitment not just to the ERM but also to EMU and political union. As a country prone to inflationary pressures and political crises engendered

[19] Eichengreen, *International Monetary Arrangements*, 99–100.
[20] 'Italian Lira: The Sick Currency of Europe', *Financial Times*, 22 July 1992, 2.
[21] Bruce Johnston, 'Sick Italy Chokes on Economic Medicine', *Sunday Times*, 6 Sept. 1992, Section 1, p. 10.
[22] Robert Graham, 'Italy Takes the Offensive in Battle for its Currency', *Financial Times*, 11 Sept. 1992, 2.

by chronic deficits in the national finances, there was a widespread perception among Italian politicians and officials that the country had a great deal to gain from the monetary and fiscal discipline that would stem from EMU. As a result, the 1992 crisis rather than weakening the government's resolve to continue an association with the EMS, actually strengthened their determination eventually to rejoin the system. To expedite this it was necessary to implement a series of drastic economic and political reforms designed to help balance the national budget and improve the competitiveness of the Italian economy.

What eventually transpired was a 1993 budget proposal which was the most Draconian since the 1950s, involving sharp cuts in state health and pension provision as well as a freeze on public-sector employment. It provoked mass demonstrations and a series of protest strikes. It also almost certainly contributed to the dramatic advances made by regional and protest parties in the local and municipal elections in 1992 and in 1993.[23] By early October the lira had effectively been devalued by 20 per cent in relation to the Deutschmark, thus fuelling fears of further inflation. The government's austerity plan was eventually approved by the Italian Parliament and the lira did stabilize on the exchanges by the end of the year. The seriousness of the crisis should not be underestimated, however. Political disintegration was a real possibility in 1992, and, some would argue, remains so. Certainly, at the time of the crisis the EU was widely perceived by all the main political parties and by industrial interests as an essential external force that would help goad Italy's cumbersome political process into action. Indeed at one stage unelected officials from the EC Monetary Committee were actually laying down conditions to the Italian government on how it should act to reduce the deficit and inflation.[24]

The mood of the time is summed up accurately by a *Financial Times* editorial:

> Most important, ERM membership is the most available signal of Italy's European commitment. Without the EC, Italy's reform process might not have come this far. For the Italian state, it remains the best insurance against political collapse and hyperinflationary suicide.[25]

[23] 'Hell Damnation and an Earthquake or Two', *The Economist*, 10 Oct. 1992, 43–4; 'Italy Redraws Political Map', *Financial Times*, 16 Sept. 1992, 3; 'Italy Lops Off More Dead Wood', *The Economist*, 27 Nov. 1993, 47–8.

[24] Wolfgang Munchau, 'EC's Intervention Lays Bare Italy's Economic and Political Malaise', *Financial Times*, 15 Sept. 1992, 21.

[25] 'Italy's Fight for Credibility', *Financial Times*, 12 Nov. 1992, 20.

Spain

Spain joined the wider 6 per cent band of the ERM in June 1989 and abolished all capital controls in February 1992. Following Maastricht, the Socialist government of Felipe Gonzalez was determined that Spain would not be left behind with Greece (and possibly Portugal) by failing to meet the convergence criteria. Accordingly, the government embarked on an austerity programme designed to cut public expenditure and bring inflation under control. This decision carried with it serious political risks, for between 1992 and the end of 1994, Spaniards would have voted in municipal, regional, general, and European elections. Moreover, the Spanish Socialists had a record of increasing public spending prior to elections. When, therefore, the Finance Minister, Carlos Solchaga, announced the austerity package in the spring of 1992 he was specifically assigning a higher priority to meeting the Maastricht targets than to winning elections.[26] On the face of it, Spain's position was less serious than Italy's. The public sector debt had historically been held at relatively low levels and the Socialist government was widely regarded as more responsible than the fragile coalition governments typical of Italian politics. However, Spain's budget deficit had risen alarmingly in 1992 and inflation was high at over 6 per cent. The government also had to contend with a still powerful labour movement which called a general strike in response to the austerity measures.

Although the strike was widely regarded as a failure,[27] the government's position remained vulnerable and while the peseta was not the first target on the foreign exchange markets in September it eventually came under pressure and forced a 5 per cent devaluation on 16 September—the first devaluation of the Spanish currency since 1982. In order to dampen any inflationary effects and ensure that Spain was not left behind in a 'two speed' Europe, the government announced a tough new budget for 1993 involving further expenditure cuts and curbs on public sector pay. Again, these measures were taken in the knowledge that they might be electorally damaging—the general election had to be held by October 1993. Gonzalez announced, somewhat disingenuously, that 'I remain to be convinced that there is any electoral advantage to be gained in hiding the truth and not doing what is necessary . . . what has to be done is to demonstrate that one is making progress in controlling

[26] Peter Bruce, 'The Strain and Pain in Spain', *Financial Times*, 27 May 1992, 18.
[27] 'Damp Strike', *Financial Times*, 29 May 1992, 16.

the deficits and that we are going to do that soon and efficiently.'[28] This was not sufficient to stop the run on the peseta, however, and the authorities were forced into further measures, including interest rate hikes and the reimposition of partial exchange controls. A further devaluation was none the less necessary in November. Eventually, the government brought forward legislation that would effectively tie its hands in monetary policy by granting to the Bank of Spain a degree of independence similar to that enjoyed by the German Bundesbank.[29]

Spain's final crisis came in May 1993 when a further and final devaluation of the peseta by 8 per cent occurred amid uncertainties about the outcome of the imminent general election. What the Spanish case demonstrates very nicely is the extent to which a government of the left was prepared to go in order to conform to the Maastricht convergence criteria. Remaining in the ERM and avoiding devaluations were accorded the very highest priorities by the Socialist government. Other values, including reducing unemployment and, indeed, maximizing their chances of re-election, were clearly secondary to these main objectives. In the event, the markets proved too powerful to prevent what amounted to three devaluations of the peseta. The response to the crises by the Spanish government was intimately related to the ultimate goal of monetary and political union. For the Spanish, the federal bargain at Maastricht brought considerable benefits, with what they thought would be relatively few costs. Even after the events of 1992 and 1993 the authorities remained absolutely committed to monetary union. Indeed, the official view of the Bank of Spain was that:

> the monetary storm has highlighted the problems inherent to the transition towards monetary union, problems which are all the greater the more uncertain the plans and timetable for union are. Resolving the ERM crisis is thus inextricably linked to negotiating the obstacles to monetary union. To do so, a degree of stability within the ERM must be restored.[30]

France

France's position within the ERM was, initially, considered to be secure. Following the policy volte-face in 1983, the French authorities

[28] Peter Bruce and Andrew Gowers, 'A Testing of Spanish Mettle', *Financial Times*, 5 Oct. 1992, 14.

[29] 'Bank of Spain to Control Monetary Policy', *Financial Times*, 30 Dec. 1992, 1.

[30] 'A Spanish Perspective: The Official View of the Bank of Spain', in Temperton, *The European Currency Crisis*, 229.

had supported the idea of the *franc fort* or a determination to make the franc an anchor currency within the ERM alongside the Deutschmark. Moreover, compared with Britain, Italy, or Spain, the French economy was, in terms of foreign exchange perceptions, relatively healthy. Inflation in 1992 was below the German level and the budget deficit of minus 2.3 per cent was one of the lowest in the EU. On 19 September 1992 just after the turmoil in the foreign exchanges, *The Economist* gave France a 'grade' of 9 out of 10 as a devaluation risk, better than any country bar Ireland (Italy was awarded a 1).[31] The narrow victory in support of ratification of the Maastricht Treaty in the referendum of 20 September at first calmed the markets, and intervention by the French and German central banks together with a rise in French interest rates proved sufficient to protect the franc.[32]

The costs to the French economy of maintaining this policy were high. By the spring of 1993 unemployment had reached 11.5 per cent and was rising, output was falling, and corporate debt–income ratios were deteriorating. As Eichengreen points out, however, in the absence of further attacks on the exchanges, the French government would almost certainly have persisted with this policy—as indeed the British would have in the absence of the September 1993 onslaught on sterling.[33] For the French, achieving inflation and budget deficit figures superior to those of the Germans was evidence enough that the French could become an anchor currency within the ERM as a prelude to monetary union. However, the markets thought otherwise and renewed their attack on the franc in July 1993. To counter the selling of the franc, the Bank of France more than exhausted its reserves, but was still unable to prevent the currency from sinking below its ERM floor. There then followed a temporary suspension of the EMS system followed by a move to the much broader plus or minus 15 per cent bands which prevailed at least until the end of 1995.

As in Italy and Spain, a left of centre government was prepared to go to extreme lengths at considerable economic and political cost to fulfil the most fundamental of the Maastricht convergence criteria—exchange rate stability without experiencing 'severe tensions'. Unlike Italy and Spain, French economic management was disciplined and effective. Even so, the markets sensed that limits existed to how far a

[31] 'A Ghastly Game of Dominoes', *The Economist*, 19 Sept. 1992, 115.

[32] In the week ending 23 Sept. a total of 160 billion French francs (about $32 billion) was spent in the currency's defence. Quoted in Eichengreen, *International Monetary Arrangements*, 97.

[33] Ibid. 100.

government would go to defend its currency, and they proved to be absolutely right.[34] Also as in Italy and Spain politicians from all the major political parties (except the more nationalistic of the Gaullists), continued to believe that monetary union was the only longer-term solution to currency stability and therefore to inflation.

The Non-EU Nordic Countries

When the federal bargain was concluded at Maastricht certain countries were, for historical reasons, excluded from the agreement, even 'though their participation would have been acceptable to other members of the EU'. These included two countries, Austria and Switzerland, who had long enjoyed strong currencies and, should they have joined, would undoubtedly have qualified for membership of the core, Deutschmark-dominated heart of the European Union. Three Nordic countries, Sweden, Norway, and Finland, were in a somewhat different situation. Finland had traditionally opposed membership because of its close association—and fear—of the Soviet Union. Political élites in Sweden and especially the leaders of the dominant Social Democratic Party had long believed that their much-valued welfare state and full employment were best protected by economic and political neutrality. Norway had, of course, formally applied for membership along with the UK in 1971, but this decision was reversed in a national referendum in September 1972. Most Norwegian politicians considered the people's verdict binding for the foreseeable future.[35] By the early 1990s, however, political élites in all three countries had been converted to the new macroeconomic discipline and had become convinced that the only way to harness inflation was through membership of the EMS, and, eventually, through political union. Let us look at this transformation in each of the countries.

[34] There is in fact a self-fulfilling element to the market attacks. As Eichengreen puts it: 'An attack forcing a devaluation might disqualify a country from participating in Europe's monetary union. This in turn would remove the government's incentive to persist with policies whose benefits resided in qualifying the country for monetary union. A rational government might shift towards more accommodating policies only if attacked, and knowledge of this fact could give traders the incentive to undertake such an attack.' Eichengreen, *International Monetary Arrangements*, 100 n. 8. While logical, this analysis cannot account for the huge sacrifices made by governments over long periods to ward off attacks. If they *knew* that attacks would in the end be successful, they would have capitulated to the markets immediately and abandoned the ERM. No country did this, however, demonstrating the extent of the political commitment to the system.

[35] Gunnar Helgi Krissinsson, 'Iceland and Norway: Peripheries in Doubt', in John Redmond (ed.), *Prospective Europeans: New Members for the European Union*, London, Harvester Wheatsheaf, 1994, 92.

Sweden

In May 1991 Ingvar Carlsson, the Social Democratic Prime Minister, announced that the Swedish krona would be pegged to the ECU (in effect to the Deutschmark). This was the first step in a campaign to control inflation as a prelude to full EU membership. It had become increasingly obvious during the 1980s that Sweden could not maintain its industrial competitiveness, continue to finance an enormous public sector (over 60 per cent of GDP), and enjoy full employment all at the same time. The result was a rapidly increasing budget deficit and rising inflation. To make matters worse, deregulation during the 1980s had led to a speculative boom in property prices which came to an end following a sharp increase in interest rates in 1991. The resulting crash in values placed the whole banking system in jeopardy and threatened an effective collapse of the country's financial infrastructure.[36]

By 1992 the Social Democrats had been replaced by a centre-right minority government led by Premier Carl Bildt. Faced with deepening economic crisis, Bildt declared that the only solution to the country's ills was a tight money policy, further cuts in government expenditure, and membership of the EMS. Devaluation was regarded as unacceptable because of its inflationary consequences. In this context it is not surprising that the Swedish krona came under sustained attack during the currency turmoil of September 1992. Following the first wave of selling, the Swedish central bank raised its marginal lending rate (the overnight rate charged to banks) to 75 per cent and on 16 September to a staggering 500 per cent. For most longer-term borrowers this translated into an average of around 38 per cent.[37] This drastic measure was followed by a further austerity package agreed by all the political parties involving expenditure cuts and tax increases equivalent to around 2 per cent of GDP. The agreement also transferred the funding of Sweden's enormously expensive health insurance system from the state to both sides of industry.[38] Parliament approved the package on 30 September by which time the marginal interest rates had fallen to 24 per cent.

In spite of all these efforts, renewed speculation against the krona later in the autumn forced the Bank of Sweden to float the currency on

[36] 'Toughing it Out', *The Economist*, 19 Sept. 1992, 52.

[37] 'Swedish Marginal Lending Rate Hits 500%', *Financial Times*, 17 Sept. 1992, 2.

[38] 'Sweden Unveils Rescue Package', *Financial Times*, 21 Sept. 1992, 22; Robert Taylor, 'Swedes Untie Welfare Apron Strings', *Financial Times*, 23 Sept. 1992, 2.

19 November. This move surprised even the Prime Minister who declared: 'You cannot run an economic policy with a floating exchange rate. European countries cannot be floated against each other. It won't work. I do not believe in this policy.'[39] Capitulation to the markets followed the failure to win all party support for yet a third austerity package presenting the Prime Minister with a choice of devaluing or losing a vote of no confidence in Parliament.

What is interesting about the Swedish case is that at 2 per cent inflation was already very low in 1992. This had been won at a considerable price—industrial production had fallen 15 per cent in three years and unemployment was rising very rapidly. It is also significant that no change of policy direction accompanied the floating of the krona. Membership of the EMS and support for Swedish participation in a single currency remained the objectives of all the leading political parties. Near consensus on the restructuring of the Swedish welfare state and of the economy remained. By early 1994 Swedish unemployment had reached 9 per cent—higher even than during the 1930s.

Finland

By 1991 Finland's economy was, if anything, more fragile than Sweden's. A collapse in trade with its main trading partner, the former Soviet Union, had led to a deep recession with output falling 6.1 per cent in one year and unemployment rising rapidly. Like Sweden, however, the Finns had pegged their currency to the ECU and were intent on eventual membership of the EMS. Having devalued the markka in November 1991 it was the declared policy of the four-party centre-right governing coalition that the value of the currency would thereafter be maintained in preparation for entry into the EU. Accordingly in April 1992, following market pressure on the markka, the government announced an austerity package involving a sharp rise in interest rates and, coincidentally given the later Swedish experience, expenditure cuts and tax increases of the equivalent of 2 per cent of GDP.[40] So amid the worst recession in recent history the government embarked on a deflationary course to defend the currency and ensure low inflation.

By June the government was making firm declarations to the effect that the economy would be 'put in order' prior to EU membership. This

[39] 'Sweden Admits Defeat in Battle for Krona', *Financial Times*, 20 Nov. 1992, 2.
[40] 'Finland Cuts Spending to Avoid Devaluation', *Financial Times*, 6 Apr. 1992, 16.

involved the abolition of capital controls by the end of 1992 and further cuts in public expenditure.[41] By August, however, pressure on the markka returned, prompting a rise in the rate at which commercial banks could borrow to 16 per cent. Yet further cuts in expenditure to the equivalent of 1.3 per cent of GDP were announced in August and on 8 September the Finnish markka was detached from the ECU and allowed to float free. Devaluation had been prompted by a massive outflow of capital which threatened the banking system. As in Sweden, the devaluation was followed by sombre pledges to cut government spending further and to return to a fixed exchange rate regime as soon as was practicable.[42] Also as in Sweden a succession of austerity measures had been taken during a deep recession when inflation was low and unemployment rising very rapidly. A final similarity is that the main opposition party, the Social Democrats, although critical of the government, were unable to provide a coherent alternative policy.

Norway

In October 1990 the Norwegians linked their krone to the ECU and by 1992 the ruling Labour Party had declared its intention to reapply for EU membership as soon as possible. In the previous twelve years the Labour Party had transformed itself from a leftist interventionist and protectionist party to one favouring free trade and the liberalization of the economy.[43] Unlike its Nordic neighbours the Norwegian economy had been partly insulated from recession by its oil revenues and the Norwegian krone was not the first target of the foreign exchange markets in September 1992. None the less interest rate hikes were necessary to defend the currency and by November the krone was under heavy pressure, prompting the central bank to increase its overnight rate to 25 per cent on 22 November. Both the Labour Finance Minister and the Governor of the Bank of Norway publicly stated that they would use 'every weapon available' to defend the currency.[44] Interest rates were raised again in late November with one month rates reaching 45 per cent following Sweden's decision to float their krona. Eventually, aware of the price paid by the Swedes in defence of their currency, the Norwegians decided to float the krone in early December.

[41] David Dodwell, 'Finland Aims to put its House in Order Ahead of EC Entry', *Financial Times*, 9 June 1992, 7.

[42] 'Minister Reassures over Markka's Float', *Financial Times*, 10 Sept. 1992, 2.

[43] See Kristinsson, 'Iceland and Norway', 92–8.

[44] 'Norway Overnight Lending Rate up Again', *Financial Times*, 23 Nov. 1992, 2.

Although the Norwegians were not forced into the severe austerity measures taken by their neighbours, they did tolerate very high interest rates over an extended period amid the worst recession since the 1930s. Unemployment continued to rise to nearly 8 per cent by the end of 1992. Like their neighbours, the Norwegian authorities had managed to bring inflation down to below 3 per cent, but this was not enough to protect their currencies on the international exchanges. Also like Sweden and Finland, the main political groupings supported the link to the EMS and eventual EU membership. The opposition Conservative Party was strongly in favour as were the leaders of the ruling Labour Party.[45]

This account of the events of 1992 and 1993 would not be complete without some reference to the response of the German Bundesbank to the crisis. Amid the first wave of selling on the foreign exchanges in September 1992 the Bundesbank cut its interest rates for the first time in five years. However, both the size and the precise timing of the cut suggested that the Germans were less than serious about their attempts to prevent major realignments within the ERM. On Sunday, 13 September the Bundesbank announced that it would cut its rates the following day. However the actual cut (one quarter of one per cent for the key rate) implemented on the Monday was so small that it signalled to the markets that the Germans were not intent on maintaining existing parities within the ERM. Later a major row broke out between the British and Germans following British claims that the Bundesbank, rather than helping sterling's plight, actually precipitated the crisis. Government and Bank of England officials were quick to point to the contrast between the Bundesbank's public support for the French franc compared with its attitude towards the plight of the British pound. As a British Treasury statement put it: 'The UK Government has never claimed that the Bundesbank did not comply with its technical obligations under the ERM. We have simply noted the very public way in which statements of support for the [French] franc were made in contrast to the undermining statements made in relation to sterling.'[46] In fact the Bundesbank had made it all too clear that it wanted a realignment within the ERM as it considered the Deutschmark undervalued.[47] German politicians did

[45] Although many Labour Party voters opposed EU membership, as was demonstrated in the subsequent national referendum which narrowly rejected Norway's entry into the EU.

[46] 'Fresh Anglo-German Row Breaks Out Over ERM', *Financial Times*, 1 Oct. 1992, 1.

[47] 'Mayhem', editorial, *The Economist*, 19 Sept. 1992, 13–14.

not dissent from this view. This sequence of events supports the argument of the last chapter that the German perception of the federal bargain was much more limited than the perceptions of those countries, including Italy, Spain, and Britain, who believed they had much to gain from association with a strong anchor currency—initially the Deutschmark and eventually a single currency. In contrast, the Germans had little to gain from association with the weak currencies of the high inflation countries and were prepared to make only limited sacrifices on behalf of France, a country which might eventually qualify for the Deutschmark 'core' of the EU. Also as argued in Chapter 4, the Germans may have had other, non-economic reasons to preserve the Franco-German relationship, but they had little incentive to do so in the case of the British. It is also significant that when the franc came under unsustainable pressure in the summer of 1993, the preferred solution was not devaluation or a French departure from the EMS, but a complete overhaul of the system which at least retained the semblance of unity and equality between the two main members, France and Germany.

CONCLUSIONS

The main argument of this chapter is that the enormous economic and political sacrifices endured by a range of European countries during the exchange rate turmoil of 1992 and 1993 can only be understood in the context of the federal bargain concluded at Maastricht. A wide range of politicians and officials from all the main political groupings believed that price stability could only be achieved in a fixed exchange rate regime, and that this was the first step towards full monetary union. They also believed that the costs of the bargain would be short term. In the longer term the macroeconomic discipline required by the convergence criteria would result in improved competitiveness and sustained economic growth. The alternative—floating exchange rates—would, in the worst possible scenario, lead to import-led inflation and eventually to economic and political collapse. Certainly this was the view among politicians in Italy, Spain, and the smaller, more vulnerable economies.

The three Nordic countries are of particular interest. For a variety of historical reasons, they had long been jealous of their political and economic neutrality and had played only a very limited part in the postwar moves towards European integration. By the early 1990s, however, changes in the world economy (together with the collapse of the Soviet Union) had convinced them that economic and political salvation lay in close association with the EMS as a prelude to full membership of the European Union. So convinced were the Nordic élites that this was the only way to stabilize their fragile finances that they deliberately deflated their economies amid deepening recession and rapidly rising unemployment. In other words, as with the signatories of the Maastricht Treaty, they became convinced that the only way to tackle actual or potential domestic inflation was through monetary union. In the Swedish case, the events of 1992 amounted to that country's most serious political crisis in modern history. Having successfully defended their independence in earlier eras with Imperial Russia and Nazi Germany, the Swedes found themselves powerless in the face of the international currency markets. Fearing the social and political costs of attempting to go it alone, they scrambled, almost in a state of panic, to be included in the European federal bargain.

Perhaps the most remarkable feature of the 1992 and 1993 currency crises was the degree of consensus across political parties that there was no alternative but to defend exchange rate parities. Often, the most Draconian deflationary measures were taken by parties of the left, parties whose historical appeal lay in promises to maintain full employment and provide a social safety net for the disadvantaged. In case after case, however, they found themselves pursuing policies which were to have precisely the opposite effects. As telling was the fact that for all the incumbent governments, whether of the left, centre, or right, the actions taken were electorally irrational. Indeed, in almost every case the political costs were to become apparent in subsequent local, regional, and national elections. In many cases deflationary policies led to a move away from the main political parties and towards smaller, protest, and populist parties.[48] It is also significant that even after devaluations or a move to floating rates, governments continued to preach the benefits of the ERM of the EMS and of the need for monetary union.

One final point. In no instance was it necessary that the perceptions

[48] Following the events of November, general elections were held in Italy, France, Spain, Norway, and Ireland during the remainder of 1992 and 1993. In France, the Socialists suffered a 15.5 per cent drop in support while the *divers gauche* and Greens saw a 7 per cent increase and the National Front a 3 per cent increase. In total, the main parties (Socialist, UDF, RPR) attracted just 60 per cent of the total on a historically low turnout (60 per cent of the valid vote). In Spain, while the Socialists suffered a minor drop in their support, the right wing Popular Party increased its vote by 9 per cent taking it to within 4 per cent of the Socialist total. Support for the centrist CDS party collapsed

of politicians and officials involved in these decisions were objectively correct. Recall Riker's insistence that what is important in any federal bargain is that the parties *believe* that the costs and benefits fall the right way. The point of this chapter has been to provide evidence in support of the view that the signatories to the Treaty as well as the Nordic johnny-come-lately applicants, were convinced that the benefits of the ERM of the EMS and thus eventually of EMU outweighed the costs. Why else would they have sacrificed so much in 1992 and 1993? Of course it could be that they were objectively wrong and that the benefits of the EMS and EMU were or will be outweighed by the costs. Whatever the case, by late 1995 governments in all the EU countries bar Britain remained committed to membership of a revamped EMS. And as mentioned earlier even the British refused to rule out eventual membership both of the EMS and of EMU.[49]

to 1.8 per cent. In Norway turn-out in the 1993 election was the lowest since 1927 (75.9 per cent). Only the Centre Party experienced a significant rise in support (an increase of 10.3 per cent). Labour saw small gains, while the Conservatives suffered a 5.2 per cent drop. The small Centre Party opposed EU membership. In Ireland both the main parties, Fianna Fail and Fine Gail, suffered significant falls in support while the small Labour Party increased its share of the vote by 9.8 per cent. Although Labour supported EU membership it had been vocal in its criticism of the austerity measures introduced in the previous year. Mention should also be made of the Italian election of April 1992 which, although it preceded the currency crisis of later that year, did occur in the midst of a general economic crisis. Again the traditional parties lost out in relation to populist and protest groups including the Northern League (plus 7.4 per cent). In all these countries unemployment and austerity measures dominated the elections. In some the relationship between these and the EU was prominent (Norway, Spain). All figures from the *European Journal of Political Research Political Data Handbook*, vol. 23, 1993, and vol. 24, 1994.

[49] David Smith, 'Britain May be Dragged Screaming Back to ERM', *The Sunday Times*, 3 Sept. 1995, 7.

PART II

On the Viability of Political Unions

6

Theory

INTRODUCTION

Few commentators on the institutional structure of the European Union dissent from the view that a 'democratic deficit' exists. Indeed this has been the perception during the whole history of European integration. From the very beginning, the EC was driven by bureaucratic and policy objectives; democratic representation and accountability followed rather than preceded these objectives. Debate on this issue is, therefore, almost always couched in terms of how the union should proceed to 'catch up' in terms of democratic institutions and processes. Thus there are repeated calls for further strengthening of the European Parliament (EP), standardizing electoral systems, providing for the protection of human rights, and extending the jurisdiction of the Court of Justice.[1] A related debate dwells on the issue of subsidiarity, or that division of powers between the central or federal level and the national or regional levels which will optimize efficiency and democratic accountability. What is interesting about these proposals is that for the most part they are treated as addenda to the specific provisions of the various European Treaties, including Maastricht. It is assumed that the EU will have an increasingly wide and complex policy brief and therefore it is important that its democratic institutions and procedures are strengthened. It may be, however, that the politicians and others involved in 'correcting' the democratic deficit have no choice in the matter. That rather than the removal of the democratic deficit being a matter for concerned élites intent on imposing democratic procedures on the EU, the nature and extent of democratic representation will be determined by what the

[1] For example the influential—and pro- EU—European Community Studies Association Second World Conference was devoted to the question of subsidiarity and democracy. The proceedings of the conference are available from the Commission of the European Community, Brussels, 1994. On the need for standardized elections, see Vernon Bognador, 'Direct Elections, Representative Democracy and European Integration', *Electoral Studies*, 8, 1989, 205–16.

EU attempts to do in policy terms. The main argument of this chapter is that monetary union brings with it a degree of economic centralization which, under certain circumstance, requires a high degree of political centralization. Whether such political centralization is acceptable to the citizens and political leaders of the component states depends on the costs and benefits implicit in the particular federal bargain under discussion. This argument will be presented in theoretical terms only; the objective is to provide a conceptual framework with which to judge the viability of political unions in general and the EU in particular. Chapter 7 will apply this framework specifically to the European case by comparing the economic and political conditions of the EU with those prevalent in other unions and in particular the United States. The chapter will be divided into two parts. Part one will review those theories drawn from the literature on the viability of federations which are relevant for our purposes. Part two will identify the logical links between economic and political centralization and what this might mean in the European case.

THE VIABILITY OF POLITICAL UNIONS

Perhaps surprisingly, given the experience of the former Soviet Union and Yugoslavia, theoretical work on the viability of federations is quite limited in volume and in scope. Very generally there are three broad approaches to the subject—legal, administrative, and political. The legal perspective argues that the federal bargain is in effect a contract or covenant between the participating parties. If the parties to the federation entered into the contract or agreement voluntarily there is at least the implication that any one party could leave the federation voluntarily should they believe that the conditions of the contract have been violated.[2] Yet no federal constitution bar that of the former Soviet Union actually permits secession.[3] When countries come together to form political unions they do so in the expectation that the arrangement will be permanent. They are not concluding a traditional treaty from which

[2] See S. Rufus Davis, *The Federal Principle*, Berkeley and Los Angeles, University of California Press, 1978, ch. 1; Preston King, *Federalism and Federation*, London, Croom Helm, 1982, chs. 8 and 9.

[3] Secession was only possible if the departing state adhered to Marxist/Leninist principles, and secession was in fact impossible in practical terms until the decay of the CPSU during the 1980s.

they may withdraw at a later stage; they are creating a new nation state. Moreover, as Preston King has stressed, voluntary secession is actually quite rare in modern federations. Of the leading twentieth-century federations—the USA, Australia, Canada, Brazil, India and the USSR—only the USSR has experienced secession, which led, of course, to the break up of the state as a federal entity. Other breakups or secessions have been non-voluntary and have involved bloody civil wars (Yugoslavia, Pakistan, and Bangladesh) or the threat of major ethnic violence (Malaysia's expulsion of Singapore). In other cases again, a dominant state in the federation, seeing no advantage in association with weaker states, decides to leave the union unilaterally (Jamaica and the West Indies Federation). In effect, then, the legal or contractual status of the bargain is irrelevant as to whether or not the bargain is kept.

A second perspective argues that what maintains federations is the nature and extent of the federal government's powers, or the degree of administrative centralization. Although the nature and extent of the federal powers are obviously an important element in any one federation—of which much more later—even the most casual review of the world's federations shows that there is no clear correlation between any particular allocation of powers to the centre and the maintenance of federations.[4] Hence it is possible to discern a great deal of variation in this measure between successful federations (the USA, Canada, Switzerland) and between successful and unsuccessful federations (Switzerland is decentralized, the USSR was highly centralized). Even more telling is the fact that constitutionally unitary systems are sometimes as, or by some measures more, decentralized than federal systems (Spain compared with the United States or Germany). Moreover, what is often invoked as the main *raison d'être* for a clear division of powers between the centre and the periphery—the protection of regional, cultural, linguistic, and religious loyalties—is often as well performed by unitary systems (Spain, the United Kingdom, Italy) as by federal systems (the USSR, Brazil).[5]

This accepted, it is difficult to accept Riker's contention that what actually transpires in any system in terms of which powers are held at the centre and which at the periphery is simply a matter of chance and

[4] For an account of this perspective see William H. Riker, *Federalism: Origins, Operation, Significance*, Boston, Little Brown, 1964, ch. 3.

[5] For a discussion of this point see Riker, 'Federalism', in Fred I. Greenstein and Nelson Polsby, *The handbook of Political Science*, vol. v: *Government Institutions and Processes*, Reading, Mass., Addison Wesley, 1975, 93–172.

administrative convenience.[6] There is, for instance, no example of a modern state delegating certain fundamental powers, including control of macroeconomic policy, to the states or regions. As we will see, once this is conceded, it carries with it profound political implications for the functioning of the federal state.

The third perspective on the maintenance of federations assigns pride of place to politics and to political institutions. In terms of the Rikerian federal bargain elaborated in earlier chapters, the 'political' could simply mean whether or not the conditions of the original federal bargain hold. If, for example, a federation is 'forced' on a group of countries by an external power—much as with the British in the West Indies or in East Africa—but there is no internal or external threat or opportunity contributing to the calculus in the federal bargain, then the federation will simply dissolve following independence.[7] A variant on this theme would be the creation of a federal state which quickly and successfully overcomes an external threat and thus removes the *rationale* for continuing the bargain. Empirical examples of this sequence are hard to find, but it could be assumed that had Britain and France formed a federation in 1940 (see Chapter 3, pp. 36–37) they may well have dissolved the union had they subsequently defeated Germany. Similarly, the Southern confederacy may have decided on state sovereignty had they defeated the Unionists during the American Civil War.

There are, however, many examples of federations enduring for many years after the conditions of the original bargain have passed. Most scholars agree that in such cases a degree of common interest emerges which helps bind the federation together. To put it another way, the citizenry acquire a loyalty both to the centre and to the state or provincial level which is articulated through mediating political institutions.[8] Hence in the United States, both external and internal threats to the nation had passed by the last third of the nineteenth century, but the union was maintained by citizen loyalty to the federal government as expressed through Congress and a popularly elected President.[9] Riker, in particular, insists that the key institutions in this maintenance process

[6] Ibid. 141–5.

[7] For a discussion of these cases, see A. H. Birch, 'Approaches to the Study of Federalism', *Political Studies*, 14/1, 1966, 15–33.

[8] Riker, *Federalism*, chs. 3 and 4. See also Michael Burgess, 'Federalism and Federation', in Michael Burgess and Alain-G. Gagnon (eds.), *Comparative Federalism and Federation: Competing Traditions and Future Directions*, London, Harvester Wheatsheaf, 1993, 3–14.

[9] Riker, *Federalism*, ch. 4.

are the political parties, for it is the parties that provide the essential connective tissue in an institutional structure designed to balance provincial interests with those of the centre. How parties operate in a federal system is the best measure of the degree to which that system is centralized. In effect, the party system provides an accurate measure of federalism. As he puts it:

> In a variety of governments, then, the structure of parties parallels the structure of federalism. When parties are fully centralized, so is federalism (e.g. in the Soviet Union and Mexico). When parties are somewhat decentralized, then federalism is only partially centralized. Because of this perfect correlation of, at least, the two extreme categories of federalism with party structure, the inference is immediate: one can measure federalism by measuring parties. The structure of parties is thus a surrogate for the structure of the whole constitution.[10]

By implication, at least, the viability of the federal system will be challenged if citizen loyalty at the provincial level is so strong that the party system is itself highly decentralized. If the trend is towards greater provincial loyalty, such as seems to be the case in modern-day Canada, then there is the possibility that the federation could become peripheralized or assume the status of a collection of *de facto* unitary states. The great advantage of this model is that it makes a clear conceptual distinction between *political* centralization and what might be called *technological* centralization. There is a tendency both among political scientists and economists to assume that technological change leads to economic and social centralization and thus to the need for central institutions capable of regulating and adjudicating the conduct of economic and social affairs. Hence the assumption that all modern federations (and indeed all modern societies) have become more politically centralized over the last several decades. Clearly, however, there is nothing inevitable about the link between economic and political centralization. In the United States, economic and social centralization have indeed resulted in a degree of political centralization as is evidenced by enhanced federal government powers.[11] In other countries where provincial loyalties are stronger (Canada) or historically have been repressed (the former Yugoslavia and the Soviet Union), economic centralization has not led to a linear-like development of political centralization.

[10] Riker, 'Federalism', 137, and sources cited.

[11] On the tendency for the government in the USA to become centralized see Theodore Lowi and Alan Stone (ed.), *Nationalizing Government: Public Policies in America*, Beverly Hills, Calif., Sage, 1978, also Samuel Beer, 'Federalism, Nationalism and Democracy in America', *American Political Science Review*, 74, 1978, 9–21.

Indeed in the case of the former Communist states, all the alleged advantages of a centralized economy have been sacrificed in order to achieve full political decentralization.

While the distinction between political and technological centralization is useful in any analysis using the original Rikerian framework where an internal or external military threat or opportunity is the *only* basis for the federal bargain, it is clearly of less use when, as in the European case, there is an intimate link between technological (or economic) concerns and the basis of the federal bargain. Uniquely in the history of federation-building, the Europeans agreed on the creation of a political union with the specific intention of centralizing the main economic function of government. In previous cases the only essential centralizing function of the new states was the raising of armies—a task that, depending on the circumstances in individual cases, could be achieved with a greater or lesser degree of taxation levied by the centre. In all the cases prior to this century this was accomplished in the absence of all the complex interventionist apparatus typical of the modern welfare state. Provincial loyalties could continue relatively unhampered by the new central government whose main (perhaps only) job was national defence.[12] This was broadly true even of some of the twentieth-century federations involving poorer countries where neither state nor central governments had traditionally provided extensive welfare and other benefits for their citizens.

Europe is different. In all the member states of the EU, governments play a major role in economy and society. While this takes many and complex forms, it consists in the main either in providing for redistribution across regions and/or social groups, or in stabilizing the economy in response to the behaviour of the business cycle or in reaction to economic or political shocks. Crucially, in what are mature democracies, citizens *expect* governments to perform these functions. Indeed it would not be going too far to argue that the redistributive and stabilizing role of government is central to the modern conception of citizenship. Governments are defeated in elections if they are perceived to have failed to perform these functions adequately. The obvious question in the European case, therefore, is: what are the likely economic and political consequences of monetary union for the redistributive and

[12] As recently as 1929 federal US government spending accounted for just 2.5 per cent of GNP of which almost half was spent on defence. State and local government spending amounted to 7.3 per cent of GNP, Advisory Commission on Intergovernmental Relations, *Significant Features of Fiscal Federalism, 1978/9*, Washington, ACIR, 1979, Table 1.

stabilizing role presently performed by national governments? More specifically, will the capacity of erstwhile national governments be reduced, and if so, what will be the political/institutional consequences of transferring some or all of this role to the federal level?

THE POLITICAL ECONOMY OF MONETARY UNION

Curiously, although the *economic* consequences of monetary union has attracted a considerable amount of attention among applied economists,[13] the link between these economic factors and *political* institutions and processes has inspired little interest among political scientists. This lacunae is all the more surprising given that almost all the economists writing on the subject point to the inextricable linkages between the economic and the political. Most treat the latter as a residual category which, unsurprisingly for professional economists, is treated as crucial to any understanding of monetary union, but which is essentially beyond their competence. A sample of quotes from economists working in this area makes the point.

> The decision to go ahead with monetary union has clearly been inspired by the political objective of European unification. In this dynamic towards political union, many objections expressed by economists, and formulated in this and in previous chapters, have been brushed aside. Whether this is a wise decision only the future will tell for sure. (Paul De Grauwe)[14]

> The single European currency, with monetary policy controlled by Eurofed . . . is a fairly drastic decision to impose formal restrictions that effectively take away national control of fiscal policy even when individual countries are vulnerable to fluctuations that are distinct from the Community average. To do so may create political as well as economic strains. (J.-P. Fitoussi *et al.*)[15]

> [The unanswered questions] refer to the costs and benefits of EMU in a Community which is still characterized by a high degree of economic diversity and relatively little political cohesion; and also in a Community where political

[13] There is a vast economics literature on this subject. For a summary, see Michael Emerson *et al.*, *One Market, One Money*, Oxford, OUP, 1992, and sources cited. One attempt to synthesise the political and economic—although not using federal theory—is Barry Eichengreen and Jeffrey Frieden (eds.), *The Political Economy of Monetary Unification*, Boulder, Colo., Westview Press, 1994.

[14] Paul De Grauwe, *The Economics of Monetary Integration*, Oxford, OUP, 2nd edn., 1994, 210.

[15] J.-P. Fitoussi *et al.*, *Competitive Disinflation: The Mark and Budgetary Politics in Europe*, Oxford, OUP, 1993, 89.

institutions fall far short of economic ambitions. EMU constitutes a long term and, perhaps also, a high risk strategy in which wider political objectives have always counted more than strict economic ones. (Loukas Tsoukalis)[16]

I can understand . . . that there are those that are willing to accept . . . adverse economic effects in order to achieve a federalist political union that they favour for other, non-economic reasons. What I cannot understand are those who advocate monetary union but reject any movement towards a federalist political structure for Europe. This is a formula for economic costs without any of the supposed political benefits. (Martin Feldstein)[17]

This is not an unrepresentative sample. Virtually all the economists working in this area are aware that monetary union brings with it potential economic costs as well as benefits, and that union has potentially profound political implications.[18] At the heart of the economists' analysis is a concern for the economic effects of removing macroeconomic policy from national governments and assigning it to the federal level. By so doing, the capacity of national (or what eventually might be considered state or regional) governments to perform their traditional redistributive and counter-cyclical functions would be reduced. Except with regard to small, highly dependent economies with currencies linked to those of powerful neighbours,[19] macroeconomic policy becomes a vital tool in response to asymmetric regional or global shocks. If this function is transferred to the federal level, political pressures will also force a centralization of fiscal policy.

THE ECONOMIC DIMENSION

To understand this dynamic all that is necessary is to note what happens in existing federal states—or indeed in the constituent regions of unitary states, the same logic applies—when an economy or part of that economy is exposed to external shocks, to the vagaries of the business cycle, or to changes in taste and technology. If, for example, the United

[16] Loukas Tsoukalis, *The New European Economy: The Politics and Economics of Integration*, Oxford, OUP, 1993, 227.

[17] Martin Feldstein, 'The Case Against EMU', *The Economist*, 13 June 1992, 26.

[18] For a literature review on the economic costs and benefits, see De Grauwe, *The Economics of Monetary Integration*, chs. 1–4; Emerson *et al.*, *One Market, One Money*, Part B.

[19] On the role of a 'hegemonic' economy in a monetary union, see Benjamin Cohen, 'Beyond EMU: The Problem of Sustainability', in Eichengreen and Frieden (eds.), *The Political Economy of European Monetary Unification*, 149–66.

States is hit by a global shock such as the oil crises of the 1970s, or goes into recession during a downturn in the business cycle, individual states are unable to respond by devaluing their currencies, increasing their money supplies, or changing interest rates, as all these functions are vested in the federal government. Given the size and high degree of specialization in the American economy, every downturn or change in taste or technology affects different states in different ways (in this sense all shocks are, to a greater or lesser extent, asymmetric in character when they hit an economy with different regions specializing in different products and services). A sudden increase in oil prices may boost economic activity in oil-producing states, but depress the economies of non-oil-producing manufacturing states. Noting the effects of the downturn or the shock, the responsibility of the federal authorities is to adjust monetary policy in ways which are in the best interests of the economy as a whole. During a general recession a reduction in interest rates may be advisable for the whole economy, even although parts of that economy (say, Texas in the mid-1970s) is hardly affected by recession. Conversely, the general economy may be overheating and thus require a tightening of monetary policy, even although some states may remain mired in recession.

In response to such events governments in all modern countries have developed a wide range of policy instruments to compensate adversely affected regions. Most of the more important of these are triggered automatically. Unemployment compensation and other income maintenance measures involve a large and automatic redistribution from wealthier areas to distressed areas. Federal taxation facilitates these transfers and, crucially, citizens are prepared to pay these taxes because they have acquired a loyalty to the centre—in the American case this means that they accept the status of citizens of the United States of America. Of course these fiscal transfers are limited by the amount that citizens are prepared to pay in general taxation—a point which is the very essence of modern American politics,[20] and by the general state of the national finances. If, as is the case in the United States, the federal budget is perceived to be in chronic deficit, pressures exist to correct this state of affairs. *How* this is corrected, and the distributional consequences of any action taken, is a matter for the democratic process.

[20] Concerns with federal government spending are central to the decline in trust in government in the USA and the emergence of divided government, see David McKay, 'Divided and Governed?: Recent Research on Divided Government in the United States, *British Journal of Political Research*, 24, 1994.

Again, this is the very stuff of politics in the USA, and while fierce controversy exists over the extent of the federal government's role in this process, few dissent from the view that it *is* the proper job of federal government to police the national finances. It was not always so. During the first half of the nineteenth century great political battles were fought over whether there should be a national bank with such responsibilities.[21] But to repeat the point, no modern state allows its states or provinces to conduct their own macroeconomic policies.[22]

If the centre is weak and fiscal transfers are correspondingly low, adversely affected states and regions will be obliged to fall back on their own resources either by indulging in deficit financing or by increasing taxation in order to finance their own redistributive programmes. Although both do occur among American states, deficit financing (should it be permitted constitutionally) increases the debt-servicing burden on the state and limits the future scope of fiscal policy. The alternative of increasing taxation will act as a disincentive for capital investment. Its extent will also be limited if the state (say West Virginia) is generally poor and depressed. The citizens of a West Virginia and other permanently or temporarily depressed states and regions do have an alternative, however, even in the context of federal fiscal transfers. They can move to another state less adversely affected by the economic downturn. A further feature of modern federations, therefore, is a high degree of both capital and labour mobility. Again using the American analogy, few cultural, linguistic, or administrative barriers to labour and capital mobility exist among the states. Moving to a new job in another state is commonplace and universally accepted. An automatic component also exists in this process. For a downturn in West Virginia will depress local wages, thus providing workers with an incentive to move to a more prosperous state. If, for some reason, they cannot move and fiscal transfers from the centre are very limited, the result, given that the government of West Virginia cannot adjust its interest rates to the appropriate 'West Virginia' level nor devalue the 'West Virginia dollar' to increase competitiveness, will be progressively falling prices and wages, or, the immiseration of the local population in relation to

[21] Stephen Skowronek, *The Politics Presidents Make*, Cambridge, Mass., Harvard University Press, 1993, chs. 4 and 5.

[22] Even the secessionist Quebecois concede that an independent Quebec would continue with the Canadian dollar. The extent to which Quebec would be genuinely independent under such an arrangement is open to some doubt.

the rest of the federation.[23] Even if the level of economic inequality among the states is low (as generally was the case in pre-unification West Germany) redistribution via fiscal centralization may still be needed. For some shocks are sector specific and may have an important spatial dimension even in a relatively homogeneous economy. In the German case, for example, a shock affecting the car industry would adversely affect Bavaria compared with North Rhine Westphalia, thus triggering transfers from the latter to the former.

As we will see in the next chapter, economists have elaborated a number of variations on this theme. Some believe that factor mobility—and in particular labour mobility—will remain low in Europe and therefore will confirm that the EU does not constitute an optimum currency area.[24] Others believe that EMU will induce a significant increase in factor mobility and regional specialization and thus produce pressures for fiscal centralization.[25] Almost none of the economists working in the area believe that EMU can be accommodated without some degree of economic policy centralization.

The crucial variables when assessing the costs and benefits of any proposed monetary union are, therefore:

1. The extent to which the economies of the component states differ from one another in terms of prices and outputs and product specialization.
2. The sensitivity and vulnerability of each of the component states to asymmetric 'shocks'. These may be country specific, sector specific, or common to the whole federation; they may be temporary or permanent. Although by definition their effects are economic they may be caused by political, environmental, or economic phenomena.[26]
3. The feasibility of using fiscal transfers from the centre to the component states to facilitate adjustment following economic shocks.
4. Labour mobility and flexibility between the component states.[27]

[23] Economists commonly use the United States as a comparison; see De Grauwe plus Martin Feldsetin's article in *The Economist*, 'The Case Against EMU', Paul Krugman, 'Lessons of Massachusetts for EMU', in Francisco Torres and Francesco Giavazzi (eds.), *Adjustment and Growth in the European Monetary Union*, Cambridge, CUP, 1993, 241–69.

[24] Tamin Bayoumi and Barry Eichengreen, 'Shocking Aspects of European Integration', in Torres and Giavazzi, *Adjustment and Growth*, 193–240.

[25] Paul Krugman, 'Lessons of Massachusetts for EMU', in Torres and Giavazzi, *Adjustment and Growth*, 241–69.

[26] For a comprehensive analysis of asymmetric shocks see Michael Emerson *et al.*, *One Market, One Money*, ch. 6.

[27] Paul Krugman, 'Policy Problems of a Monetary Union', in Paul de Grauwe and L. Papademos (eds.), *The European Monetary System in the 1990s*, London, Longman, 1990.

Although economists disagree on the question of where, precisely, the EU would fit in terms of these variables should a single currency be adopted, they accept that *some* degree of fiscal centralization would follow from EMU. As will be shown in Chapter 7, the balance of argument among economists favours scenarios involving quite substantial redistributions from the centre to the component states.[28]

The Political Dimension

As suggested in the American case, fiscal centralization is accepted by American voters because they have acquired a loyalty to the centre or to the federal government. The fairly massive redistribution characteristic of the system may be a matter of political controversy in terms of the level of federal taxation, but few citizens are concerned with the spatial consequences of the redistribution. In other words, although voters in (say) Connecticut may be aware that their tax dollars are funding the poor of West Virginia and some may even be resentful of this fact, most are not, and none are so concerned with what is in effect a permanent redistribution that they favour secession or the expulsion of West Virginia from the union. In other unions—and indeed in many unitary states—such resentments are much stronger and have resulted in the breakup of the country (Czechoslovakia) or in serious strains which threaten the viability of the federation (Canada).

What actually determines the degree of centralization in any federal system will naturally depend on unique circumstances. This accepted, it is possible to make some broad theoretical statements about the level of centralization. As noted earlier, the political party system is one of the best indicators of how and to what extent a federal system develops in a centralizing or a decentralizing direction. Drawing largely on the American experience, a number of scholars have long recognized the relationship between party organization and ideology on the one hand and the level of political centralization on the other. In contrast to British or French parties, parties in the USA have historically acquired little in the way of ideological unity; they are also characterized by a low level of control over personnel by central organizations—indeed the central organizations are remarkably weak.[29] The USA has on occasion

[28] See Eichengreen, 'Fiscal Policy and EMU', in Eichengreen and Frieden (eds.), *The Political Economy of Monetary Unification*, 167–90.

[29] An excellent historical perspective on the decentralized nature of the American party system is provided by William Nisbet Chambers and Walter Dean Burnham (eds.), *The American Party Systems: Stages of Political Development*, Oxford, OUP, 1975.

displayed a centralizing characteristic, however: parties in control of the federal government sometimes also control the state governments. Moreover, during centralizing periods such as the New Deal, a dominant party not only controlled the Congress and the presidency and most of the states, it was also able to achieve an unusually high degree of ideological cohesion over fundamental economic and social reforms.[30]

Riker has formalized these statements by constructing an index of disharmony based on the following two measures:

> 1. Whether or not the party in control of the national government is in control of the constituent governments. If the nationally controlling party cannot win in state and provincial elections (as often happens in the United States and usually happens in Canada), then it can hardly hope to bring about a centralized party structure of a centralized constitution.
>
> 2. Whether or not party discipline exists on legislative and executive matters. If party members can act together, then they can hope to centralize, otherwise not.[31]

As the disharmony index rises so 'the central government is less and less likely to be able to control policy in the constituent governments simply because there is no formal connection between the levels'. If the index measure falls 'the central government is more and more likely to be able to control policy in the constituent governments, simply because there is some kind of informal partisan connection between levels'.[32] Political and social pressures at any one time in history may, as with the New Deal, add to party cohesion and lead to centralization, while at other times pressures may weaken the parties and strengthen the periphery. In modern-day Canada, for example, federal-level parties have weakened to the point where a real possibility of disintegration exists.[33] Given these historical variations it is not surprising that for any one country the index of disharmony varies quite widely over time.[34]

What the federal government actually does at any one time will be determined by this historical pattern of centralization and decentralization. In the most extreme case, such as the former Soviet Union, a non-democratic but hegemonic political party (the CPSU) ended up with a near monopoly of central power. In democratic federations the crucial

[30] See Chambers and Burnham, *The American Party Systems*, ch. 11 and sources cited.

[31] Riker, 'Federalism', 137. [32] Ibid. 139.

[33] David Milne, ' "Whither Canadian federalism": Alternative Constitutional Futures', in Burgess and Gagnon (eds.), *Comparative Federalism*, 203–26.

[34] William H. Riker and Ronald Schaps, 'Disharmony in Federal Government', *Behavioural Science*, 2, 1957, 276–90.

variable is the loyalty of the citizenry to the centre as opposed to the periphery. When this is high and the party system is more centralized (the New Deal) the federal government takes on new policy functions. When it is low (in the Reconstruction era following the Civil War), the party system decentralizes and the federal government's powers are reduced in relation to those of the states. In other words, over time, the original federal bargain is constantly being renegotiated.

Uniquely in the history of federations, the bargain underpinning the European Union was policy driven and, as has been argued, will certainly produce pressures towards fiscal centralization. In every other democratic federation this process has been facilitated by a centralizing party or parties operating through well-developed central political institutions. Politics has, therefore, been driving policy, rather than policy driving politics. What the rather dry and analytical term 'fiscal centralization' actually means is, of course, the willingness of the citizens of the component states of the EU to pay taxes to a federal government intent on redistributing revenues to disadvantaged countries and regions. This may be a permanent redistribution; the rich may never be paid back. The key questions for the future of the EU are, therefore:

1. What is the nature and level of support for the EU among the citizens of the component states? What evidence is there that citizen loyalties to EU central institutions are changing and in what direction?

2. What is the nature of the evolving European party system? What are the links, if any, between Europe-wide parties and existing national parties? Is the trend towards decentralization or centralization in these party systems?

Chapter 7 will attempt to answer these questions and will also attempt to answer the economists questions relating to the existence of pressures which might lead to fiscal centralization.

7

Applications

INTRODUCTION

As indicated in the last chapter, economists disagree as to the precise effects of EMU on national economies in general and national finances in particular. We also concluded, however, that the economic effects of EMU could, under certain circumstances, have important policy implications. The purpose of this chapter is to elaborate on these likely policy ramifications. The main argument will be that almost all the scenarios provided by a range of respected economists produce pressures for fiscal centralization. The first part of the chapter will review the policy implications of competing economic scenarios and the second part will place these implications in political context by assessing the capacity of the European party system and institutional structure to accommodate them. Ultimately this capacity depends on the level of public support for and identity with the federal (or central) government. Relevant survey data on levels of support for EU institutions will also be reviewed, therefore.

Obviously this exercise must be speculative in nature. No one knows for sure what the consequences of EMU will be. Given the importance of the issue, however, educated guesses on the likely outcome are necessary. Certainly economists have been quick to develop a large body of work in this area. They have also used existing federal monetary unions as comparisons in their studies, with the United States serving as the most appropriate comparator case. Curiously, political scientists have not repeated this exercise with respect to the political dimension. Again, although this must of necessity involve speculation, it remains crucially important that policy makers and citizens alike are aware of the likely political consequences of ceding control of macroeconomic policy to a federal authority, and we can only make such speculations through comparisons with other political systems.

THE ECONOMIC AND POLICY IMPLICATIONS OF EMU

Economic Implications

A good starting-point in any discussion of the economic and policy consequences of EMU is the theory of optimum currency areas.[1] First elaborated by Mundell in 1961 the theory claims that in some instances basic economic differences between a particular group of countries can only be efficiently reconciled through changes in the exchange rate.[2] The most important of these differences are: shifts in demand, different preferences about inflation and unemployment, and variations in labour market institutions. Should these differences be low it is conceivable that the benefits of monetary union (mainly in the form of lower transaction costs) will exceed the costs. If they are high then welfare losses rather than gains would follow from monetary union. Labour market flexibility and mobility are important variables because in the absence of the freedom to devalue, a shift in demand away from (say) British goods to German goods means that competitiveness can be only be restored if wage rates fall.

Alternatively, the work-force could move to an adjacent country (or state) where the demand for labour remains high. Adjustment following a shift in demand would also be aided by a centralized fiscal system, which could redistribute tax revenues from the high demand to low demand area in the short term, thus easing the pain of adjustment. As will be discussed later, centrally collected taxes are also recognized as a useful adjustment mechanism should countries be the victims of asymmetric supply shocks. It is now fashionable to argue that in the long run different preferences about inflation and unemployment are irrelevant because the natural rate of unemployment is independent of the inflation rate. However, all economists agree that if two countries with different inflation rates join a monetary union, the trade-offs in the short-term Philips curve between unemployment and inflation remains

[1] This analysis of optimum currency area is based partly on Paul De Grauwe's *The Economics of Monetary Integration*, Oxford, OUP, 2nd edn., 1994, chs. 1 and 2.

[2] R. Mundell, 'A Theory of Optimal Currency Areas', *American Economic Review*, 51, 1961. See also R. McKinnon, 'Optimal Currency Areas', *American Economic Review*, 53, 1963, 717–25; P. Kene, 'The Theory of Optimal Currency Areas: An Eclectic View', in R. Mundell and A. Swobodaa (eds.), *Monetary Problems of the International Economy*, Chicago, University of Chicago Press, 1969.

operative, in which case the high inflation country will suffer higher unemployment in the 'short' term following union. We do not know, of course, how short this will be.

Labour market institutions are important because the degree of centralization in wage bargaining has an important effect on the level of wage inflation following a supply shock (such as the oil price shocks of the 1970s). As De Grauwe has summarized, countries with highly decentralized bargaining and highly centralized bargaining will adjust more efficiently (i.e. with lower levels of wage-induced inflation) than those with intermediate levels of wage bargaining. Unions in the highly centralized countries will know that excessive wage claims will lead to inflation and thus will have no incentive to outbid each other. In highly decentralized states, although unions have an incentive to claim high awards, to do so would damage firms' competitiveness. Fear of unemployment, therefore, will keep claims low. In intermediate cases unions are less likely to fear that their demands will lead to unemployment, and because they remain numerous they will not see that their demands will lead to general inflation. Some empirical evidence in support of these hypotheses exists,[3] and all three cases are represented within the EU states. (Austria, Sweden, and Denmark are highly centralized; Italy is decentralized; France, the Netherlands, and Belgium are intermediate cases.)

The optimal currency area theory has been subject to a number of criticisms over the last twenty years. It tends to ignore the fact that some governments use devaluations as policy instruments, which leads to ever higher levels of inflation without any compensating improvement in output and employment as firms and unions constantly anticipate future devaluations. By definition these costs would disappear in a monetary union. There is, additionally, considerable evidence that the more open the economy (in terms of factor flexibility and mobility) the more quickly will a country adjust following the creation of a monetary union. So even if economic differences between countries are great, these may be irrelevant if the economies involved are characterized by a high degree of openness.[4] However, after reviewing the relevant literature, De Grauwe concludes that: (*a*) not all governments use devaluations irresponsibly. Often, as with France, Belgium, and Denmark

[3] De Grauwe, *The Economics of Monetary Integration*, 24.

[4] On the relationship between the openness of economies and economic policy, see R. Barro and D. Gordon, 'Rules, Discretion and Reputation in a Model of Monetary Policy', *Journal of Monetary Economics*, 12, 1983, 101–21.

during the 1980s, devaluations helped these countries adjust with a loss in employment and output that was lower than would have occurred in the absence of devaluation. (*b*) Economies are never completely open, and regional (national) variations in openness are likely to persist. In other words, differences in industrial structures and the labour and capital markets will always be there. Given these differences, the use of the exchange rate as an instrument to help countries adjust to shocks is likely to remain an important policy option. Without it, a new equilibrium may be reached at a lower level of output and employment. Whether or not this is the case obviously depends on the empirical evidence, to which we now turn.[5]

Very generally, empirical studies have been of two sorts: those comparing the historical characteristics and performance of the EU countries in response to asymmetric shocks; and those which project the likely behaviour of the EU countries following the introduction of EMU.

In their article 'Shocking Aspects of European Monetary Integration', Bayoumi and Eichengreen attempt to measure the extent of economic difference in GDP growth and inflation across the eleven main members of the EC and the eight major regions of the United States. They then measure the incidence, size, and responsiveness of the two economic areas to shocks (measured in terms of changes in prices and output) from 1963 to 1988.

Not unsurprisingly, given the level of integration among the American regions, they found a significantly greater level of price and output coherence among US regions than among the EU countries. They also found a higher correlation (or symmetry) of shocks across US regions than across the EC states. In both the USA and the EC a core of regions (countries) were characterized by high correlations between shocks. In other words the shocks affecting the EC core (Germany, France, the Netherlands, Belgium, Denmark, and Luxemburg) were fairly evenly distributed among these states, compared with the uneven effects of shocks on the periphery (the UK, Italy, Spain, Portugal, Ireland, and Greece). The US core (Eastern Seaboard, the Mid West, and the Far West) showed higher correlations than the EC core. Only when the EC core was compared with all eight US regions were similar correlations found.[6]

[5] De Grauwe, *The Economics of Monetary Integration*, 59.

[6] Tamim Bayoumi and Barry Eichengreen, 'Shocking Aspects of European Monetary Integration', in Francisco Torres and Francesco Giavazzi, *Adjustment and Growth in the European Monetary Union*, Cambridge, CUP and the Centre For Economic Policy Research (CEPR), 1993, 202–15.

They also looked at the size of shocks and the speed of the different economies' response to them. In both instances a similar pattern was found. The shocks affecting the EC were larger than in the USA and the adjustment to them was lower. Again the core EC states were less vulnerable than the periphery, but the US economy was, as a whole, less vulnerable even than the EC core.[7]

Bayoumi and Eichengreen acknowledge that higher levels of factor mobility, and especially labour mobility, greatly aid the adjustment process between US regions—even in the absence of the 'automatic' adjustment implicit in floating exchange rates. Their work is, of course, based on historical patterns and they concede that the incidence and size of shocks may well change during the 1990s and after.

Paul Krugman, however, has attempted to predict what the likely consequences of EMU will be on economic performance. In a stimulating article comparing the fortunes of Massachusetts in the US economy with likely fortunes of EC regions affected by an asymmetric shock, he claims that following EMU, the EU will be even more vulnerable to region-specific shocks as product specialization increases from its present relatively low level. EU regions will also show greater variation in output and growth as labour and capital leave adversely affected areas in favour of growth regions. In effect this is what happens in the US with a state like Massachusetts shedding labour in response to the downturn in demand for high technology products in the early 1990s.[8]

Krugman's analysis depends, however, on the highly contentious claim that labour mobility in the EU will increase following EMU. All the empirical studies point to low levels of labour mobility in the EU,[9] and it is likely that cultural, linguistic, and other barriers will continue to prevent any dramatic increase in intra-EU labour mobility—in spite of the fact that it is official EU policy to remove all barriers to labour mobility.

The work of these American scholars is part of a broad consensus among economists that: (*a*) the EU is not an optimum currency area and is more vulnerable than the USA to asymmetric shocks; and (*b*) the main reason for this is low labour mobility and flexibility compared with comparable economies and especially the USA.[10]

[7] Ibid. 215–21.

[8] Paul Krugman, 'Lessons of Massachusetts for EMU', in Torres and Giavazzi, *Adjustment and Growth*, 241–61.

[9] See Bayoumi and Eichengreen, 'Shocking Aspects', 197–9, and sources cited.

[10] See De Grauwe, *The Economics of Monetary Integration*, refs. at p. 87.

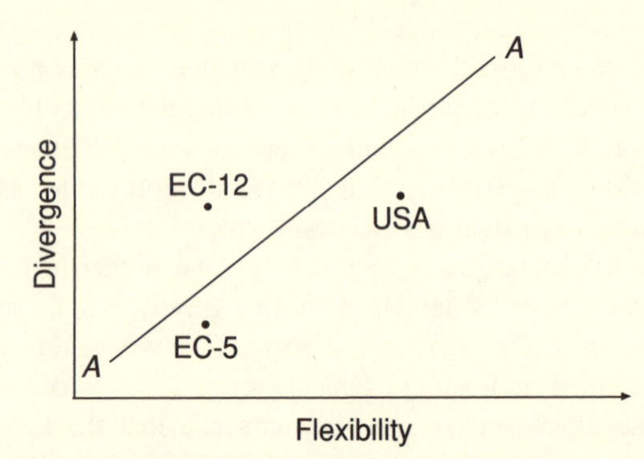

Source: Paul De Grauwe, *The Economics of Monetary Integration*, Fig. 4.4.

FIG. 7.1. Real divergence and labour market flexibility in monetary unions

Paul de Grauwe has expressed this in graph form (Fig. 7.1). The vertical axis measures the extent to which output and employment diverge in response to asymmetric shocks. The horizontal axis measures the degree of labour market flexibility (labour mobility and wage flexibility). Economies above line *AA* would lose (in terms of total welfare) from monetary union while those below would gain. The high degree of divergence in the USA reflects the high level of product specialization typical of that country. With full monetary union and further economic integration it would be expected that product specialization would also increase in Europe which, *in the absence of significant increases in labour market flexibility*, would have the effect of moving the EC-12 further above line *AA*. It might also move the EC-5 above line *AA*. Put another way, the more integrated the EU economies become, the greater will be the variations in output and employment in reaction to asymmetric shocks. Of course we do not *know* for sure that further integration would result in greater product specialization, but a large body of evidence from other countries strongly suggests that this usually follows from integration.[11] Nor do we know how extensive and serious asymmetric shocks will be. If they are external supply shocks such as the oil price increases of the 1970s, adjustment may be painful but relatively short lived. If they are more permanent demand shocks resulting from changes in taste and technology, the consequences may be longer term and involve more traumatic adjustments. As governments are intimately involved in this adjustment process this leads

[11] Krugman, 'Lessons from Massachusetts', and sources cited.

us to the policy implications of this large body of economic research. As might be predicted, because the likely economic outcomes of EMU are in dispute, so the policy implications vary from study to study. This accepted, EMU clearly will have important policy consequences and it is the aim of the next section to outline these and to link them to the political viability of a single currency union.

Policy Implications

All of the above scenarios have important policy implications. Starting with the Krugman thesis, there is no question that high product specialization combined with high labour mobility (as exists in the USA) would bring intense pressures for fiscal centralization. The reasoning here is simple. Should a region experience a shift away from its specialist product (say coal in West Virginia), much of the labour force will leave in search of jobs elsewhere. They will not, however, do this immediately. There will always be a lag between the occurrence of the shock and the labour market response to it. Unemployment will, therefore, rise rapidly in the short term and will remain high in the longer term given that the labour force is never perfectly mobile. Pressure for the alleviation of the resulting hardship by governments will be intense, but the government of the state of West Virginia can do little, given its eroded tax base. It could indulge in deficit financing (should this be permitted constitutionally), but even this option is limited in the longer term as the capital markets downgrade the state's credit rating.

The alternative is transfers from the federal government. In all modern states there is an automatic element in this process. Unemployment, social security, and other benefits flow automatically as recession hits. These will become a permanent redistributive flow given that the remaining West Virginian population will be older and more dependent than the national average. It is estimated that for the USA something between 35 per cent and 40 per cent of regional output shocks are absorbed by the federal government, or for every dollar in income lost as a result of a shift in demand, the local economy is compensated by between 35 and 40 cents.[12] A single currency European union characterized by high

[12] See, in particular, Xavier Sala I. Martin and Jeffrey Sachs, 'Fiscal Federalism and Optimum Currency Areas: Evidence for Europe from the United States', in Matthew Canzoneri, Vittorio Grilli, and Paul R. Masson, *Establishing a Central Bank: Issues in Europe and Lessons from the United States*, Cambridge, CUP, 1992, 195–227, and sources cited.

product specialization and labour mobility would, therefore, lead to similar pressures for fiscal centralization. In many cases the redistribution would be permanent. Just as West Virginia or North Dakota have become areas whose tax contributions to the federal purse are always exceeded by monies they receive from Washington, so some regions (or countries) in an open EU would become the permanent beneficiaries of tax revenues collected in other regions (or countries). By 1993 EU revenues accounted for just 1.22 per cent of total member state GDP and more than half of this amount was devoted to agricultural subsidies. Moving even part way towards the American level of fiscal redistribution (which is, compared with the already large redistributions operative *within* many of the EU member states, quite modest) would, therefore, represent a very radical change in EU responsibilities.

In one respect, the extent of fiscal centralization required in a united Europe may be greater than in contemporary America, because one of the objectives of redistributive fiscal policy is to reduce labour mobility by giving workers, through the social security system, an incentive to stay where they are. It is highly unlikely that (say) the British or Italian people (or their governments) would be prepared to tolerate a mass movement of their populations to other states in the way that (say) the people and governments of North Dakota or West Virginia have. The reason for this is, simply, that American citizens have a relatively weak attachment to state identity compared with their identities as Americans. As will be discussed later, the opposite is true in Europe. National identities are stronger than European identities.

What are the policy consequences if, as seems more likely, labour mobility remains low following EMU? Economic theory suggests that in the absence of factor mobility and denied the freedom to devalue, economies will be obliged to adjust by reducing relative prices and labour costs. In theory, at least, this should eventually restore competitiveness. As with the high factor mobility scenario, however, there will be serious short-term disruptions leading to high unemployment and therefore pressures for redistribution via the tax system. When discussing the likely size of this redistribution and whether it will be provided by national (or regional) governments or by the EU, economists seriously disagree. Indeed, work in this area is riven with dispute. In 1992 fifty leading European economists signed a document in support of EMU claiming that because labour mobility after EMU would remain low, the required level of fiscal redistribution would also be low. It is worth quoting their conclusions at length:

Federations with high labour mobility need a central tax authority because differences in regional taxation can be arbitraged through migration. Not so in Europe. Therefore fiscal policy in each member country can deviate from those in others and be used to counteract regional shocks. Whilst a central fiscal authority is therefore less necessary, general transfers to poorer regions may be desirable on redistribution grounds, but are unconnected with EMU. What might be necessary is an insurance mechanism against regional shocks. Automatic fiscal transfers in case of *transitory* shocks to unemployment would be less costly than some of the structural funds of the Community if properly restricted to increases in unemployment above the EC average. Linking EMU to political union is, however, not necessary on pure economic grounds.[13]

Their declaration was in direct response to a manifesto by sixty-two leading German economists who argued the opposite:

With a common currency, the weaker members of the European Union will be exposed to greater competitive pressures, suffering growing levels of unemployment as a result of their lower productivity and competitiveness. Substantial transfer payments in the interests of financial equalization will therefore be necessary. Since no agreements have yet been reached about the structure of a political union, a sufficiently democratic system to regulate such transfers is therefore lacking. At the moment, therefore, there is no economically convincing argument in favour of superimposing from above a monetary union on a Europe which is still not united economically, socially, and in terms of political interests. Attainment of the EU internal market by no means requires or imposes a common European currency. The over hasty introduction of a European currency will expose Western Europe to powerful economic strains, which could within the foreseeable future lead to a major test of political will and thereby jeopardize the goal of integration.[14]

While this dispute cannot be resolved, some common ground exists. In particular, the dispute is not over *whether* fiscal centralization will be needed, but over the *degree* of centralization. In addition, the analysis of the EMU supporters is not always internally consistent. Let us elaborate these points in more detail.

1. All economists agree that asymmetric shocks, whether on the supply side in the shorter term or on the demand side in the longer term, occur

[13] Daniel Gros and Alfred Steinherr, 'In Favour of EMU: A Manifesto of European Economists', in Alfred Steinherr (ed.), *30 Years of European Monetary Integration: From the Werner Plan to EMU*, London, Longman, 1994, 76.

[14] 'EC Currency Union: An Acid Test for Europe: Manifesto by Sixty German Economists', in ibid. 73.

in all economies. Some evidence exists to suggest that higher levels of price and output variations among the EU states makes them more vulnerable to shocks. The historical record suggests that shocks affecting Europe have been greater and the response to them more sluggish than in the USA. But this research (Bayoumi and Eichengreen) compares Europe with an *existing* monetary union which may underestimate the adjustment benefits inherent in an integrated, politically unified state. On the other hand, product differentiation in the EU is relatively low compared with the USA. In this sense, the countries of the EU may be less vulnerable to asymmetric shocks than the USA.

2. Economists agree that in any integrated economy if labour mobility is high then pressures for fiscal centralization will emerge. All modern developed economies with high labour mobility have acquired major redistributive mechanisms to compensate those sectors of the economy affected by shifts in demand. Economists also agree that even in the absence of a high level of labour mobility, asymmetric shocks will produce adjustment problems in the short term, but considerable dispute over the extent of these problems and the proper policy response to them exists. One group, represented by the signatories to the pro-EMU document mentioned above, believe that the main adjustment burden should fall on existing national governments. In other words, in the absence of the exchange rate tool, governments should use fiscal and other means to adjust their economies. Most agree that in many cases this might involve having to use deficit financing in the short to medium term. A number of problems are raised by this alternative. First, deficit financing of this sort is incompatible with the Maastricht convergence criteria. The implication of these criteria is that countries should achieve a *permanent* convergence in economic performance including government debt. Achieving the targets and then abandoning them following monetary union is not the objective. Even if this objection is swept aside, there remains the problem of how sustainable national government debt would be. Paul de Grauwe studied the response of the Italian, Dutch, and Belgium governments to the deep recession of the early 1980s. Their policy objective was to use deficit financing and reductions in real labour costs rather than devaluation to help their economies adjust. He concludes:

> These examples vividly demonstrate the limits to the use of fiscal policies to offset negative economic shocks. Such policies cannot be maintained for very long. The experience of these countries shows that large government budget

deficits quickly lead to unsustainable dynamics from which countries find it difficult to extricate themselves. . . . once used once, it will not be possible to use these fiscal policies again until many years later.[15]

Once this dynamic is established, the alternatives are to print money (the 'Latin American' choice) which leads to hyperinflation. Or to devalue (not an option following EMU), or to deflate the economy through expenditure cuts and tax increases. But the latter would have to be Draconian indeed—and politically unsustainable—if they are to be sufficient to return the government's finances to the status quo ante and therefore enable the national authorities to use fiscal tools to deal with any subsequent shock. It is for this reason that all economists concede that some central fiscal or other economic role is likely to be assumed by the federal authorities following the implementation of EMU.

This role may be in some form of income support transfer such as unemployment compensation or social security, or in the form of a centrally funded bail-out for debt defaulters.[16] What level of transfer or of bail-out would be necessary is, of course, impossible to say. However, the arguments of those economists who insist that the extent of these transfers need not be large and therefore would not require major political changes are wholly unconvincing. The experience of all existing federations is that once central mechanisms for income redistribution are established, all potential recipient individual states and provinces will scramble furiously for inclusion.[17] Anthony Downs has put this nicely, labelling it the 'iron law of political dispersion . . . All benefits distributed by elected officials will be distributed to all parts of the constituency, regardless of the economic virtues of concentrating them upon a few parts of the constituency.'[18] The American experience suggests that redistributions triggered by threshold figures such as average unemployment levels are particularly prone to rapid growth.[19] Indeed, economists concede that such programmes are prone to 'moral hazard' problems or the possibility that they will be exploited for political

[15] De Grauwe, *The Economics of Monetary Integration*, 199.

[16] For a discussion of the problems associated with centrally organized bail-outs, see ibid. 202–8.

[17] On this phenomenon see in particular R. Kent Weaver, *Automatic Government*, Washington, Brookings Institution, 1988.

[18] Anthony Downs, quoted in David McKay, 'Industrial Policy and Non Policy in the US', *Journal of Public Policy*, 3, 1983, 45.

[19] See David McKay, *Domestic Policy and Ideology: Presidents and the American State, 1963–1987*, Cambridge, CUP, 1987, chs. 4 and 5.

rather than economic ends.[20] Crucially, the political rationale for such assistance would be quite different from that underpinning existing EU structural funds. Structural funds are used to facilitate economic growth in those countries (or regions of countries) whose incomes fall below 75 per cent of the EU average. They are not regarded as tools of economic stabilization but rather as instruments designed to help longer-term economic prospects.[21] Funds used to help countries recover from economic shocks would be of a different status. If, as suggested by most economists, they came in the form of income transfers (unemployment compensation and the like) they would soon build up a constituency of support rooted in mass politics rather than in the sort of support from government officials and business élites which is typical of the structural funds programmes.

Bail-outs of debt-ridden governments would also be problematical and might lead to a further enhancement of the role of central institutions. If a country could not fund its budget deficit and successfully appealed to the federal authorities (or the European Central Bank) for help, this would lead to inflationary pressures should the request be met without a general increase in Europe-wide tax levels. In fact, the Treaty on European Union specifically prohibits the ECB from lending to national, state, or local governments precisely because the provision of such credit would have inflationary consequences. Should this directive be implemented, therefore (and assuming the absence of a redistributive fiscal policy), then the country or region concerned would have to cope with the deficit on its own by deflating its economy during an economic downturn. This is in effect what happened during the currency crises of the early 1990s. In the context of a full monetary union, where the freedom to devalue is denied, it seems highly improbable that such a deflationary spiral would be tolerated for long. Political pressure for direct fiscal assistance from the central government would be intense. Should assistance be denied or should it be considered inadequate, the option of leaving the union may become attractive. As one supporter of the EMU has put it, 'We cannot exclude the possibility that some countries will find it very difficult to adjust.'[22]

As Barry Eichengreen has perceptively pointed out, what Maastricht

[20] See the discussion in Eichengreen, *International Monetary Arrangements for the 21st Century*, 102–9.

[21] For a discussion of EC Structural Funds, see Loukas Tsoukalis, *The New European Economy: The Politics and Economic of Integration*, Oxford, OUP, 1993, 241–8.

[22] De Grauwe, *The Economics of Monetary Integration*, 209.

does not say about fiscal policy is as significant as what it does say. In effect, the Treaty's requirement for fiscal rectitude both from national governments and the ECB is an open invitation for the creation of an elaborate system of fiscal federalism. Yet not one word of the Treaty is devoted to fiscal federalism.[23]

While the economics literature leaves most crucial issues unresolved—the level and nature of shocks, the extent of fiscal centralization, likely labour market mobility and flexibility, the capacity of national or regional economies to adjust through the price mechanism alone—it is difficult to find an economic analysis which argues that *no* centralization will occur. The logic even of the most sanguine of the studies leads to *some* fiscal centralization or to pressures for the co-ordination of national fiscal policies. Ultimately, therefore, monetary union must involve some enhancement of the federal government's tax capacity.

POLITICAL FACTORS

The crucial point about fiscal redistribution is, of course, that it involves a transfer of tax revenue from one section of the population to another. In all developed welfare states this dynamic involves a temporary component and a permanent component. In the examples cited above, demand shocks resulting from changes in taste and technology would, if accompanied by high factor mobility, lead to a permanent redistribution with a strong spatial dimension. Regions within the existing EU states which have experienced such shocks (the older industrial regions of the UK, France, and Belgium; the Mezzogiorno in Italy) have tended to become long-term net beneficiaries of central government income transfers. And as we discussed above, even if the shock (usually on the supply side) is classified by economists as temporary, this might involve a severe and possibly prolonged adjustment period. The key political question is, therefore, the willingness of the richer parts of the union to subsidize the poorer parts. At present, the EU Structural Funds amount (in 1992) to just 27 per cent of the total EU budget, or less than .4 per cent of the total EU GDP.[24] Although quite

[23] Barry Eichengreen, 'Fiscal Policy and EMU', in Barry Eichengreen and Jeffrey Frieden (eds.), *The Political Economy of European Monetary Unification*, Boulder, Colo., Westview Press, 1994, 188.

[24] Tsoukalis, *The New European Economy*, 245.

significant for the smaller net recipient states—structural funds accounted for 3.5 per cent, 2.9 per cent and 2.3 per cent of the GDP of Portugal, Greece, and Ireland respectively in 1992—the amounts involved constitute tiny proportions of the GDP of the major donor states (Germany and France in particular).[25] As a result, the political salience of the programme is low. Few voters in the larger countries bemoan their tax francs or Deutschmarks being diverted to the Greeks or Portuguese. If, however, the transfers were much larger and, as the economists advise, part of an automatic redistribution linked directly to payments to individuals, the political salience of the issue would increase considerably. If, additionally, it was widely perceived that this redistribution was likely to continue in the longer term, then it would require the political support of voters in the donor countries.

Recall Riker's insistence that federal political arrangements can only be sustained through the operation of political institutions serving constituencies at both the federal and the state or regional levels. The successful functioning of these institutions is in turn determined by popular loyalty to these different levels of government. If popular support is concentrated at the regional level the federation will be 'peripheralized'. If it is concentrated at the federal level, the system will be centralized.[26] Riker also uses party systems as a surrogate for popular support—if parties control both federal and regional government and they act in a disciplined way at both levels, this reflects a high degree of loyalty to the centre. If different parties control regional and federal governments and discipline is low, this reflects a high degree of loyalty to the state or regional level.

Although in the case of the EU there is a broad consensus that a 'democratic deficit' exists, this is almost always characterized in terms of the institutional structure of the EU, rather than in terms of the nature of the party system or popular support for different levels of government. In other words, EU decision-making is regarded as insufficiently accountable to voters in the member states. Thus the limited, mainly advisory, powers of the directly elected European Parliament (EP), and the broad legislative powers of a Council of Ministers which is not directly accountable, are usually identified as the core of the

[25] Tsoukalis, *The New European Economy*, 245.

[26] William Riker, *Federalism: Origins, Operation, Significance*, Boston, Little Brown, 1964, ch. 5; see also his 'Federalism', in Fred I. Greenstein and Nelson Polsby (eds.), *The Handbook of Political Science*, vol. v: *Governments Institutions and Processes*, Reading Mass., Addison Wesley, 1975, 137–41.

democratic deficit problem.[27] It may be, however, that the EU institutional structure could be quite easily adapted to ensure greater accountability. Certainly the powers of the EP were increased with the adoption of the SEA and Maastricht, and further moves along the path towards the creation of a genuine European legislature are likely to be taken at the Intergovernmental Conference in 1996 and beyond. The extent to which this occurs will in part be determined by the extent to which the powers of the EU are expanded. For although, in some policy areas, the existing regulatory powers of the Union are considerable, the budget accounts for a mere 1.22 per cent of the combined GDP of the member states. A democratic deficit may exist, but for the vast majority of EU citizens, it is a deficit limited to just a small part of the total government activity affecting their daily lives. Should the activities of the Union expand to include redistributive income transfers of a magnitude necessary to cushion regions and countries against the effects of negative economic shocks, then the pressure for institutional reform will be greatly increased.

Such redistributive measures will, of course, follow directly from monetary union. Representatives from aggrieved countries (or regions of countries) will demand assistance to help economies adjust. If conceded, these measures will have to be financed by an enhanced EU tax base, which in turn will produce calls for greater democratic accountability. As with so many aspects of the European Union, these events would follow a sequence which is quite different from those which, historically, have characterized federations elsewhere. In other federations the building of democratic institutions preceded policy; in the EU, policy has typically preceded institution-building. Put another way, in such countries as the United States, the enhancement of the federal government's powers resulted from popular pressure for centralized redistributive measures which could be accommodated within an existing constitutional and institutional structure. During the New Deal and other centralizing periods, it was changes in the party system which in turn reflected shifts in popular support for the federal government that facilitated the centralization, not changes in institutional arrangements. In terms of Riker's model, the New Deal produced both a more disciplined Democratic Party and one which was able to exercise control—albeit imperfectly—at both the national and the state levels.[28] In the

[27] A broad consensus on this exists; see e.g. Ernest Wistrich, *The United States of Europe*, London, Routledge, 1994, ch. 6.

[28] On this theme, see Steve Fraser and Gary Gerstle (eds.), *The Rise and Fall of the New Deal Political Order*, Princeton, Princeton University Press, 1989.

European case, monetary union would trigger pressures for policy centralization which would in turn produce institutional change, but unlike the United States there is no federation-wide party system worthy of the name which would provide the newly powerful federal government with a base of popular support or legitimacy. Although theoretically such a party system could develop, such evidence as exists suggests that it is unlikely to. Two admittedly limited sources of evidence can be invoked to support this claim: the functioning of political parties in the existing EP and levels of public support for the EU and its policies. Let us look at each of these in turn.

Parties in the European Parliament

Supporters of European federalism are prone to bemoan the fact that the organization of the elections to the European Parliament tends to emphasize national differences rather than promote a pan-European or federal party system.[29] Although there is some truth to this—national rather than European electoral rules prevail, and voters cast their ballots for candidates representing nationally based constituencies—these arrangements are not so unusual when compared with those prevailing in other federal systems. In the United States, for example, all members of the national legislature are elected from state-based constituencies, and the Constitution specifically leaves the determination of electoral qualifications to state governments (although over time these have been standardized by the courts).[30]

Pleas for Europe-wide constituencies reflect the fears of many federalists that the existing system reinforces the national rather than supranational identity of MEPs. By introducing pan-European constituencies federalists hope that citizens' identity with the larger project will be strengthened. Whatever the effects of such a change—and we will return to the question of European identity later—it is obviously important to examine the actual functioning of the party system in the EP and assess its relationship to national party systems. However, because to date the EP's main role is advisory rather than legislative, it is not possible to make meaningful comparisons with national party systems.

[29] See e.g. Julie Smith, *The Voice of the People: The European Parliament in the 1990s*, London, Pinter, Royal Institute of International Affairs, 1995, ch. 2. Also, Andrew Duff, 'Building a Parliamentary Europe', *Government and Opposition*, 29, 1994.

[30] For a discussion, see David McKay, *American Politics and Society*, Oxford, Blackwell, 1993, ch. 6.

Some pan-European coherence is achieved through the national groupings into which the parties in the EP are organized. However, the party groupings tend to be fluid. For example, the main conservative grouping, the European People's Party (EPP), consists of a core of mainly Christian Democratic parties with the Danish and British Conservatives 'allied' to the grouping. The largest grouping represented by the Party of European Socialists (PES) is more coherent, although not all the socialist parties, including the British Labour Party, subscribe to all aspects of the manifesto which the PES (and its predecessor, the Confederation of Socialist parties) puts out before European elections. The third largest grouping, the European Liberal Democrat and Reform Party is the most heterogeneous of the groupings, its main appeal being that it represents neither socialists nor traditional conservatives. Together with the smaller groupings[31] these parties issue pre-election manifestos. However as a cue for voters during the election campaigns, these documents make little impact. As one commentator has put it:

> In the preface to its manifesto, the PES noted that it was 'not a detailed programme, but rather a framework in which our future policies will be worked out.' Such a statement applied equally to the other parties as well: in general the documents were rather bland and uncontentious, offering few substantive policies. Of course this is not surprising when one considers that they are the product of negotiations between parties from numerous countries working in several languages and that large national parties are themselves electoral coalitions shaped by national pressures.[32]

Even if the EP's powers are limited, it is possible that the European elections could be used as a forum to debate contentious questions relating to EU policies. However, they are not. In most of the member states a broad consensus between the parties on the most fundamental aspects of the EU exists (membership and enlargement, the single market, the broad regulatory role of the Commission and monetary policy). As a result the European election campaigns are remarkably bland affairs and act more as referenda on the performance of incumbent national parties than as genuine opportunities to debate European issues. Even the British Conservative Party failed to fight the 1994 campaign on the European issue which most distinguished it from the other British political parties—monetary union.

[31] The main smaller groupings are the Left Unity, the Greens, Rainbow, Group of the European Democratic Alliance, and the Technical Group of the European Right.

[32] Julie Smith, *The Voice of the People*, 26.

Most important of all, European elections do not result in a change of government or even in a meaningful change in EP policy. If the socialist grouping were to be replaced as the single largest party by the conservatives, it is unlikely that this would *in terms of voters' perceptions* be seen to herald significant changes in policy. As was discussed earlier, attempts by political scientists to measure the degree of centralization of political parties in federal systems depend on such variables as the extent of party discipline, change of control of the central government, and the degree to which this is mirrored at the state or provincial level.[33] In the case of the EP we cannot use such measures because the legislature's powers are so limited and there is no democratically elected central government.

Given this situation it is not possible to measure in any meaningful way the interpenetration of national and European parties. Only when the EP is given real powers will the extent of the connections become apparent. Another way of putting this, of course, is that at present the European party system is highly decentralized—it is the all-powerful Council rather than the EP which is dominated by national governments, and the composition of the Council is determined by national parties in national elections. When attempting to predict the potential for building a European party system we are forced to fall back on such evidence that exists on the level of public support for a European identity. If this is high, or at least the potential for it is high, so the chances of a more centralized party system are enhanced. If it is low, the chances are that any future European party system will be decentralized, in which case the federation will become (or remain) peripheralized.

Support for a European Identity

The question of European identity has attracted a great deal of attention from scholars and politicians alike.[34] In the main this concern is rooted in the belief that if the countries of Europe are to develop into a genuine union, it is essential that the citizenry regard European-level institutions as legitimate. Many supporters of union see the conscious creation of such legitimacy as a major political objective. All that is needed is

[33] Riker, 'Federalism', 138–9.

[34] See William Wallace, *The Transformation of Western Europe*, London, Pinter, Royal Institute of International Affairs, 1990; A. Smith, 'National Identity and the Idea of European Unity', *International Affairs*, Jan., 1992; Ernest Gellner (ed.), *Culture, Identity and Politics*, Cambridge, CUP, 1987; Garcia Soledad (ed.), *European Identity and the Search for Legitimacy*, London, Pinter, Royal Institute of International Affairs, 1993.

TABLE 7.1. Electoral turn-out in national and European elections, EU countries, 1994 EP elections, and latest national election (%)

	EP Election	National Election
Belgium	90.7	92
Denmark	52.5	76.7
Germany	60.1	79.1
Greece	71.2	81.5
Spain	59.6	77.3
France	52.7	69
Ireland	44	68.5
Italy	74.8	86.1
Luxemburg	88.5	88.3
Netherlands	35.6	78.3
Portugal	35.6	68.2
UK	36.4	77.7

Source: Jan Erik Lane, David McKay, and Kenneth Newton (eds.), *The Political Data Handbook*, Oxford, OUP, 1996.

to enlighten the people of Europe, through education and information, on the advantages of full integration.[35] In reality, no matter how enthusiastically the federalists might *wish* legitimacy, the level of support for European institutions will ultimately depend on how the *interests* of the various peoples of the union are affected by European policies.

It is in this light that survey and other data relating to public levels of support for the EU and its institutions should be judged. One of greatest current concerns, for example, is the low level of turn-out for European elections compared with national elections (Table 7.1).

This data is altogether unsurprising, however, given how little the EP actually does. EP elections are, in fact, almost the inverse of elections in the United States where turn-out for that level of government deemed by the voters to be the most important (the federal government) is higher than for state governments.[36] Table 7.1 does reveal very wide variations in turn-out between member states, which may reflect varying citizen attachments to European institutions. Unfortunately, however,

[35] See e.g. Karlheinz Reif, 'Cultural Convergence and Cultural Diversity as Factors in European Identity', in Garcia (ed.), *European Identity*, 148–9.

[36] For US voter turnout figures at the state and national levels see 'The Book of the States, Volume 30, 1994/5, Lexington, Council of State Governments, 1995, Tables 5.8 and 5.9.

the data shows no particular pattern. Variations among the core states (Germany, Netherlands, Luxemburg, France, and Belgium) are almost as great as among the peripheral states; turn-out among the larger net beneficiaries of EU funds (Ireland, Portugal, Greece, Spain) shows as great a variation as among the main contributor nations. In sum, turn-out data almost certainly reflects peculiar national electoral factors, as much as any identification with European institutions.

More interesting is survey data relating to public attitudes towards the EU and its institutions and policies. At the most basic level attitudes towards place reveal a weak attachment to the EC and Europe compared with town, region, or country (Table 7.2). This data shows relatively few variations among the member states; most people admit to a low or moderate attachment both to Europe and the EC, and a strong attachment to country, region, and locality.

More specific questions relating to membership of the Union and whether respondents believe that membership brings benefits and would regret dissolution show a gradual increase in support during the 1980s followed by a decline during the early and mid-1990s (Figure 7.2). This data almost certainly reflects the recession of the early 1990s and the turmoil on the foreign exchanges during 1992.

A similar pattern can be discerned from data relating to the desirability of membership, a European single currency, central bank, and common defence policy or organization (Tables 7.3, 7.4, 7.5, and 7.6).

Note that as far as monetary questions are concerned, the support among the core countries, although higher than in the periphery, is tempered by very low levels of support among the Germans. On the defence question, however, support among all the core countries, and especially by the Germans, is high. In the periphery countries, Britain and Denmark are clear outriders on the monetary questions and to some extent on the question of the costs and benefits of membership.

When attempting to assess the significance of this data, two things stand out. The first is the fall in support for EMU during the 1990s as the possible costs and benefits of union became more apparent. Turmoil in the EMS and the resulting political and economic fall-out no doubt helped fuel fears that EMU would be deflationary. Indeed, those who admit to being 'fearful' of EMU and the Single Market, have cited unemployment (33 per cent of the fearful) as the main source of their worries with higher prices coming second at 23 per cent.[37] Second, the

[37] Quoted in Reif, 'Cultural Convergence', 148.

TABLE 7.2. Feeling attached to a place (1990)

Question: People may feel different degrees of attachment to their town or village, to their region, to their country, to the EC or to Europe as a whole. Please tell me how attached you feel to . . . ?

	B	DK		G		GR	E	F	IRL	I	L	NL	P	UK	EC12	EC12
			West		East											
Town/Village																
Very attached	49	56	60	60	56	81	73	40	60	59	48	28	75	42	54	54
Fairly attached	33	28	27	29	33	12	20	41	29	29	33	36	19	38	31	31
Not very attached	10	11	10	10	8	5	5	10	8	7	11	27	4	14	10	10
Not at all attached	5	2	1	1	1	2	1	8	1	4	5	8	1	6	4	
Don't know	3	3	1	1	1	0	2	1	1	0	4	1	2	0	1	1
TOTAL	100	100	99	101	99	100	101	100	99	99	101	100	101	100	100	100
Region																
Very attached	41	67	62	62	62	87	71	41	62	50	52	34	69	56	55	55
Fairly attached	40	25	32	31	31	10	23	40	27	36	28	39	22	32	32	32
Not very attached	11	4	4	4	4	2	4	6	7	7	5	19	4	10	7	7
Not at all attached	5	1	0	0	1	1	1	3	1	3	3	5	1	3	2	2
Don't know	3	2	2	2	3	0	1	11	3	3	13	3	3	2	4	4
TOTAL	100	99	100	99	101	100	100	101	100	99	101	101	99	101	100	100

TABLE 7.2. (*cont.*)

Question: People may feel different degrees of attachment to their town or village, to their region, to their country, to the EC or to Europe as a whole. Please tell me how attached you feel to . . . ?

	B	DK		G		GR	E	F	IRL	I	L	NL	P	UK	EC12	EC12
			West		East											
(OUR COUNTRY)																
Very attached	30	84	47	47	45	86	62	46	72	55	60	40	70	58	54	53
Fairly attached	44	14	40	40	40	11	27	44	23	34	32	41	24	31	35	35
Not very attached	17	2	10	10	11	3	6	5	4	7	4	14	4	8	8	8
Not at all attached	7	0	1	1	2	0	3	3	0	3	2	4	0	2	2	2
Don't know	2	1	3	3	2	0	3	2	1	1	3	0	2	0	1	2
TOTAL	100	101	100	101	100	100	101	100	100	100	101	99	100	100	100	100
The EC																
Very attached	13	9	9	9	8	15	18	12	9	18	16	4	11	6	12	12
Fairly attached	34	33	35	33	27	34	40	42	27	43	39	24	36	29	36	36
Not very attached	28	36	37	38	42	28	26	24	34	17	26	50	36	35	30	30
Not at all attached	19	19	14	14	15	19	10	14	27	13	12	19	11	27	16	16
Don't know	7	2	6	7	8	5	5	9	3	10	7	3	7	2	6	7
TOTAL	101	101	101	101	100	101	101	100	100	100	101	99	100	99	100	101

Europe as a whole																
Very attached	11	15	11	11	11	16	18	10	8	19	15	5	8	8	12	12
Fairly attached	36	46	35	35	31	36	34	40	26	40	37	26	33	29	35	35
Not very attached	27	27	34	34	36	25	28	24	32	16	25	46	31	32	28	28
Not at all attached	20	10	13	13	15	20	13	16	28	14	15	20	22	29	18	18
Don't know	6	2	6	7	8	4	7	11	6	10	8	3	6	3	7	7
TOTAL	100	100	100	100	101	101	100	101	100	99	100	100	100	101	100	100

Source: Karlheinz Reif, 'Cultural Convergence and Cultural Diversity', in Soledad Garcia (ed.), *European Identity and the Search for Legitimacy*, Table 8.3.

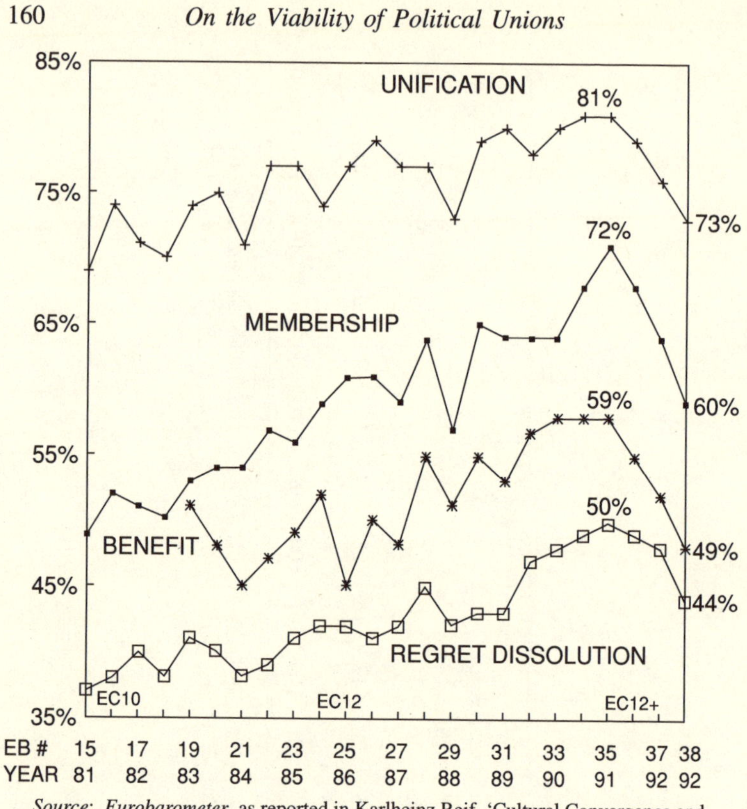

Source: *Eurobarometer*, as reported in Karlheinz Reif, 'Cultural Convergence and Cultural Diversity', Fig. 8.5.

FIG. 7.2. Support for European unification in the EC, 1981–1992

antipathy of the Germans to EMU but their support for a common defence policy fits nicely into the theoretical perspective outlined in earlier chapters. A Union-wide single currency and central bank might involve 'importing' inflation from the periphery countries. It might also involve an increase in the German contribution to central EU funds. Strong German support for a European defence policy appears to confirm the claim that German motivations in striking a federal bargain were as much to do with diplomatic aggrandizement as related to a fear of inflation.

As with almost all the analysis in this chapter, the significance of this data as indicators of citizen identity with European institutions must

TABLE 7.3. Opinion on membership of the European Union

Country	1973			1980			1990			1994		
	Good	Bad	No opinion	Good	Bad	No opinion	Good	Bad	No opinion	Good	Bad	No opinion
Belgium	57	5	19	57	2	25	69	5	20	56	10	30
Denmark	42	30	19	33	29	28	49	25	23	53	26	18
Germany	63	4	22	65	6	18	62	7	25	50	12	33
Greece				42	22	26	75	5	14	64	9	20
Spain				58	5	13	65	8	21	50	14	31
France	61	5	22	51	9	32	63	7	25	50	13	33
Ireland	56	15	21	52	19	22	74	8	12	72	7	16
Italy	69	2	15	74	3	16	75	3	13	68	5	20
Luxemburg	67	3	22	84	3	10	72	8	16	71	9	17
Netherlands	63	4	20	75	3	16	82	3	10	77	5	16
Portugal				24	6	11	62	4	21	54	13	32
United Kingdom	31	34	22	21	55	15	52	19	24	43	22	29
Totals	509	102	182	636	162	232	800	102	224	708	145	295
Averages	56.5	11.3	20.2	53	13.5	19.3	66.6	8.5	18.6	59	12.1	24.6

TABLE 7.3. (*cont.*)

Country	1973			1980			1990			1994		
	Good	Bad	No opinion	Good	Bad	No opinion	Good	Bad	No opinion	Good	Bad	No opinion
CORE												
Belgium	57	5	19	57	2	25	69	5	20	56	10	30
Germany	63	4	22	65	6	18	62	7	25	50	12	33
France	61	5	22	51	9	32	63	7	25	50	13	33
Luxemburg	67	3	22	84	3	10	72	8	16	71	9	17
Netherlands	63	4	20	75	3	16	82	3	10	77	5	16
Totals	311	21	105	332	23	101	348	30	96	304	49	129
Averages	62.2	4.2	21	66.4	4.6	20.2	69.6	6	19.2	60.8	9.8	25.8
PERIPHERAL												
Denmark	42	30	19	33	29	28	49	25	23	53	26	18
Greece				42	22	26	75	5	14	64	9	20
Spain				58	5	13	65	8	21	50	14	31
Ireland	56	15	21	52	19	22	74	8	12	72	7	16
Italy	69	2	15	74	3	16	75	3	13	68	5	20
Portugal				24	6	11	62	4	21	54	13	32
United Kingdom	31	34	22	21	55	15	52	19	24	43	22	29
Totals	198	81	77	304	139	131	452	72	128	404	96	166
Averages	49.5	20.3	19.3	43.4	19.9	18.7	64.5	10.3	18.3	57.7	13.7	23.7

Source: *Eurobarometer*, various years.

TABLE 7.4. Support for a single European currency

Country	1976		1985		1988		1991		1992		1993		1994	
	For	Against	For	Against	For	Against	For	Against	For	Against	For	Against	For	Against
Belgium	53	21	46	23	72	15	62	18	65	23	64	27	62	28
Denmark	21	56			27	49	35	54	35	60	26	69	29	65
Germany	33	54	14	54	46	40	45	32	36	53	32	58	33	55
Greece					52	14	61	14	71	14	71	14	65	21
Spain					61	12	58	18	63	22	60	20	65	17
France	52	27	49	20	74	14	64	18	59	33	59	31	65	25
Ireland	38	43			64	17	54	17	66	20	68	19	68	19
Italy	67	18	55	15	77	8	69	12	79	11	80	13	74	13
Luxemburg	66	16	43	29	67	21	48	35	67	24	65	25	65	27
Netherlands	51	34	27	35	61	23	58	31	61	30	56	33	59	32
Portugal					52	13	53	15	59	17	59	24	47	34
United kingdom	30	53	12	64	29	58	40	42	30	58	27	63	35	56
Totals	411	322	246	240	682	284	647	306	691	365	667	396	667	392
Averages	45.6	35.7	35.1	34.3	56.8	23.6	53.9	25.5	57.6	30.4	55.5	33	55.6	32.6
CORE														
Belgium	53	21	46	23	72	15	62	18	65	23	64	27	62	28
Germany	33	54	14	54	46	40	45	32	36	53	32	58	33	55
France	52	27	49	20	74	14	64	18	59	33	59	31	65	25
Luxemburg	66	16	43	29	67	21	48	35	67	24	65	25	65	27
Netherlands	51	34	27	35	61	23	58	31	61	30	56	33	59	32
Totals	255	152	179	161	320	113	277	134	288	163	276	174	284	167
Averages	51	30.4	35.8	32.2	64	22.6	55.4	26.8	57.6	32.6	55.2	34.8	56.8	33.4

TABLE 7.4. (*cont.*)

Country	1976		1985		1988		1991		1992		1993		1994	
	For	Against	For	Against	For	Against	For	Against	For	Against	For	Against	For	Against
PERIPHERY														
Denmark	21	56			27	49	35	54	35	60	26	69	29	65
Greece					52	14	61	14	71	14	71	14	65	21
Spain					61	12	58	18	63	22	60	20	65	17
Ireland	38	43			64	17	54	17	66	20	68	19	68	19
Italy	67	18	55	15	77	8	69	12	79	11	80	13	74	13
Portugal					52	13	53	15	59	17	59	24	47	34
United Kingdom	30	53	12	64	29	58	40	42	30	58	27	63	35	56
Totals	156	170	67	79	362	171	370	172	403	202	391	222	383	225
Averages	39	42.5	33.5	39.5	51.7	24.4	52.9	24.6	57.6	28.9	55.9	31.7	54.7	32.1

Source: *Eurobarometer*, various years.

TABLE 7.5. Support for a European Central Bank

Country	1991		1992		1993		1994	
	For	Against	For	Against	For	Against	For	Against
Belgium	59	16	69	16	74	15	70	19
Denmark	47	40	52	41	51	44	47	42
Germany	55	23	59	30	56	33	60	29
Greece	63	10	71	13	76	10	69	13
Spain	56	16	68	16	66	13	69	14
France	61	16	67	23	63	25	72	18
Ireland	52	15	68	16	67	15	70	13
Italy	62	14	83	7	84	9	76	10
Luxemburg	48	29	70	18	74	15	68	20
Netherlands	67	19	74	14	75	12	73	15
Portugal	57	11	65	10	71	14	60	21
United Kingdom	39	41	45	42	45	41	48	37
Totals	666	250	791	246	802	246	782	251
Averages	55.5	20.8	65.9	20.5	66.8	20.5	65.2	20.8
CORE								
Belgium	59	16	69	16	74	15	70	19
Germany	55	23	59	30	56	33	60	29
France	61	16	67	23	63	25	72	18
Luxemburg	48	29	70	18	74	15	68	20
Netherlands	67	19	74	14	75	12	73	15
Totals	290	103	339	101	342	100	343	101
Averages	58	20.6	67.8	20.2	68.4	20	68.6	20.2

TABLE 7.5. (*cont.*)

Country	1991		1992		1993		1994	
	For	Against	For	Against	For	Against	For	Against
PERIPHERY								
Denmark	47	40	52	41	51	44	47	42
Greece	63	10	71	13	76	10	69	13
Spain	56	16	68	16	66	13	69	14
Ireland	52	15	68	16	67	15	70	13
Italy	62	14	83	7	84	9	76	10
Portugal	57	11	65	10	71	14	60	21
United Kingdom	39	41	45	42	45	41	48	37
Totals	376	147	452	145	460	146	439	150
Averages	53.7	21	64.6	20.7	65.7	20.9	62.7	21.4

Source: *Eurobarometer*, various years.

TABLE 7.6. Support for a common defence organization

Country	1988		1992		1993		1994	
	For	Against	For	Against	For	Against	For	Against
Belgium	77	12	77	12	81	13	78	12
Denmark	36	42	48	46	47	48	50	44
Germany	66	20	81	12	82	11	81	13
Greece	62	14	75	12	75	14	71	19
Spain	63	14	76	13	70	12	71	13
France	80	10	81	12	74	17	79	13
Ireland	60	19	50	32	55	27	52	26
Italy	84	8	81	9	83	12	75	13
Luxemburg	80	12	84	6	79	10	75	13
Netherlands	74	13	80	12	83	11	83	11
Portugal	68	4	67	8	79	10	67	16
United Kingdom	71	18	70	20	74	17	70	20
Totals	821	186	870	194	882	202	852	213
Averages	68.4	15.5	72.5	16.2	73.5	16.8	71	17.8

TABLE 7.6. (*cont.*)

Country	1988		1992		1993		1994	
	For	Against	For	Against	For	Against	For	Against
CORE								
Belgium	77	12	77	12	81	13	78	12
Germany	66	20	81	12	82	11	81	13
France	80	10	81	12	74	17	79	13
Luxemburg	80	12	84	6	79	10	75	13
Netherlands	74	13	80	12	83	11	83	11
Totals	377	67	403	54	399	62	396	62
Averages	75.4	13.4	80.6	10.8	79.8	12.4	79.2	12.4
PERIPHERY								
Denmark	36	42	48	46	47	48	50	44
Greece	62	14	75	12	75	14	71	19
Spain	63	14	76	13	70	12	71	13
Ireland	60	19	50	32	55	27	52	26
Italy	84	8	81	9	83	12	75	13
Portugal	68	4	67	8	79	10	67	16
United Kingdom	71	18	70	20	74	17	70	20
Totals	444	119	467	140	483	140	456	151
Averages	63.4	17	66.7	20	69	20	65.1	21.6

Source: *Eurobarometer*, various years.

TABLE 7.7. Fiscal equalization and party centralization in five federations

	Ranking of interregional equalization	Centralization of party system
Switzerland	5	5
USA	4	3
Canada	3	4
Germany	2	2
Australia	1	1

Source: The interregional equalization figures are taken from Michael Emerson *et al.*, *One Market, One Money: An Evaluation of the Potential Costs and Benefits of Forming an Economic and Monetary Union*, Oxford, OUP, 1992, Table 6.4. The party centralization rankings are the authors.

ultimately be a matter of speculation. We cannot know how citizens will respond to further centralization in the EU, including how they will react to the likely fiscal centralization which would follow from full monetary union. An informed guess would indicate, however, that: (*a*) over the last several years support for the EU and its policies has been highly variable, both across countries and across issues. It would be logical to assume that this uneven pattern of support will continue should EMU be achieved. (*b*) The experience of the early and mid-1990s would indicate that as the costs and benefits of union become more apparent, so the political salience of membership will increase. It is feasible to assume that should large-scale fiscal redistribution be deemed necessary following EMU, support for the whole European project will decline in the net contributor countries.

It could be argued, on the other hand, that the relationship between the centralization of the party system and citizen support on the one hand, and the extent of fiscal equalization on the other, is not always positive. Canada does more in the way of income equalization than the USA, but with a more decentralized party system. A ranking of fiscal redistribution and party centralization in federations suggests in fact that Canada may be the odd country out. Generally, the more centralized the party system the greater the redistribution. In other words, decentralized federations can still achieve a high degree of redistribution (Table 7.7). But redistribution in Canada is facilitated by a stronger attachment to the centre by the richer donor provinces than by one of the major net recipient provinces (Quebec). Indeed it could be argued that redistribution has occurred at least in part to keep the federation viable. It is highly unlikely that a similar pattern would emerge in Europe. While we cannot know for sure who the net recipient countries would be in a system of fiscal federalism, they are less likely to be the richer core states and more likely to be the poorer periphery states. What survey evidence we have (Table 7.3) suggests no particular pattern in terms of citizen support between these two groups.

CONCLUSIONS

Writing in 1993, the Head of the Eurobarometer surveys run by the European Commission lamented that

> the new controversy over Europe has . . . increased mass public opposition. This shows the need to give citizens more say in EC affairs but also, above all, to give them more information. A significant part of this new opposition to closer European integration appears to be based on misunderstanding and lack of information on the part of the general public, but also on the part of national political elites.[38]

The major objective of this chapter has been to provide just such information on the likely political consequences that would stem from monetary integration in Europe. Unlike the Head of the Eurobarometer, however, the analysis has not assumed, a priori, that a lack of information must always lead to misunderstanding and therefore to opposition to European political union. On the contrary, the chapter has attempted to show that by using (albeit limited) information in an analytical way, some of the recent opposition to EMU, whether emanating from élites or from mass publics, may have a sound foundation. All the economists working in the area concede that EMU would bear economic costs as well as benefits, and all accept that some degree of fiscal centralization would follow from monetary union. The political consequences of such a centralization of economic policy would be profound, and the viability of the whole project would ultimately depend on the level of public support for European institutions. Although we are obliged to rely on a limited base of data, there is little evidence to suggest that, as a whole, the peoples of Europe have acquired a level of identity with

[38] Reif, 'Cultural Convergence', 149.

European institutions that is in any way equivalent to their identification with existing nation states and regions. Worse, there is evidence of some weakening of a European identity over recent years. The fact that a European identity is quite highly developed in some countries might be a source of comfort for some, but there is no reason to believe that such sentiments will be diffused among the other member states through 'education or information'. In the final analysis, the viability of the union will be determined by the particular mix of costs and benefits which flow over time. Ultimately, it will be the willingness of some states and regions to subsidize others that will determine whether the union stands or falls.

8

Prospects for the European Federal Bargain

ORIGINS OF THE EUROPEAN FEDERAL BARGAIN

In Chapter 1 the process of European integration culminating in the Maastricht Treaty was described as 'an intellectual puzzle'. Never before had a group of rich and powerful nations voluntarily come together and consciously planned to cede control over monetary policy to a supranational authority. Macroeconomic policy is one of the two essential pillars of nationhood, and federation-building in the past had always been based on the second pillar, national defence. Central to the argument of this book has been the assumption that political leaders do not cede control of either of these defining functions of nationhood unless they believe that the benefits of doing so outweigh the costs. Given the fundamental nature of the governmental functions being ceded to a higher authority, the perceived costs and benefits involved must be high. In the case of defence, the costs are, ultimately, measured in terms of military or diplomatic threats. In the European case, monetary union was seen as the solution to a quite different sort of threat—that stemming from a perception that, with the internationalization of capital, governments were increasingly unable to control inflation. The experience of the 1970s and early 1980s had convinced government and opposition parties alike not only of the evils of inflation, but also that the problem had to be solved through the imposition of some external discipline. For most of signatories to the Treaty on European Union, therefore, the striking of the federal bargain involved the sacrifice of control over monetary policy in exchange for a guarantee of price stability. For the Germans, the bargain was almost certainly more limited. They hoped for diplomatic aggrandizement, or the ability to play a role in international affairs commensurate with their economic power. In exchange, they were prepared to cede control over monetary policy to the proposed European Central Bank, although their insistence on very strict convergence criteria almost certainly meant that the EMU would be confined to a small Deutschmark-dominated core of countries, whose economies would pose very little threat to price stability in what would be a smaller, more cohesive union.

It was also established that when striking a federal bargain, there is no requirement that the perceptions of the participants be objectively correct. It is sufficient that they *believed* that their cost benefit calculus fell the right way. Until the full adoption of EMU we cannot tell whether they were right or not. Taking the performance of the ERM of the EMS as a surrogate for full EMU, for example, provides at least a suggestion of how prices may move, but no more. Inflation rates among the EMS members when it was perceived to be working (1987–92) did appear to converge—although only in the inflationary context of German unification. Since the effective collapse of the system in 1992 and 1993, inflation rates appear to have returned to their historical pattern—higher in the UK, Italy, and Spain; lower in Germany, France, Belgium, and the Netherlands.[1] What we do know, however, is that although support for EMU is now weaker in some countries, and most notably Germany, than it was in 1991, no country has fundamentally changed its position since Maastricht. Even the British Conservatives, pressured as they are from within their own party, continue not to rule out the possibility of membership should the conditions be right. And apart from protest parties of the right and left, all the major political parties in all the member states, whether in government or not, continue to support, if sometimes only in principle, membership of EMU.

As was established, alternative explanations of Maastricht ranging from the influence of national and international interest groups, to the commitment of an ideologically dedicated group of national and supranational Europhiles, to claims that the Treaty was a logical successor to the spillovers from the SEA and earlier initiatives, are simply inadequate given that the Treaty represented a fundamental departure from previous EC policy. The SEA was a major step towards the creation of a customs union, but not towards the creation of a new federal state.[2]

[1] By late 1995, the average inflation rates in the core countries was 1.7 per cent and in the periphery states, 3.9 per cent.

[2] Some economists would argue that a genuine single market would require such a high degree of labour and capital mobility that it would require political unification. See the discussion by Benjamin J. Cohen, 'Beyond EMU: The Problem of Sustainability', in Barry Eichengreen and Jeffrey Frieden (eds.), *The Political Economy of European Monetary Unification*, Boulder, Colo., Westview Press, 1994, 149–65. However, few politicians or economists expected that the SEA would, at least for many years, achieve this

It was not necessary to subject the SEA to a politically charged ratification process because it was widely accepted that by agreeing to the Act individual states were giving little away. Most telling, perhaps, was the fact that the British, who were the most serious of the Maastricht detractors, were also one of the most enthusiastic supporters of the SEA.

An adapted Rikerian framework also has the advantage of placing Maastricht in historical and comparative context. In terms of the interests of the negotiating parties, the trade-off did not fall the right way for the creation of a union prior to the 1980s—not even in the early 1950s, when an external threat was palpable and when federalist ideology was at its most influential. Similarly, neither in East Asia nor in North America is it in the interests of the dominant economic powers to advance the idea of economic and political union. Moves towards the removal of trade barriers as represented by such arrangements as the North American Free Trade Agreement are of a quite different order, and can be quite easily explained in terms of the perceived advantages of free trade—an arrangement which, in one form or another, has been the dominant model in international economics since the Second World War.

This study has made little attempt to disaggregate the motives of the main participants at Maastricht. Research devoted to such a project concludes that the motives of the participants were complex and varied and therefore no one explanation of the Maastricht phenomenon is adequate.[3] However, the participants at Maastricht came to the meeting with the question of monetary union already on the agenda. What followed was discussion and debate on a range of complex technical questions which, although clearly related to participants' motivations, did not in themselves tell us why EMU dominated the agenda. Analysis of the Federalist Papers on the US Constitution tells a great deal about the disagreements over the proper role of government in the new republic, but not why representatives from the states decided on the creation of a new federal state in the first place. To claim, as one commentator has put it, that there was 'an overwhelming consensus' at Philadelphia in favour of a stronger national government, is quite compatible with the doubts, disputes, and arguments about the role of government that

status. Instead, the objective was to remove all remaining trade barriers between the members, and to work towards increases in the mobility of labour.

[3] See in particular, Kenneth Dyson, *Elusive Union: The Process of Economic and Monetary Union in Europe*, London, Longman, 1994.

followed.[4] Similarly, at Maastricht a range of national leaders were convinced that monetary union would solve a range of problems, but they were in considerable dispute over the technicalities of how and when to achieve union. Only the British were serious dissenters and their refusal to commit themselves to the new arrangements was in some ways analogous to the refusal on the part of Rhode Island to agree to the new Constitution. The interesting aspect of the British position was not the (quite transparent) division in the Conservative Party which limited the negotiators' room for manœuver, but the fact that in spite of a deep hostility to Europe from within the party, the government refused to rule out EMU membership in the longer term.

The events on the currency markets during 1992 and 1993 tended to confirm the extent of the commitment to EMU with a successful EMS regarded as an essential prelude to the introduction of a single currency. Events in the Nordic states during this period can also be explained by the Rikerian perspective. None of the Nordic EU applicants had acquired the sort of extensive institutional and personal linkages with EU members which, so some of the federalist ideologues would have it, are the essential pre-conditions for federation. Instead, they saw in the exchange rate stability of the EMS (and eventually of EMU) an opportunity to achieve price stability and thus protect a vital national interest. They struck the federal bargain very quickly and in the absence of intra-EC 'spillovers' from the SEA or other earlier European treaties.

VIABILITY OF THE EUROPEAN FEDERAL BARGAIN

Part of the remaining puzzle of European union relates to the apparently extensive and increasing role which the Community plays in citizens' lives. Even if monetary union fails, surely this role will gradually be enhanced and eventually lead to the emergence of a *de facto* federal state, especially given the presence of a supranational institutional framework? Although the competence of the EU in such areas as environmental protection, competition policy, and regulatory aspects of the labour market has undoubtedly increased in recent years, the sum of this competence is not remotely equivalent to the powers of a nation

[4] James Madison, Alexander Hamilton, and John Jay, *The Federalist Papers*, Harmondsworth, Penguin, 1987, Introduction by Issac Kramnick, p. 33.

state. The EU is indeed an odd species of government, but in the absence of monetary union (or indeed a single foreign and defence policy) it can be seen in terms of a general trend towards international co-operation and regulation where supranational organizations impinge on the traditional prerogatives of nation states.[5] In the European case, the powers of the supranational government happen to be more complex and organizationally diffuse than those of other international organizations. In aggregate they do resemble those of a government, but they have yet to play a role equivalent to the highly intrusive powers which an organization such as NATO may have exercised during the Cold War, or the IMF did indeed exercise in such cases as the bail-out of the British economy in 1976.

It is significant that the one occasion when an EU institution did play both an extensive and intrusive role—the functioning of the EMS during 1992 and 1993—related to preparations for EMU. These events also greatly increased the political salience of the European Union in the minds of citizens.

None of this is to deny the uniqueness of the European case, or to suggest that the EU is somehow equivalent to other supranational organizations. Clearly it is not. At the same time it has not evolved into something resembling a nation state. At best it is a highly peripheralized union. Only when a single currency is adopted (or a single foreign and defence policy instituted) will it qualify as a species of federal state.

Our discussion of the viability of the EU following such a development emphasized the intimate link between the economic and the political. Redistribution via the tax system is at the heart of the relationship between governments and citizens in modern welfare industrial societies. When spatially defined, such redistributions can cause tensions within nation states if the loyalty of the donor states and provinces to the centre is weak. Following the adoption of a single currency, the balance of economic opinion suggests that pressures for economic centralization will emerge as national fiscal resources prove inadequate as defences against economic shocks. Denied the power to devalue or use monetary policy as instruments of stabilization and redistribution, governments will come under intense pressure from voters to seek help from the EU or the ECB. Redistribution via the ECB could only occur if the ECB reneges on its mandate banning lending to member states. Such

[5] See in particular the collection edited by Peter B. Evans, Harold K. Jacobson, and Robert D. Putnam, *Double Edged Diplomacy: International Bargaining and Domestic Politics*, Berkeley and Los Angeles, University of California Press, 1993.

lending would be inflationary unless funded by Union-wide taxation. More likely is a programme or programmes of redistribution using fiscal rather than monetary devices. The most efficient stabilization policies provide monies directly to individuals via such benefits as unemployment compensation and social security.[6] By making comparisons with the USA and other federations, some economists believe that the level of such transfers required to help economies adjust would be high. And even among the more sanguine observers who believe that the size of such programmes need only be small, there is an acceptance that once fiscal redistribution is established as an instrument of stabilization (rather than, as with the EU Structural Funds, to aid economic growth), problems of 'moral hazard' or the expansion of such programmes for non-economic reasons, remain.

In democracies extensive programmes of fiscal federalism can only be sustained if citizen loyalty to the centre is high. More often than not this is reflected in the extent to which the party system is centralized. Because the powers of the EP are so limited, we cannot measure in any meaningful way the degree of centralization in the embryonic European party system. As exercised through the Council of Ministers, real power in the EU is nationally based, and thus reflects the power of national parties in national elections. Survey evidence tends to confirm a weak loyalty on the part of most of the citizens of the EU to European institutions. Such loyalty cannot somehow be 'created' through education and information. It will follow only if governments and citizens see in a united Europe benefits which are unavailable through national action alone. If the cost of the price stability which it is widely accepted would result from monetary union is further unemployment and deflation in some countries without compensating income equalization, the whole project may fail.

As of the mid-1990s all the evidence points to the creation of a smaller, more cohesive union based on a core of states dominated by the German economy—Austria, Belgium, Luxemburg, and the Netherlands. This group may also include France but is extremely unlikely to include the high-inflation peripheral states such as Britain, Italy, and Spain.

[6] Monies transferred to countries and regions in the form of grants, as with the existing structural funds, are generally considered less efficient in part because of the problem of corruption. On this see Giorgio Basevi, 'Discussion of Shocking Aspects of European Integration', in Francisco Torres and Francesco Giavazzi (eds.), *Adjustment and Growth in the European Monetary Union*, Cambridge, CUP, 1993, 230–5.

THE RUSH TO UNION

When striking federal bargains, the politicians representing sovereign nation states are involved in complex calculations. They have, first, to avert an external or internal threat which national action alone cannot accomplish. Following the traumas of the 1970s and the early 1980s, politicians in a range of countries had become convinced that only a European monetary policy could guarantee a level of price stability that was compatible with economic, and, by implication, political order. Unfortunately, while federation-builders may make sensible calculations about the costs and benefits involved in such decisions, they can never know exactly how the trade-off will fall until after the new state is created. Mistakes are likely to be made, especially if their decisions are taken in the absence of good information, or are driven more by ideology than by practical calculation.

No one now disputes that mistakes were made at Maastricht. Economists have produced a collective howl of protest at the restrictiveness of the fiscal arrangements in the Treaty. Mass publics showed a deep suspicion of the Treaty during the ratification process. The events on the foreign exchange markets in 1992 and 1993 exposed the very different vulnerabilities of member state economies to external forces. In these respects, Maastricht did indeed represent a 'rush to union'. It now looks inevitable that the remainder of the decade of the 1990s will be devoted to a renegotiation of the original federal bargain. It also looks likely that only a core of the existing EU states will eventually agree to the creation of a genuine federal state.

BIBLIOGRAPHY

Alesina, A., and Summers, L., 'Central Bank Independence and Macroeconomic Performance: Some Comparative Evidence', *Journal of Money, Credit and Banking*, 25, 1993.

Alt, James E., and Alec Chrystal, K., *Political Economics*, Berkeley and Los Angeles, University of California Press, 1983.

Arter, David, *The Politics of European Integration in the Twentieth Century*, Aldershot, Dartmouth, 1993.

Baldwin, David A., *Neorealism and Neoliberalism: The Contemporary Debate*, New York, Columbia University Press, 1993.

Barro, R., and Gordon, D., 'Rules, Discretion and Reputation in a Model of Monetary Policy', *Journal of Monetary Economics*, 12, 1983.

Basic Statistics of the EC, Eurostat.

Bayliss, John, *Anglo-American Defence Relations 1939–1984*, London, Macmillan, 2nd edn., 1984.

Beer, Samuel H., 'Federalism, Nationalism and Democracy in America', *American Political Science Review*, 74, 1978.

—— *To Make A Nation: The Rediscovery of American Federalism*, Cambridge, Mass., Harvard University Press, 1993.

Bell, Daniel, and Huntingdon, Samuel (Contributions by) in Special Edition of *Public Interest*, 41, 1975.

Beveridge, William, *Peace by Federation*, London, Royal Institute of International Affairs, World Order Papers no. 3, 1940.

Bidwell, Charles, *Maastricht and the UK*, London, PACE, 1993.

Birch, A. H., 'Approaches to the Study of Federalism', *Political Studies*, 14/1, 1966.

Bogdanor, Vernon, 'Direct Elections, Representative Democracy and European Integration', *Electoral Studies*, 8, 1989.

Bosco, Andrea, 'What is Federalism: Towards a General Theory of Federalism', Paper Before the Second ECSA World Conference on Federalism, Subsidiarity and Democracy in the European Union, Brussels, 5–6 May 1992.

Brittan, Samuel, 'The Economic Contradictions of Democracy', *British Journal of Political Science*, 5, 1975.

Bruce, Peter, 'The Strain and Pain in Spain', *Financial Times*, 27 May 1992.

—— and Gowers, Andrew, 'A Testing of Spanish Mettle', *Financial Times*, 5 Oct. 1992.

Buchanan, James M., *et al.*, *Europe's Constitutional Future*, London, Institute of Economic Affairs, 1990.

Bullock, Alan, *Ernest Bevin: Foreign Secretary 1945–1951*, London, Heinemann, 1983.

Burgess, Michael, *Federalism and European Union: Political Ideas, Influences and Strategies in the European Community 1972–1987*, London, Routledge, 1989.

—— and Gagnon, Alain-G. (eds.), *Comparative Federalism and Federation: Competing Traditions and Future Directions*, London, Harvester Wheatsheaf, 1993.

Canzoneri, Matthew, Grilli, Vittorio, and Masson, Paul R., *Establishing a Central Bank: Issues in Europe and Lessons from the United States*, Cambridge CUP, 1992.

Chambers, William Nisbet, and Burnham, Walter Dean (eds.), *The American Party Systems: Stages of Political Development*, Oxford, OUP, 1975.

Corbett, Richard, *The Treaty of Maastricht: From Conception to Ratification: A Comprehensive Reference Guide*, London, Longman, 1993.

Cuckierman, A., *Central Bank Strategy, Credibility and Independence: Theory and Evidence*, Cambridge, Mass., MIT Press, 1992.

Curry, William, *The Case For Federal Union*, Harmondsworth, Penguin, 1939.

Curtice, John, 'Failures That Will Outlast a Change of Face', *Independent*, 6 Apr. 1994.

De Grauwe, Paul, *The Economics of Monetary Integration*, Oxford, OUP, 1994.

—— and Papademos, L. (eds.), *The European Monetary System in the 1990s*, London, Longman, 1990.

Demopoulos, G., Katsimbris, G., and Miller, S., 'Monetary Policy and Central Bank Financing of Government Budget Deficits: A Cross Country Comparison', *European Economic Review*, 31, 1987.

Deutsch, Karl, *et al.*, *Political Community in the North Atlantic Area*, Princeton, Princeton University Press, 1957.

Dickson, Tim, 'Genscher Call for Closer European Monetary Links', *Financial Times*, 21 Jan. 1988.

Dodwell, David, 'Finland Aims to Put its House in Order Ahead of EC Entry', *Financial Times*, 9 June 1992.

Duchacek, Ivo D., *Comparative Federalism: The Territorial Dimension of Politics*, New York, Holt, Rinehart and Winston, 1970.

Duchene, François, *Jean Monnet: The First Statesman of Interdependence*, New York, Norton, 1994.

Duff, Andrew, 'Building a Parliamentary Europe', *Government and Opposition*, 29, 1994.

—— Pinder, John, and Pryce, Roy (eds.), *Maastricht and Beyond: Building the European Union*, London, Routledge, 1994.

Duroselle, J.-P., 'General de Gaulle's Europe and Jean Monnet's Europe', in C. Cosgrove, and K. Twitchett (eds.), *The New Institutional Actors: The UN and the EEC*, London, Macmillan, 1970.

Dyson, Kenneth, *Elusive Union: The Process of Economic and Monetary Union in Europe*, London, Longman, 1994.

—— Featherstone, Kevin, and Michalopolous, George, 'The Politics of EMU: The Maastricht Treaty and the Relevance of Bargaining Models', Paper before the Annual Meeting of the American Political Science Association, New York, 1994.

Economist, The, 'A Ghastly Game of Dominoes', 19 Sept. 1992.

—— 'Mayhem', Editorial, 19 Sept. 1992.

—— 'Toughing it Out', 19 Sept. 1992.

—— 'Hell Damnation and an Earthquake or Two', 10 Oct. 1992.

—— 'Italy Lops Off More Dead Wood', 27 Nov. 1993.

Eichengreen, Barry, 'Is Europe an Optimum Currency Area?', CEPR Discussion Paper, 1990.

—— *International Monetary Arrangements for the 21st Century*, Washington, Brookings Institution, 1994.

—— and Frieden, Jeffrey, 'The Political Economy of European Monetary Unification', *Economics and Politics*, 5, 1993.

—— —— (eds.), *The Political Economy of Monetary Unification*, Boulder, Colo., Westview Press, 1994.

El-Agraa, Ali M., *The Economics of the European Community*, London, Harvester Wheatsheaf, 4th edn., 1994.

Elkins, Stanley, and McKitrick, Eric, *The Age of Federalism: The Early American Republic, 1788–1800*, New York, OUP, 1993.

Emerson, Michael *et al.*, *One Market, One Money: An Evaluation of the Potential Benefits and Costs of Forming an Economic and Monetary Union*, Oxford, OUP, 1992.

European Journal of Political Research Political Data Handbook, vols. 23 (1993) and 24 (1994).

Evans, Peter B., Jacobson, Harold K., and Putnam, Robert D., *Double Edged Diplomacy: International Bargaining and Domestic Politics*, Berkeley and Los Angeles, University of California Press, 1993.

Featherstone, Kevin, *Socialist Parties and European Integration: A Comparative History*, Manchester, Manchester University Press, 1988.

Feldstein, Martin, 'The Case Against EMU', *The Economist*, 13 June 1992.

Financial Times, 'Finland Cuts Spending to Avoid Devaluation', 6 Apr. 1992.

—— 'Damp Strike', 29 May 1992.

—— 'Italian Lira: The Sick Currency of Europe', 22 July 1992.

—— 'Major is Committed to Keeping Strong Pound', 3 Aug. 1992.

—— 'Minister Reassures over Markka's Float', 10 Sept. 1992.

—— 'Italy Redraws Political Map', 16 Sept. 1992.

—— 'Swedish Marginal Lending Rate Hits 500%', 17 Sept. 1992.

—— 'Sweden Unveils Rescue Package', 21 Sept. 1992.

—— 'Fresh Anglo-German Row Breaks Out Over ERM', 1 Oct. 1992.

Financial Times, 'Italy's Fight for Credibility', 12 Nov. 1992.

—— 'Sweden Admits Defeat in Battle for Krona', 20 Nov. 1992.

—— 'Norway Overnight Lending Rate up Again', 23 Nov. 1992.

—— 'Bank of Spain to Control Monetary Policy', 30 Dec. 1992.

Fitoussi, J.-P., *et al.*, *Competitive Disinflation: The Mark and Budgetary Politics in Europe*, Oxford, OUP, 1993.

Franck, T. M. (ed.), *Why Federations Fail: An Enquiry into the Requisites for Successful Federalism*, New York, New York University Press, 1968.

Fraser, Steve, and Gerstle, Gary (eds.), *The Rise and Fall of the New Deal Political Order*, Princeton, Princeton University Press, 1989.

Friedman, Milton, 'Inflation and Unemployment', *Journal of Political Economy*, 85, 1977.

Friedrich, Carl J., *Trends of Federalism in Theory and Practice*, London, Pall Mall Press, 1968.

Gamble, Andrew, 'The Labour Party and Economic Policy Making', in Martin J. Smith and Joanna Sear (eds.), *The Changing Labour Party*, London, Routledge, 1990.

Garber, Peter, 'The Collapse of the Bretton Woods Fixed Exchange Rate System', in Michael D. Bordo and Barry Eichengreen (eds.), *A Retrospective on the Bretton Woods System*, Chicago, University of Chicago Press, 1993.

Gellner, Ernest (ed.), *Culture, Identity and Politics*, Cambridge, CUP, 1987.

Gilpin, Robert, *US Power and the Multinational Corporation*, New York, Basic Books, 1975.

—— *The Political Economy of International Relations*, Princeton, Princeton University Press, 1987.

Goodhart, C. A. E., *EMU and ESCB After Maastricht*, London, LSE Financial Markets Group, 1992.

Graham, Robert, 'Italy Takes the Offensive in Battle for its Currency', *Financial Times*, 11 Sept. 1992.

Grant, Charles, *Delors: Inside the House that Jacques Built*, London, Brealey, 1994.

Greenstein, Fred I., and Polsby, Nelson, *The Handbook of Political Science*, vol. v: *Government Institutions and Processes*, Reading, Mass., Addison Wesley, 1975.

Grieco, Joseph M., 'The Maastricht Treaty, Economic and Monetary Union and the Neorealist Research Programme', *Review of International Studies*, 21, 1995, 21–40.

Haas, Ernest B., *The Uniting of Europe: Political, Social and Economic Forces 1950–1957*, Stanford, Calif., Stanford University Press, 1968.

Haas, Peter (ed.), 'Knowledge, Power, and International Policy Coordination', Special Issue of *International Organisation*, 46/1 (1992).

Hall, Peter, *Governing the Economy: The Politics of State Intervention in Britain and France*, New York, OUP, 1986.

Hirsch, Fred, and Goldthorpe, John H. (eds.), *The Political Economy of Inflation*, Oxford, Martin Robertson, 1978.

Holland, Martin, *European Integration: From Community to Union*, London, Pinter, 1994.

Jefferson, Michael, Mann, Thomas, Dickson, Andrew, and Rostow, Walt, *Inflation*, London, John Calder, 1977.

Jennings, Ivor, *A Federation for Western Europe*, Cambridge, CUP, 1940.

Johnston, Bruce, 'Sick Italy Chokes on Economic Medicine', *Sunday Times*, 6 Sept. 1992.

Juberias, Carlos Flores, 'The Break Up of the Czechoslovak Federation: Political Strategies and Constitutional Choices', Paper Before the ECPR Joint Sessions of Workshops, Bordeaux, 27 Apr.–2 May 1995.

Katzenstein, Peter J. (ed.), *Between Power and Plenty*, Madison, Wisc., University of Wisconsin Press, 1978.

Kenen, Peter B., *Understanding Interdependence: The Macroeconomics of the Open Economy*, Princeton, Princeton University Press, 1995.

Keohane, Robert O., 'Neo-Orthodox Economics, Inflation and the Role of the State: Political Implications of the McCracken Report', *World Politics*, 27, 1977.

—— *After Hegemony: Co-operation and Discord in the World Political Economy*, Princeton, University of Princeton Press, 1984.

—— and Hoffman, Stanley (eds.), *The New Community of Europe: Decision Making and Institutional Change*, Boulder, Colo., Westview Press, 1991.

—— —— *Institutional Change in Europe*, .

—— and Nye Jr., Joseph S., *Power and Interdependence: World Politics in Transition*, Boston, Little Brown, 1977.

—— —— *Power and Interdependence: World Politics in Transition*, Boston, Little Brown, 2nd edn., 1989.

Kindleberger, Charles, *The World in Depression 1929–1939*, Berkeley and Los Angeles, University of California Press, 1973.

King, Anthony, 'Overload: Problems of Governing in the 1970s', *Political Studies*, 23, 1975.

King, Preston, *Federalism and Federation*, London, Croom Helm, 1982.

Krugman, Paul, 'Target Zones and Exchange Rate Dynamics', *Quarterly Journal of Economics*, 51, 1991.

—— *Peddling Prosperity: Economic Sense and Nonsense in an Age of Diminished Expectations*, New York, Norton, 1994.

The Labour Party Programme 1973, Labour Party, London.

Lange, Peter, and Regina, Marino (eds.), *State, Market and Social Regulation: New Perspectives on Italy*, Cambridge, CUP, 1989.

Lehmbruch, Gerhard, and Schmitter, Phillippe C., *Patterns of Corporate Policy-Making*, London, Sage, 1982.

Lister, L., *Europe's Coal and Steel Community*, New York, Wiley, 1960.

Lowi, Theodore, and Stone, Alan (eds.), *Nationalizing Government: Public Policies in America*, Beverley Hills, Calif., Sage, 1978.

McCracken, Paul, *et al.*, *Towards Full Employment and Price Stability*, Paris, OECD, 1977.

McKay, David, 'Industrial Policy and Non Policy in the U.S.', *Journal of Public Policy*, 3, 1983.

—— *American Politics and Society*, Oxford, Blackwell, 1993.

—— 'Divided and Governed?: Recent Research on Divided Government in the United States', *British Journal of Political Research*, 24, 1994.

Mackay, R. W. G., *Federal Europe*, London, Michael Joseph, 1940.

McKinnon, R., 'Optimal Currency Areas', *American Economic Review*, 53, 1963.

Madison, James, Hamilton, Alexander, and Jay, John, *The Federalist Papers*, Harmondsworth, Penguin, 1987.

Malcolm, Noel, 'The Case Against Europe', *Foreign Affairs*, Mar./Apr. 1995.

Milner, Helen, 'The Domestic Political Economy of International Economic Co-operation: A Comparison of the NAFTA Accord and the Maastricht Treaty', Paper Before the 22nd Joint Sessions Workshops of the ECPR, Madrid, 1994.

Milward, Alan S., *The Reconstruction of Western Europe 1945–1952*, London, Unwin, 1984.

—— *The European Rescue of the Nation State*, London, Routledge, 1994.

Moravcsik, Andrew, 'Preferences and Power in the European Community: A Liberal Intergovernmentalist Appreach', *Journal of Common Market Studies*, 31, 1993.

Mundell, R., 'A Theory of Optimal Currency Areas', *American Economic Review*, 51, 1961.

—— and Swobodaa, A. (eds.), *Monetary Problems of the International Economy*, Chicago, University of Chicago Press, 1969.

Munchau, Wolfgang, 'EC's Intervention Lays Bare Italy's Economic and Political Malaise', *Financial Times*, 15 Sept. 1992.

Paoa-Schioppa, Tommaso, *The Road to Monetary Union in Europe: The Emperor, the Kings and the Genies*, Oxford, OUP, 1994.

Pohl, Karl Otto, 'Prospects of the European Monetary Union', in James Buchanan (ed.), *Europe's Constitutional Future*, London, Institute of Economic Affairs, 1990.

Pollock, Mark A., 'Creeping Competence: The Expanding Agenda of the European Community', *Journal of Public Policy*, 14 Apr.–June 1994.

Porter, Bernard, *The Lion's Share: A Short History of British Imperialism*, London, Longman, 1984.

Pryce, Roy (ed.), *The Dynamics of European Union*, London, Croom Helm, 1987.

Redmond, John (ed.), *Prospective Europeans: New Members for the European Union*, London, Harvester Wheatsheaf, 1994.

Riker, William H., *Federalism: Origins, Operation, Significance*, Boston, Little Brown, 1964.

—— 'Federalism', in Fred I. Greenstein and Nelson Polsby (eds.), *The Handbook of Political Science*, vol. v: *Government Institutions and Processes*, Reading, Mass., Addison Wesley, 1975.

—— and Schaps, Ronald, 'Disharmony in Federal Government', *Behavioural Science*, 2, 1957.

Ross, George, *Jacques Delors and European Integration*, Oxford, Polity, 1995.

Rufus Davis, S., *The Federal Principle: A Journey Through Time in Quest of a Meaning*, Berkeley and Los Angeles, University of California Press, 1978.

Sanders, David, *Losing an Empire, Finding a Role: British Foreign Policy Since 1945*, London, Macmillan, 1990.

Sandholz, Wayne, 'Choosing Union: Monetary Politics and Maastricht', *International Organisation*, 47/1, Winter 1993, 1–39.

—— and Zysman, John, '1992: Recasting the European Bargain', *World Politics*, 42, 1989.

Sassoon, D., *The Strategy of the Italian Communist Party from the Resistance to the Historic Compromise*, London, Pinter, 1981.

Serfaty, Simon, *France, de Gaulle and Europe: The Policy of the Fourth and Fifth Republics Towards the Continent*, Baltimore, Johns Hopkins Press, 1968.

—— and Gray, Lawrence (eds.), *The Italian Communist Party: Yesterday, Today and Tomorrow*, London, Aldwych Press, 1980.

Shaw, Eric, *The Labour Party Since 1979*, London, Routledge, 1994.

Skowronek, Stephen, *The Politics Presidents Make*, Cambridge, Mass., Harvard University Press, 1993.

Smith, A., 'National Identity and the Idea of European Unity', *International Affairs*, Jan. 1992.

Smith, David, 'Britain May be Dragged Screaming Back to ERM', *Sunday Times*, 3 Sept. 1995.

Smith, Julie, *The Voice of the People: The European Parliament in the 1990s*, London, Pinter, Royal Institute of International Affairs, 1995.

Soledad, Garcia (ed.), *European Identity and the Search for Legitimacy*, London, Pinter, Royal Institute of International Affairs, 1993.

Stein, Herbert, *Presidential Economics: The Making of Economic Policy From Roosevelt to Reagan and Beyond*, New York, Simon and Schuster, 1984.

Steinherr, Alfred, *30 Years of European Monetary Integration: From the Werner Plan to EMU*, London, Longman, 1994.

Taylor, Robert, 'Swedes Untie Welfare Apron Strings', *Financial Times*, 23 Sept. 1992.

Temperton, Paul (ed.), *The European Currency Crisis: What Chance Now for a Single European Currency?*, London, Probus, 1993.

Thurow, Lester, *Head to Head: The Coming Economic Battle Among Europe and America*, New York, William Morrow, 1992.

Torres, Francisco, and Giavazzi, Francesco (eds.), *Adjustment and Growth in the European Monetary Union*, Cambridge, CUP, 1993.

Tsoukalis, Loukas, *The New European Economy: The Politics and Economics of Integration*, Oxford, OUP, 1993.

Tufte, Edward, *Political Control of the Economy*, Princeton, Princeton University Press, 1978.

Urwin, Derek W., *The Community of Europe: A History of European Integration Since 1945*, London, Longman, 1991.

Wallace, William (ed.), *The Dynamics of European Integration*, London, Pinter, Royal Institute of International Affairs, 1990.

—— *The Transformation of Western Europe,* London, Pinter, Royal Institute of International Affairs, 1990.

Walters, A. A., *Britain's Economic Renaissance: Margaret Thatcher's Reforms 1979–1984*, OUP, Oxford, 1984.

—— *Sterling In Danger: The Economic Consequences of Pegged Exchange Rates*, London, Fontana Collins, 1990.

Watts, R. L., *New Federations: Experiments in the Commonwealth*, Oxford, OUP, 1966.

Weigall, David, and Stirk, Peter (eds.), *The Origins and Development of the European Community*, Leicester, Leicester University Press, 1992.

Wheare, Kenneth C., *What Federal Government Is*, London, OUP, 1941.

—— *Federal Government*, Oxford, OUP, 3rd edn., 1956.

Wistrich, Ernest, *The United States of Europe*, London, Routledge, 1994.

Wildavsky, Aaron, 'Government and the People', *Commentary*, Aug. 1973.

World Development Report, World Bank, Washington.

Yannopoulos, G., *Greece and the European Economic Community: Integration and Convergence*, London, Macmillan, 1986.

Zurcher, Arnold, *The Struggle to Unite Europe*, Westport, Conn., Greenwood, 1958.

Zysman, John, *Governments, Markets and Growth: Financial Systems and the Politics of Industrial Change*, Ithaca, NY, Cornell University Press, 1983.

INDEX